Learnership

Raising the status of learning
from an act to an art
in your school

James Anderson

'I have looked long and hard for a great book on how to include the teaching of learning strategies in the classroom – and finally found it. Anderson uses the latest research coupled with a deep classroom understanding of merging thinking and learning WITH the curriculum to empower teachers and students with the optimal strategies for success.'

John Hattie, Melbourne Laureate Professor Emeritus

'James Anderson has been inspiring educators across NZ through his delivery of workshops on what great teaching and learning looks like … the information he shares is thought-provoking, relevant, purposeful and inspiring. James challenges teachers to reflect on their practice and think about how they can create effective learning opportunities in their classrooms. A skillful and engaging facilitator, James has thoughtfully shaped the learning experience in each and every one of his workshops.'

Faye Huawai, Learning Network NZ

'James's work always focuses on student growth and learning, and opens up ways of thinking for teachers to consider. We appreciate the way he stretches thinking, keeps a student focus and is an ever-evolving, lifelong learner who shares his wisdom with others. James is creative and innovative, a deep thinker, futuristic and data driven. The way he integrates concepts such as Habits of Mind, growth mindset and deliberate practice is just amazing.'

Pat Mullikin, Educational Consultant, Adaptive Schools & Cognitive Coaching Training Associate, Habits of Mind Consultant, Director, Tri-County Teacher Center

Juanita Henry, Educational Consultant, Adaptive Schools & Cognitive Coaching Training Associate, Habits of Mind Consultant, Director, Genesee Region Teacher Center

'I am thrilled to endorse the exceptional work our school has undertaken in collaboration with James Anderson. His approach to education goes beyond traditional teaching methods, emphasising a profound focus on learning and the process required for learning. James has a remarkable ability to connect content with our staff in a way that is truly exciting, relevant and engaging. Through his innovative strategies, we are successfully transforming our classrooms into dynamic learning environments where students actively participate and flourish. His passion for education is contagious, and he has empowered our teachers to think creatively and foster a love for learning among our students. James Anderson's contributions have undoubtedly enriched our school community and ignited a passion for lifelong learning. As a result, our school vision is no longer about Being Our Best, rather Bettering our Best!'

Carl Allan, Principal, Glenview Primary School

'Working with James Anderson has been a transformative journey, focused on the concepts of Learnership, growth mindset and Habits of Mind. A highlight of our collaboration lies in James's ability to engage and motivate our staff, cultivating a team of dedicated individuals who eagerly embraced their new learning opportunities. Through his unique approach, James has helped us refine our school's vision, mission and values, fostering a school culture centred on strong morale and shared beliefs. What sets James apart is his exceptional willingness to co-design learning experiences tailored to our staff's needs, while effectively contextualising them for the entire school, from Prep to Year 6.'

Trish Hollands, Principal, Ipswich Central State School

'As an educational leader, working with James Anderson has been highly impactful in shaping my understanding of the relationships between teaching and learning as complementary but very different crafts. While teachers obviously have skills that make them good teachers, do students have well-developed skills to be good learners? His guidance to shift our instructional focus from how we teach to prioritise how students learn has enabled us to empower students as accountable stakeholders in their educational journeys. Through our partnership with James, we understand where to put our instructional energy to balance the teaching and learning equation and help our students to grow their agency.'

Jan Stone, Principal, Pinjarra Senior High School

'I am writing this endorsement with great enthusiasm and pleasure to express my sincere appreciation for the exceptional work and significant impact that James Anderson has had during three years of collaboration with our school. James has played a crucial role in helping me become a better leader. His professional guidance and mentorship have enhanced my understanding of growth mindset principles and equipped me with effective strategies to foster a culture of continuous improvement. Through his empowering approach, we developed a future-focused school community that strives towards excellence.

'I wholeheartedly endorse James Anderson's book. His extensive knowledge, dedication, and unique approach to fostering a growth mindset have significantly impacted our school. James's book will empower and inspire countless educators and parents, enabling them to create environments that foster a growth mindset and maximise the potential of every learner.'

Elizabeth Amvrazis, Principal, Asquith Girls High School

'Inspirational. This is the most exciting thing in my 30 years of teaching. It's the single thing in my 14 years of being a principal where every single staff member is on the journey and changing the way they think – in order to bring change with our students. It's so, so cool. It's the one thing I think could really make a difference with teenagers in our current culture. And that's saying something!'

Rosey Mabin, Principal, Inglewood School

'We engaged James Anderson as a keynote for a conference that was held online. Right from the start James was professional in his communication with us, and flexible in helping us design a program that allowed the themes of his keynote to flow through the sessions that followed. James's presentation was highly professional, varied and informative. He used great models, props and examples to get his messages and ideas for change and improvement across clearly to teachers. James helped us out through the day in various sessions, providing his own time and expertise to remain part of the entire day, as both participant and leader in education. We really valued James's contribution, including his engaging and natural presentation style, and encourage others to take advantage of James abilities!'

Peter Saffin, CEO, Mathematical Association of Victoria

'James Anderson's keynote at our recent Mathematics conference was engaging, insightful and exceptionally well delivered. His presentation was well paced and was the perfect starting point for the day. James also joined in on some of the workshops that followed, which was very appreciated by participants who were keen to take a deeper dive into his work. His presentation sparked great discussion, and feedback from participants was very positive. I would highly recommend him as a keynote speaker.'

Deb Carmichael, Senior Advisor, Independent Schools Victoria

OTHER BOOKS BY JAMES ANDERSON

Succeeding with Habits of Mind

The Agile Learner: Where Growth Mindset, Habits of Mind and Practice Unite

The Learning Landscape: How to increase Learner Agency and become a lifelong learner

The Mindset Continuum: How to implement Growth Mindsets and increase Learner Agency

Available from www.jamesanderson.com.au and through online retailers

Acknowledgements

I want to acknowledge all the incredible educators I've had the privilege to work with. Those who guided and encouraged me as a beginning teacher. You challenged me to teach students not just to think, but to think well. Those who mentored me and encouraged me. You taught me how to multiply my impact through leadership. And all those that have invited me to work with their school communities over the last 25 years. Your passion for learning and your dedication to raising the aspirations and improving the lives of our youth is a constant source of inspiration and energy for me.

I'd also like to acknowledge the many thought leaders, researchers and academics who have helped shape my thinking over the years. There are too many to name, but several stand out for their keen observation of the human condition and their insights into how we achieve growth. Key among these are Art Costa and Bena Kallick for their work describing the Habits of Mind and understanding what to do, when we don't know what to do. Anders Ericsson for helping me understand the processes behind developing expertise. Carol Dweck for the way she shed light on the importance of understanding our capacity to grow. And Nicholas Taleb for describing what it means to become antifragile and to thrive on disruption. Your 'thought prints' can be found throughout this book.

Writing a book is so much more than putting words on a page. Thank you for the invaluable contribution of my coach, and friend, Andrew Griffiths, who consistently guided and pushed me to be a better author. Thank you also to Michael Hanrahan and the team at Publish Central for helping create the best book possible. This book is so much richer and more valuable than I could have created on my own.

To my daughter Lucy, who is becoming such a strong, capable young woman.

And to my partner in life, Fiona, whose love and support I draw on constantly.

Thank you all.

First published in 2023 by James Anderson
www.jamesanderson.com.au
james@jamesanderson.com.au

© James Anderson 2023

The moral rights of the author have been asserted.

All rights reserved. Except as permitted under the *Australian Copyright Act 1968* (for example, a fair dealing for the purposes of study, research, criticism or review), no part of this book may be reproduced, stored in a retrieval system, communicated or transmitted in any form or by any means without prior written permission.

All inquiries should be made to the author.

A catalogue entry for this book is available from the National Library of Australia.

ISBN: 978-0-6459129-0-6

Printed in Australia
Book production and text design by Publish Central
Cover design by Julia Kuris
Author photo (back cover) by Fiona Basile

The paper this book is printed on is environmentally friendly.

Disclaimer: The material in this publication is of the nature of general comment only, and does not represent professional advice. It is not intended to provide specific guidance for particular circumstances and it should not be relied on as the basis for any decision to take action or not take action on any matter which it covers. Readers should obtain professional advice where appropriate, before making any such decision. To the maximum extent permitted by law, the author and publisher disclaim all responsibility and liability to any person, arising directly or indirectly from any person taking or not taking action based on the information in this publication.

Contents

Let's begin xiii

PART I: THE NEED FOR AGENCY

Chapter 1: How well are we preparing students for their future?   5
Chapter 2: We don't have a teaching problem, we have a learning problem   14

PART II: MINDSET IS THE FOUNDATION FOR LEARNERSHIP

Chapter 3: Your autopilot for learning   31
Chapter 4: It's about having a choice   43
Chapter 5: Changing mindsets: a nudge in the right direction   54
Chapter 6: The value is in the backstory   66

PART III: WHAT IS LEARNERSHIP?

Chapter 7: Transforming learning from an act to an art   81
Chapter 8: Learnership: the skill of learning   87

PART IV: THE FIVE ESSENTIAL ELEMENTS OF LEARNERSHIP

Chapter 9: Challenge: the pathway to growth   101
Chapter 10: Habits of Mind: actions for growth   115
Chapter 11: Mistakes: finding information for growth   126
Chapter 12: Feedback: seeking information for growth   134
Chapter 13: Effort: the currency of growth   141

PART V: THE SIX LEVELS OF LEARNERSHIP

Chapter 14:	The Learnership Matrix	161
Chapter 15:	Non-Learners	167
Chapter 16:	Beginning Learners	170
Chapter 17:	Performance Learners	174
Chapter 18:	Learnership and learner agency	179
Chapter 19:	Directed Learners	184
Chapter 20:	Independent Learners	189
Chapter 21:	Agile Learners	196
Chapter 22:	Why the world needs Agile Learners	201

PART VI: CREATING A CULTURE FOR LEARNERSHIP

| Chapter 23: | Assessing your learning culture | 215 |
| Chapter 24: | Creating a culture of learning and growth | 244 |

PART VII: BUILDING A LEARNING COMMUNITY

| Chapter 25: | Addressing the needs of teachers | 263 |
| Chapter 26: | Showing teachers the future | 270 |

PART VIII: HOW TO DEVELOP LEARNERSHIP

| Chapter 27: | Teaching for Learnership | 283 |

| Where to now? | 301 |

Let's begin

Imagine walking around your school and seeing engaged and enthusiastic students and teachers. Everybody is focused on learning and growth. In the classroom, students are engaged. In the staffroom, teachers are excited about their next lesson and are sharing ideas. There's not a complaint to be heard. Parents appreciate the wonderful results and the confident people their children are becoming. Students, teachers and the wider community all understand themselves as learners. It's a place where students are not simply learning, they are becoming skilful lifelong learners.

This is what we all wish every school was like. But we also know it's a rarity.

School leaders know we have a problem. Teachers are under-resourced, overworked and burnt out, while students are not learning or being prepared as well as we'd want them to be for today's rapidly changing world.

For years the solution to just about every educational issue has been to focus on teaching practices. In this environment, students have increasingly sat back and done less and less, becoming passive learners, their classroom performance a function of teaching, rather than their own ability to learn and grow.

As educational leaders we are charged with ensuring students have both the will and power to act in the world and to be confident in their ability to overcome the challenges and adversity that will come their way. In short, for them to have agency in their lives.

In these pages we open a new chapter in education. A chapter that addresses these problems. One that recognises the skill of learning as being at least as important as the skill of teaching, and probably more so. One that challenges educators to ensure students become masters of *how* they learn, not just *what* they learn. One that recognises Learnership as the *skill of learning*.

For school leaders, *Learnership* provides a pathway for raising student achievement. But it does so much more than that. It shows you how to create a school culture that increases the agency students have in the world, and to raise their aspirations to set them confidently on a path to succeed in school and thrive in life.

WHAT'S IN THIS BOOK?

This book is broken up into eight parts, each a step on the journey towards building a true learning community.

In part I we take a brief look at the world we are preparing our students for. A world where the only certainty is uncertainty, and the only constant is change. A world that demands students are not only continuously learning, but also continuously improving.

If we are to build a culture of learning and growth and create true learning communities, every person in the community needs to understand themselves as a learner. So, in part II we explore how we build the foundation of our culture by nurturing a growth mindset. I introduce you to the Mindset Continuum and show you how to 'nudge' your learners, and your culture, towards a more growth-oriented mindset.

We then take a deep dive into Learnership in parts III, IV and V. We begin by defining Learnership, and I then challenge the way you think and talk about learning – to shift the paradigm from learning being something students simply do, to something that can be done well. To transform learning from an act to an art in your school.

And I describe the pinnacle of Learnership: the Agile Learner. This is someone who embraces challenges and cultivates their Habits of Mind in a way that makes them antifragile, essentially futureproofing themselves against challenges and uncertainty.

In parts VI and VII we turn our attention to your school culture and ask, 'How is learning done at your school?' I invite you to assess the environment in your school using my Learnership Diagnostic, which provides enormous insight into your learning culture and points the way to developing a more growth-oriented system.

Finally, in part VIII, we take a practical look at how to teach for Learnership. I share how to structure your Learnership program in a way that supports and nurtures your culture of learning and growth, creating a true learning community.

Throughout the book you'll find QR codes like this. Scan these codes to watch short videos where I explain each 'nudge' and give short examples of how they might be applied to nudge teaching practice and your school culture. I provide a full explanation of how nudges work in chapter 5.

WHO IS THIS BOOK FOR?

This book is for principals and senior school leaders, although of course teachers will also find it hugely valuable. It is for senior people in decision-making positions, who are thinking about school-level issues. The school leaders who are concerned about the limited aspirations and opportunities passive and ineffective learners have in life. Leaders who are waking up to the fact that they have been trapped in a teaching and performance culture.

In these pages I provide a clear understanding of what you didn't know was missing: a focus on the skill of learning. I give you a way to recognise it. A way to understand how to develop a culture around it. In doing so, I will help you hit your short-term curriculum outcomes while also preparing students for life after school. A life in a world that is rapidly changing, and increasingly complex.

As leaders, it us up to us to raise the standard of learning, not just the learning outcomes, in our school community. We all need to become better learners. We all need to develop Learnership. Our students, our teachers, our leaders and ourselves.

So please join me as we share this journey of Learnership.

Part I
The need for agency

What is happening in your school today that will benefit students in 20 years' time?

We begin our Learnership journey by briefly exploring the bigger purpose of education. Your job as a school leader is to prepare students for a rapidly changing and increasingly complex and challenging world. Your students must learn how to be the masters of their circumstances, not victims. To be powerful in the face of change, not powerless. In short, you are responsible for developing students who have agency in the world. The question I'd like to begin with is, how well is our current system of education allowing you to do this?

We then look at a system that has become almost obsessed with teaching. In schools we regularly discuss quality teaching, the most effective teaching strategies, and how we can measure the impact of teaching on student learning. But I ask, where is the role of students in their own learning? We have a clear understanding of what skilful teachers do, but do we have the same level of clarity around what skilful learners do?

Chapter 1
How well are we preparing students for their future?

Students must be the masters of their circumstances, not victims.

THE BIGGEST CHALLENGE OF SCHOOL LEADERSHIP TODAY

I was listening to Karl, a principal in a small secondary school, when he described the challenge of school leadership like this:

> I want my students to approach life with an attitude of 'I'm capable of finding a way'. Otherwise they are stuck with the way they are now. And that's not good enough. I worry that too many of our young people don't have the self-belief to get them beyond how they view the world today.
>
> I want to raise their aspirations and improve outcomes for all my students, so they can thrive at school and in life after school.
>
> I want to create a school culture – the way we do business around here – that will get maximum growth for young people, and my teachers. Put them on a path that sets them up to succeed in school and thrive in life.

Like so many of the school leaders I work with, Karl has a deep social conscience. He wants to make a *real* difference to the lives of his students, so they can create a better world for themselves and others. He's trying to establish a school culture that sets students up for life *after* school, not just the life *of* school.

I hear that idea repeated over and over.

Carl, a primary school principal, described how he worried his students weren't extending themselves. On paper the school did well, but he felt he should have a higher percentage of students who were exceeding expectations, not just meeting them. His students were not in the habit of pushing themselves. Too many of them were content to sit back and wait for school, and life, to happen to them. Passive learners who coast through, doing 'well enough'.

Elizabeth, frustrated with how the system and the community values education, told me she had stopped paying much attention to her students' year 12 results. Many of them were receiving university offers before they even sat their exams. She told me: 'The system itself is limiting students' aspirations and ability to achieve in life … The real measure of school achievement is not what students achieve in one year, it's how they are succeeding in 20 years!'

Jan, another principal, commented that the system has trapped teachers into focusing on short-term goals. It's a system that places all the responsibility on teachers to achieve outcomes. In fact, she felt her teachers were so focused on short-term outcomes, they'd either lost sight of their long-term goals or simply didn't have the space to address them. She wanted her teachers, her community and the culture she created to recognise that school is about more than content delivery and standards. It's about preparing students for the future.

Deb, another leader, echoed this frustration with the system's narrow focus on what students are learning. She said: 'We need to shift away from what we *teach*, to how people *learn*. What's going to matter to these kids is not simply what they have learned at school, but that they know how to learn. We rarely teach that, and never measure it. But it's the most important part.'

A future that will be very different

All these leaders are concerned about preparing students well for the future they will be living in, which has always been what education should really be about. The challenge they are recognising is that the current system wasn't designed for the future today's students will have. It's a future that will be very different from the one envisioned when we left school, and unrecognisable compared to the one our parents imagined when they were at school.

Perhaps there was a time when schools could teach students everything they needed to know and then send them off fully prepared for the future. But that's certainly not now. Our youth are growing up in a world that's more volatile, uncertain, complex and ambiguous (VUCA) than ever. Not only is this generation facing more change, the complexity of the changes they face means those challenges will be more difficult to overcome. It's not just a matter of needing to consume more knowledge; they'll need to be better learners too.

A generation ago, teachers could expect that what they taught their students would last them a lifetime. Today, according to Richard Riley, former US Secretary of Education (1993–2001), we are 'preparing students for jobs that don't yet exist, using technologies that haven't been invented, in order to solve problems we don't even know are problems yet'. Our short-term curriculum outcomes that drive most of the learning in our schools are simply no longer enough.

Even the very idea of having a job, something most of us grew up taking for granted, is disappearing. In 2020 Ravi Venkatesan, Special Representative for Young People and Innovation at UNICEF, noted that there is 'no such thing as a secure job anymore. And more and more, the idea of jobs and careers feels like an artifact of the last century … our lives are looking like a series of projects.'

So, if our short-term educational outcomes – which are still important – aren't enough to prepare students for this type of world, what is? It's all very well to say we want to raise the aspirations of students and prepare them to thrive, not just survive, in the future we know they are headed for, but what does that *actually mean*?

If we use Elizabeth's measure of success as being what our students are doing in 20 years, what would that look like? Or conversely, if we fail to prepare them well for this future, what might that look like?

THE NEED FOR AGENCY

When we dig a little deeper, the idea all these school leaders (and for that matter, parents as well) are grappling with is **agency**. What we want more than good grades, more than specific content outcomes, more than any of the short-term results our system measures and values, is for our students to have agency in their lives.

'Agency' is starting to become a buzzword – one of those words people casually drop into discussions with an air of 'everyone should already know all about it'. But it's a very deep and very important idea that philosophers and others have been debating for centuries. At its heart it asks: to what extent are we in control of our lives, and to what extent are we controlled by events? To what extent are individuals able to exercise free will? This deserves much greater attention than is currently being paid to it in some circles.

The concept of agency is at the heart of what it is to lead a rich, fulfilling and meaningful life, and to be able to go out in the world and make a difference.

To understand agency, it's easier begin with what it's *not*. Someone *without* agency feels like the world happens to them. They are powerless in the face of adversity. When challenge and difficulty come along, they become the victim of their circumstances, unable to respond effectively.

> ❝ What we want more than good grades, more than specific content outcomes, more than any of the short-term results our system measures and values, is for our students to have agency in their lives.

What we fear is that our students will lack agency in their lives.

On the other hand, someone *with* agency is the master of their circumstances. The world still happens to them but they can respond effectively. They are powerful, not powerless, in the face of challenge and adversity. People with agency can shape and control their future. They become the masters of their circumstances. They become the person they want, or need, to be. Is this a fair, if broad, description of the type of life you'd like your students to be living in 20 years?

Our current focus on resiliency is a response to the number of students who feel they are acted upon by the world, and they cannot cope with the challenges and adversity they regularly face. Our concern for some students' low aspirations is based on them not believing they can act in a way that makes them powerful. Our desire to see students take advantage of opportunities in the world is the desire that they will become the masters of their circumstances.

Defining 'learner agency'

In recognition of the challenges of the world our students will be living in, the term 'learner agency' is increasingly finding its way into high-level educational policy documents around the world, such as those from the Organisation for Economic Co-operation and Development (OECD), Harvard University's Achievement Gap Initiative, the International Baccalaureate Organisation, the Victorian Department of Education and the New Zealand Ministry of Education.

As is the way when these ideas begin to filter into systems, everyone talks about the same broad ideas but comes up with their own, slightly different, definition. I've draw on the research around learner agency, and define it like this:

> Learner agency is the degree to which a person can take initiative and meaningfully influence their world, particularly in the face of challenges. It involves three interrelated and equally important elements: the environment to act, the will to act, and the power to act.

The three elements of learner agency

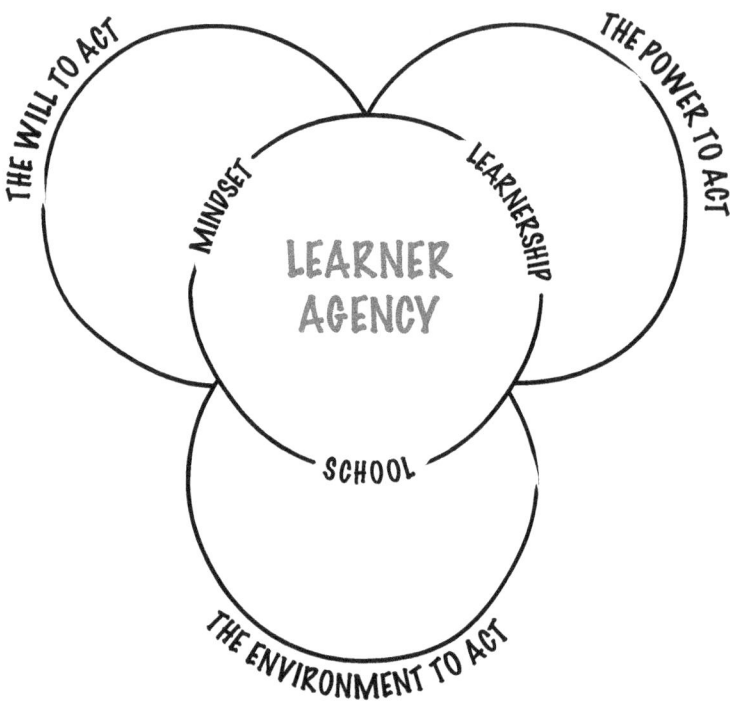

Let's break that definition down to see how it connects to our core work of preparing students for the future.

To begin with, agency happens by degrees. The question is not whether you have agency or not; it is how much agency you have. The qualities we are going to discuss throughout this book increase the agency students will have, making them increasingly powerful and increasingly able to act on the world.

Agency is about acting meaningfully. It's about having choice over the path you take in life. It's not about trivial things. It's about important things. Being able to make a meaningful difference in your life and the lives of others. Too many of the learner agency initiatives seen in school today focus on trivial choices.

The environment to act

Agency involves being in an environment to act. This is not simply the world at large, which we all experience. It's an environment rich in the challenges that are necessary to drive growth. In the context of our work in schools, it is our school and classroom environment that must challenge students and drive their growth.

Arguably, the rate of change and level of challenge in the world today means there is more opportunity for growth than there has ever been. But as the school leaders above pointed out, circumstance on its own is not enough. Our schools can provide challenging opportunities, but students must also *want* to act on that opportunity. They must have the will to act.

The will to act

Challenges can present themselves in one of two ways:

- Sometimes challenges arise and you have a choice to take them or leave them. The only consequence of choosing to let something pass you by is the lost opportunity to achieve. The choice here is *if you will* act. We refer to this as an **opportunity**.
- Then there are challenges, such as the Covid pandemic, where there is no avoiding it. The world happens to you. The issue here is not *if you will* act. The issue is *if you can* act. We refer to this as **adversity**.

We would hope our students choose to act when unavoidable circumstances arise. Even when you are forced to act, like during the pandemic, skilful learners will embrace the challenge as a once-in-a-lifetime learning opportunity. But not all people choose to act.

Why would students choose not to act on an opportunity? For some, it is one they are not interested in. It represents a direction they are *choosing* not to take. This is an exercise of free will. In many cases, that's a perfectly reasonable choice to make.

But the actual issue here is not that some students choose not to act. Rather, it is that some students, when confronted with an opportunity, don't think they *have the choice* to act.

Many students carry with them self-limiting beliefs that they aren't the 'right type of person' to take advantage of a particular opportunity. They aren't smart enough, or they are not musical, or they are only good at languages but not maths. The belief that their basic characteristics – such as their talents, abilities and intelligence – are unchangeable is what Stanford Professor Carol Dweck calls a 'fixed mindset'.

A fixed mindset limits a student's will to act, not because they are choosing not to act but because they believe they are incapable of acting. This belief limits their ability to exercise their free will.

Not taking advantage of an opportunity is one thing. The opportunity is missed. But what about when adversity comes along? For someone with a fixed mindset, when adversity comes along, they look inside themselves, asking if they have the abilities to deal with the adversity. If the answer is no, they see no way of developing those abilities. They become the victim of their circumstances.

We want students to have choices in life and exercise their free will. Students won't always make the decisions we would hope they would, but there is a big difference between not doing something because you don't want to and not doing something because you don't believe you can.

> 66 ... there is a big difference between not doing something because you don't want to and not doing something because you don't believe you can.

The foundation of the learning community you will create is a growth mindset. It is the understanding that we are capable of growth. Developing a growth mindset allows a learner to see more and more opportunities where previously they thought none existed. And it gives them the understanding that, although the world might happen to them at that moment, they can become the person who can act under such circumstances. The more growth-oriented we become, the more agency we have in the world.

The power to act

Then there is the power to act. Being in the environment that challenges you to act is one thing. Having the desire and belief in your ability to succeed at that challenge and act is another. But developing the power to act, and actually succeeding at that challenge or overcoming that adversity – that is something else again.

As I said above, agency comes in degrees, and it relates to the important things in life, not the trivial. All of us have agency over the easy things in life. In chapter 9, we'll examine 'above and below the bar' challenges. Challenges that are below the bar are within our current abilities – they are 'easy things we haven't done yet'. These are things *we already have agency over*, even though we may never have encountered them before.

It is things we encounter in life that are beyond our current abilities, both challenges and adversity, that we are interested in gaining agency over. To gain agency over things beyond our current abilities we need to change ourselves. To become someone with the necessary abilities. Agency is not something to be given. It's something learners must develop.

To increase agency the learner has to change – not just their environment. They have to understand their capacity to grow, removing any self-limiting beliefs. This is what a growth mindset is all about. And they must increase their abilities, their capacity to act on the world.

This is what Learnership is all about.

Chapter 2
We don't have a teaching problem, we have a learning problem

'Learning is not the product of teaching.
Learning is the product of the activity of learners.'

~ John Holt

A CULTURE OF TEACHING, NOT LEARNING

Something odd has been happening in education over the past 10 to 15 years. Take a look around and you'll notice we have created a culture based on the skill of teaching.

The evidence is all around us. Teachers, and the idea of quality teaching, are at the centre of almost everything we do. Take a walk around most schools, look at where the professional learning budget is being spent, listen to the conversations in the staffroom – schools have become more about teaching than they are about learning.

Take a moment to reflect on the language used in schools today. Internationally renowned learning expert John Hattie talks about the learning 'dose' teachers provide, and how they must adjust the dose to achieve the desired results. He also talks about teachers as 'activators of learning'.

If a teacher is not present to activate learning, can learning not occur?

The metaphors we use so often convey the idea that teachers act on students. We measure the *impact* of teaching *on* students. This is echoed in Hattie's famous statement for teachers to 'know thy impact'. In my home state of Victoria, the Department of Education has created a list of High Impact Teaching Strategies and proudly uses the acronym HITS. The model is based on the belief that a teacher's efforts cause learning to happen.

Learners have become the passive recipients of teaching.

Consider the role description of the Teaching and Learning Leader. This is undoubtedly one of the most important roles in your school. Chances are the position description has two key components:

- ensuring teachers are engaging in high-quality teaching strategies
- measuring the impact teachers have on learning by gathering data on student achievement.

Implicit in this description is the idea that *learning* is the outcome of *teaching*.

But where is the role of the learner in their own learning? How is that being valued, measured and improved?

Or consider how your professional learning budget has been invested over the past 15 years. If you're like most schools, you have spent much of it on teacher action, identifying the most effective teaching strategies (those with an effect size above 0.4) and how to use data on student performance to improve teacher practice.

We've invested enormous amounts in quality teaching.

Where is the investment in quality learning?

We have a system where teachers teach. When that is done well, student learning outcomes are achieved. The responsibility for achieving better learning outcomes is placed on teachers, which places enormous pressure on them and, at times, lays unfair blame at their feet when learning goals are not met.

At what point do students share responsibility for their role in their own learning?

You probably remember the traditional parent–teacher interviews. When parents and teachers met, it was simply assumed that the teacher was doing their job well. Parents and teachers would sit down and the teacher would explain what the student needed to do to improve their results. Now the roles have reversed. Parents come in questioning why their child isn't doing well and demanding to know what the teacher is doing about it.

The Australian Professional Standards for Teachers capture this idea in their statement ' ... there is a broad consensus that teacher quality is the single most important in-school factor influencing student achievement'. The dominant paradigm is that teachers act on students to achieve learning outcomes, and so to achieve better outcomes we need better teaching.

But where do we address the role of the learner in their own learning?

Please don't misunderstand me. I want quality teaching in schools. I want teachers who understand their role in the classroom. Teachers who can measure their impact and adopt the most effective strategies for improving student learning outcomes. Hattie's work, as well as the work of many others, has made an enormously valuable contribution to our understanding of what constitutes quality teaching practice. But quality teaching alone is not enough.

> ❝ This is where we have gone fundamentally wrong in education over the past 15 years. We've forgotten, or at least minimised, the role of the learner in their own learning.

International education adviser Sir Ken Robinson saw it this way: 'Whether teaching is a delivery system, or an art form, it still treats students as receivers, the part of the system that is being acted on.' This is where we have gone fundamentally wrong in education over the past 15 years. We've forgotten, or at least minimised, the role of the learner in their own learning. Our focus on teacher quality is valid and important – but it's only part of the story. Learners must, and do, play a critical role in their own learning. We have lost focus on how students engage in the process.

We have lost focus on learning.

LEARNING IS NOT THE PRODUCT OF TEACHING

I am constantly reminded of the words of American author, educator and founder of the unschooling movement, John Holt, who said: 'Learning is not the product of teaching. Learning is the product of the activity of learners.'

Take a moment to read that again. Let it sink in. *Learning is not the product of teaching. It is the product of the activity of learners.*

For years, we've been told learning is the product of teaching. It's what we measure. We adopt a new pedagogy, and we measure the impact on student learning outcomes. Teachers are a variable in the equation that matters. But are they the *only* variable in the equation that matters?

Holt's words are absolutely true. Learning is not the product of teaching. You can be the best teacher in the world. You can set appropriately challenging tasks. You can provide timely, actionable and constructive feedback. You can adopt all the most effective teaching strategies. But if the student chooses to avoid that challenge, if they refuse to listen to the feedback, if they choose not to participate in the learning process, no learning occurs and no learning outcomes are achieved.

I often ask teachers about how students are behaving in their classroom. Over and over, I hear stories about students who opt for easy tasks rather than challenging ones. Students who engage in avoidance activities. Students who are discouraged by mistakes. Students who don't listen to, or won't act on, feedback. I hear stories of students who are stubbornly unmotivated, not simply uninterested in learning but actively resistant to it (an issue we explore in part II: Mindset is the foundation for Learnership).

I invite you to spend some time in your own classrooms. Ask the teachers you lead about their observations of how students are engaging in the learning process. I guarantee you'll hear the term 'passive learners'. These are learners who have picked up on the culture we've created that's centred on the importance of teaching, and are now sitting back, waiting for learning to happen to them.

A LEARNING PROBLEM

Clearly, how students engage in the learning process is important. However, that's not the message we've been hearing. The very loud and clear message in schools today is that teachers make the difference. It's what teachers do in the classroom that matters most.

So it might surprise you to learn that in his 2003 paper 'Teachers Make a Difference: What is the research evidence?', John Hattie wrote:

> Students account for about 50% of the variance of achievement. It is what students bring to the table that predicts achievement more than any other variable.

Fifty percent of the variation in performance between one student and the next comes down to what students do. How the student engages in the learning process. Some students engage very effectively in the learning process, while others are less effective. And this is the single biggest variable in student performance.

When students account for so much of the variance in performance, why aren't we focusing more on how students contribute to their own learning? Why aren't we teaching students how to improve how they contribute to their own learning? Hattie's mantra is: *'It's through teaching the learning strategies, that students make progress, to higher achievement – in that order'*. But this has been largely misunderstood. For the most part we've focused on the teaching strategies, not the learning strategies.

Why do we treat teachers as a controllable variable in learning but not students? Especially when even the most casual observation of student behaviours in the classroom, like those described above, would suggest that these behaviours are *choices* students are making, or skillsets they haven't developed, and not fixed qualities. Surely we can teach in a way so students can engage more effectively in the learning process.

In *Visible Learning for Teachers* (2012), Hattie continued to acknowledge the role of the learner, and the need to teach them learning strategies. He wrote:

> When students invoke learning rather than performance strategies, accept rather than discount feedback, set benchmarks for difficult rather than easy goals, compare their achievements to subject criteria rather than with that of other students, develop high rather than low efficacy to learning, and effect self-regulation and personal control rather than learned helplessness in the academic situation, then they are much more likely to realise achievement gains and invest in learning. These dispositions can be taught; they can be learned.

What all of this tells us is that despite what the media might want to portray, we do not have a teaching problem in our schools. We understand what quality teaching looks like, and teachers are working hard at meeting those standards.

What we have is a learning problem.

This is largely what this book is about: getting students to engage more effectively in the learning process and become better learners. What Hattie (and others) has done for quality teaching, I do for quality learning: I define what quality learning looks like, and I outline a process for developing students as more skilful learners, developing what I call 'Learnership' – the skill of learning.

> 66 ... it's time to think of what goes on in classrooms like a partner dance or couples figure skating, with the skills of both the teacher and the student contributing equally to the overall performance.

If, as Sir Ken Robinson said, teaching is an art, surely it's time to think of what goes on in classrooms like a partner dance or couples figure skating, with the skills of both the teacher and the student contributing equally to the overall performance. At the moment what we have is the teacher taking centre stage, dancing skilfully. Demonstrating their expertise – while many of our students are led along, stumbling, or sitting on the sidelines watching the teacher at work.

Imagine a classroom where teaching and learning are both done ... *beautifully*. Like figure skaters Torvill and Dean's legendary 'Bolero' performance at the 1984 Winter Olympics. Both contributing equally and skilfully to produce an extraordinary performance that neither one could accomplish on their own.

Our recent past in education has been focused on raising the status of teaching. I love the way educational researcher Robert Marzano and others talk about the 'art and science' of teaching. Understanding and documenting what expert teachers do has been valuable. We have developed a clear, helpful guide to the art of teaching. Now we need to do the same for learning.

> 66 ... raise the status of learning from an act to an art.

I'd like to see schools raise the status of learning from an act to an art, to become places where we recognise and develop the skill of learning just as much as the skill of teaching. Places where we recognise the intimate relationship – the dance – between the teacher and the learner in achieving growth.

If our goal is to improve student learning outcomes as our system calls for, we will get the best results when we recognise the role of both the teacher and the learner in achieving learning outcomes.

We can represent this as follows:

THE LEARNING EQUATION

Growth = Skilful teaching × Skilful learning

We get maximum growth when skilful teaching is partnered with skilful learning.

THE CLASH OF SHORT-TERM OUTCOMES AND LONG-TERM GOALS

Focusing on the skill of learning alongside the skill of teaching allows us to achieve two important outcomes. It allows us to reach our short-term outcomes that are so valued by our education system, and it helps us better prepare students for the world after school.

Hattie argues that the starting point when determining what to teach should be the curriculum. When we start with our curriculum outcomes, success is nearly always measured by the achievement of those outcomes – which are important. These are the outcomes being measured by our teaching and learning leaders, reported in the media, celebrated in our schools and placed on the 'data walls' in our staffroom.

However, I'd argue that these outcomes, alone, are short sighted. Let's not lose track of what we are trying to achieve, and the reason you became a school leader. We want to do more than achieve curriculum outcomes – we have loftier long-term goals for our learners. We want to prepare students to thrive in a rapidly changing and increasingly complex world. We want students who have agency. Our measures of success go well beyond the curriculum goals achieved at the end of a unit of work. We are interested in what our learners are doing 20 years after they leave school. Focusing on our short-term curriculum outcomes alone won't achieve our long-term goals.

In chapter 7 I tell the story of a skilled teacher who, steeped in a culture of teaching and armed with many of the 'best' teaching strategies, achieves extraordinary short-term outcomes by essentially doing all the hard work of learning for her students. With the teacher in charge of learning, short-term learning outcomes are achieved. By the measures of the system the students are doing well.

But while these students were learn*ing*, they didn't become learn*ers*. They may have excelled at the short-term measures but were unprepared for life after school. This is just one example of how our focus on short-term learning outcomes can get in the way of our long-range educational goals.

THE BEST OF BOTH WORLDS

About now I can almost hear your thoughts: *But that's what we must do! We have to teach the curriculum. We have to report against these short-term outcomes. I can't abandon them.*

No-one is suggesting we abandon those short-term outcomes. In fact, I argue that we can exceed our short-term outcomes on the way to achieving our long-term goals. You can have the best of both worlds.

Learners who engage in the learning process more skilfully achieve more from every learning situation. Teachers who focus on developing more skilful learners are given their energy back and can focus on engaging in more productive pedagogy. Schools that create a culture of learning and growth develop students who not only do well in school but also thrive in the world after school.

> ❝❝ I argue that we can exceed our short-term outcomes on the way to achieving our long-term goals. You can have the best of both worlds.

This book is premised on the belief that learning is a skill. When schools value and develop that skill students not only achieve (and likely exceed) our traditional short-term educational outcomes, they are also better prepared to thrive and have agency in a rapidly changing and increasingly complex world.

To do this, and create a culture of growth and learning, students must first understand themselves as learners. They must develop a growth mindset. That's what we explore in part II.

PART I KEY TAKEAWAYS

- The world our learners will be living in is characterised by rapid change and increasing challenges.
- To thrive in this world, our learners will need to develop **agency** to become the master of their circumstances and powerful in the face of change.
- Agency has three interrelated and equally important parts: the **environment** to act (school). The **will** to act (mindset). The **power** to act (Learnership).
- Skilful teaching is important, but on its own is not enough.
- Learning is not the product of teaching. It is the product of the activity of learners. Therefore it is how students engage in the learning process that is of critical importance.
- The Learning Equation: Growth = Skilful teaching x Skilful learning.
- We have an understanding of quality teaching. What we lack is an understanding of what quality learning looks like.

Use the space below to add some of your own part I key takeaways.

- _____
- _____
- _____
- _____
- _____
- _____
- _____
- _____
- _____

DISCUSSION AND ACTION

- With your leadership team, discuss your aspirations for your students after they leave school. How much do these resemble the definition of learner agency we've explored?
- Download the 'Learner Agency: a Guide for School Leaders' and distribute it to your leadership team.
- Reflect on John Holt's quote 'Learning is not the product of teaching. Learning is the product of the activity of learners' with your leadership group. What do you notice about the activity of your learners in your school that might be inhibiting their learning?

Use the space below to add some of your own discussion and action items.

- _____
- _____
- _____
- _____
- _____
- _____
- _____
- _____
- _____
- _____
- _____
- _____

WHERE TO FROM HERE?

As we prepare our youth for this challenging and changing world we must create a learning community that guides them to become skilful learners. But before they can do that, students must first understand themselves as learners – people who can create the abilities they want or need in the face of challenges and adversity. For this to happen, we must create an environment that nurtures a growth mindset.

Part II
Mindset is the foundation for Learnership

To create and lead a community of learners, every member of that community must first understand themselves as a learner. That's what a growth mindset is about.

At its core, our mindset is a set of beliefs about our ability to change our most basic characteristics. Somewhat surprisingly, many in our learning community hold the belief that their abilities are limited. That school is about discovering these limits, and working out what they can and can't do. They are not creators but discoverers of their abilities.

Nurturing a growth mindset means developing an understanding that we do not *discover* our abilities, we *create* them. We do not work out where we fit in the world; rather, through our efforts we become the person we want or need to be in the world.

To change these beliefs I introduce you to the Mindset Continuum. I show you how we 'nudge' our community and our policies to create growth mindset movers, which move students along this continuum and nurture an increasingly growth-oriented mindset.

Developing a more growth-oriented mindset in students affects not just their learning behaviours – it impacts their motivation, aspirations and agency in the world. Importantly, it results in learners who are more willing and able to engage in the learning process, and that makes teachers' lives better, while at the same time it becomes easier to achieve both our short-term outcomes and our long-term educational goals.

All of this makes our work with growth mindset the foundation of our learning community. When we invest in creating a culture that nurtures a growth mindset, everything we do to create skilful learners becomes easier.

So let's begin to build the foundation of our learning community.

Chapter 3
Your autopilot for learning

Making productive learning behaviours automatic.

YOUR MINDSET

Stanford Professor Carol Dweck defines mindset as a person's beliefs about their ability to change their most basic characteristics, like their talents, abilities and intelligence. These are some of our most deeply held, and often unexamined, beliefs, and they powerfully influence many of our day-to-day learning behaviours. Channelled and guided correctly, mindset forms the foundation of our learning community.

> 66 Channelled and guided correctly, mindset forms the foundation of our learning community.

The reason mindset is so powerful is that it works like an autopilot for learning. Which is a very good thing ... most of the time. Let me explain.

I was on a plane recently, flying from Melbourne to Singapore to run some workshops. Traveling at around 900km/h at an altitude of around 10km is pretty crazy when you stop to think about it. But I felt pretty safe knowing that an experienced pilot was flying the plane. They had everything in hand. I could relax.

Except that wasn't true. It turns out that pilots are rarely flying the plane.

It might surprise you to know that for up to 98% of a flight it's the autopilot doing the flying. The autopilot is sensing the environment, making decisions and responding in line with its programming. It's quietly making all the decisions in the background. Most of the time, the pilot will be unaware of the actions the autopilot is taking.

A change in altitude detected? The autopilot adjusts to maintain altitude. A change in wind direction has altered the course of the plane? The autopilot adjusts to maintain the correct heading. Ice on the wings? The autopilot turns on the de-icing mechanism. The autopilot makes reliable, predictable and accurate decisions, unobtrusively guiding most of the plane's actions.

The autopilot doesn't check in with the pilot before making a decision. It doesn't ask if it's making the right decision. It relies on its programming and just does it. The pilot only notices the plane staying on course. The autopilot has been programmed to make the right decisions. It can be relied on.

Of course, the pilot can step in and override the autopilot, making a different decision in the moment. But it's important to note that intervening doesn't change the autopilot. It only changes that one decision. The next time the same circumstances come up, the autopilot will go back to its default. If you *regularly* want a different action, you have to change the autopilot's programming.

Your mindset is a lot like your own personal autopilot for learning. The plane's autopilot is a program that guides its flight behaviours. A learner's mindset guides their learning behaviours. And like an autopilot, your mindset does this easily and automatically, without you even noticing.

Mindset matters

How do you respond in the moment when you make a mistake? Do you hide or learn from it? Your mindset decides. How do you feel when your teacher is providing feedback? Do you feel criticised or take the feedback on board constructively? Your mindset drives those emotions. When you're lying in bed at night dreaming up what your future could look like, are your dreams aspirational or limited? Your mindset writes the script.

In your learning community, how would you like your learners' mindsets guiding their default actions? Would you want them to hide from mistakes, or learn from them? Feel criticised by feedback, or act on it? Would you want them to lead aspirational lives, or limited ones? These are just some ways learners' mindsets are affecting learning in your school today.

BELIEFS DRIVE BEHAVIOURS

As a leader of a learning community, it's critical you understand the beliefs that are driving learners' behaviours in your school. You will be much better placed to change students' mindsets when you can deeply empathise with their beliefs. When you can see the world through your students' eyes and recognise how, from their perspective, their actions make perfect sense. This understanding will position you to implement practices that effectively change behaviour and drive a culture of growth.

The fixed mindset – discovering your abilities

Take a moment now to see the world through the eyes of a student with a fixed mindset. Recognise how their autopilot is programmed. Remember, your mindset silently guides your actions without you noticing. It's not a conscious choice, so truly seeing the world through a different filter can be both challenging and powerful.

As a person with a fixed mindset, your autopilot is based on the belief that your most basic characteristics – such as your talents, abilities and intelligence – are fixed and unchangeable. You were born with certain abilities. These are different to other people's abilities. This means you have fixed limits. There are some things you are good at. Some things you aren't. Things you are good at come easily and naturally. In any domain or task there are people in the world who are better at it than you, and always will be, and there are people in the world you have superior abilities to.

With your fixed mindset autopilot running, this is how you see the world.

What is learning?

Learning is about discovering what your abilities are. You come to school and wonder *if* you'll be able to succeed. That you 'learn a little each day' means you are discovering a little more about yourself. You spend your life looking inwards, asking, 'who am I?' and 'what can I do?'

What is schooling about?

The purpose of school is diagnostic. To find out what you're good at. To discover your limits and to direct you towards the type of (limited) life you're best suited to. Eventually, school will tell you what you're able to do with your life. Your choices are limited, some people's more than others. School will eventually tell you where you 'fit in'.

What is potential?

Your potential is the best you can be. It's something to be achieved, but is never exceeded. Your one great hope is you will discover some untapped potential within you, some special talent or ability that will offer you close to effortless success at what you're 'meant to be'.

What does it mean to be good at something?

To be good at something means you have natural ability. It makes sense to ask, 'am I a leader?' before you take on a leadership role. Or to ask, 'am I good at maths?' before you try to solve a maths problem. You believe people spend time on the things they are good at. Not that you get good at things you spend your time on.

Indicators of a fixed mindset

Let's see how these fixed beliefs logically, sensibly and automatically influence the way learners engage in the learning process. How a fixed mindset autopilot works.

Avoids challenges

If you have a fixed mindset, a challenge is simply an opportunity to fail. A failure reveals your lack of abilities. It defines you. So from this perspective challenges are best avoided, particularly if any failure will become known to others.

Dweck notes that students who are labelled and identified as 'being' smart (or clever, or gifted, or musical, and the like) will frequently avoid challenges. From their perspective, they have everything to lose and nothing to gain from a challenge. If they succeed, they have only confirmed they are still smart. Nothing has changed. But if they fail, suddenly they are no longer smart. Their entire identity is threatened. So from their fixed perspective, it's much safer to avoid that judgement.

Similarly, students who believe they have discovered their limits will quickly identify challenges that are beyond their ability and take action to avoid what they perceive as inevitable failure. For example, if they believe they aren't smart enough, or they aren't artistic, they will avoid challenges that require them to be smart or artistic. (We explore how this belief keeps students in their comfort zone in chapter 9.)

Gives up easily

For someone with a fixed mindset, their fixed abilities mean something that is hard today will always be hard. It never gets easier. So as soon as things get difficult, it makes sense to give up. Why struggle and waste resources on something you can't do?

Worse still, in their minds, if the current level of challenge is hard, the next level is going to be even harder. The level after that is going to be harder still! Struggle is a sign they are approaching their limits and they should stop. Unfortunately, schools often reinforce this idea of increasing struggle when we tell students things like, 'If you think this is hard, just wait until next year, then it gets *really* hard.'

By giving up at the first sign of struggle, their life becomes about the path of least resistance. They search for the easy tasks. They thrive on doing things they find easy.

Dislikes effort

For someone with a fixed mindset, effort is a sign of weakness and deficit. They believe people who have abilities are capable of almost effortless performance. So any effort they have to put in is a sign they lack abilities. Effort is the necessary evil to overcome deficits.

Unfortunately, many of the strategies for growth mindset that have focused on 'praising effort' have missed the mark. After all, why would you focus on and praise someone for something they think is bad? In the ears of the student with a fixed mindset phrases like 'great effort' and 'you've really worked hard today' sound like 'you must be stupid, or you wouldn't need to work so hard'.

This highlights that learners' beliefs not only direct their actions but also how they interpret the actions of others – automatically. The teacher who said 'great effort' did not intend for the student to hear 'you must be stupid if you need to work that hard'. But through the filter of fixed beliefs, that might be what the student hears.

Avoids mistakes and ignores feedback

Students with a fixed mindset will ignore feedback. Not because they are being uncooperative or defiant, but simply because they see feedback as not being helpful. If they could have done it, they would have. Any critical or constructive feedback a teacher might offer on how to improve is seen as a way of pointing out their deficits.

They view mistakes similarly. If they had the ability, they wouldn't have made the mistake. The mistake is proof of their lack of ability, and is better avoided, hidden or ignored, lest others identify their limitations.

Someone with a fixed mindset may perceive an offer of help as evidence that they *need* help – another sign of lack of ability. Teachers often experience this in classrooms when students see the need to ask questions or to ask for help as another (public) indicator that they lack certain abilities.

Is threatened by the success of others

The success of others threatens someone with a fixed mindset. Everything someone else can do simply highlights what they can't. For them, life is about proving themselves. Competition and comparisons are a way of working out who's got more talent or ability. So another person's success is their loss. We see more of this idea when we examine how the differing mindsets of John McEnroe and Roger Federer led them to respond to the success of others in very different ways in the next chapter.

It is not a fixed mindset world

Remember, from the fixed mindset perspective students aren't choosing these behaviours – their autopilot is producing them. It's their default setting. Behaving this way just makes sense. And to be fair, if we lived in a fixed mindset world, where abilities were fixed or limited at birth, these would all be reasonable behaviours we should encourage in schools.

In that world, the role of schooling should be diagnostic – to work out which abilities students have and which they don't have. To find roles in society that each student is suited to. Potential would be something to be identified, and by accurately identifying each student's potential, we'd be saving them from the inevitable disappointment and failure of setting their sights too high.

In the fixed mindset world, school would teach students they have limited agency. That there are some things forever beyond their abilities and they'll be forever powerless to influence, and to get used to a life within those limits. Recognising this, it would become the socially responsible thing to protect these vulnerable people from the challenges of the world.

The growth mindset – creating your abilities

Now take a moment to see the world through the autopilot of the growth mindset. Try to feel the consistency. Try to recognise how the growth mindset beliefs lead naturally and easily to more productive learning behaviours. How differently you see the world when your autopilot is set to growth.

As a person with a growth mindset you understand you can change your talents, abilities and even your intelligence. You weren't born with any special abilities, other than your ability to create new abilities. Your life and efforts to this moment have created who you are. Sometimes this creation was intentional, other times it was incidental.

There are limits to the abilities you have today, but no limits to the abilities you can create in the future. As the creator of your abilities, given time you can become good at pretty much anything. But achieving that growth isn't free. You understand growth takes effort. You recognise people are different to each other, with unique abilities, but understand this is because each has invested their efforts to develop their unique abilities.

Now, ask yourself the same four questions as you did above.

What is learning?

Learning is about creating. It's a process for developing new abilities. It is your greatest asset in facing a challenging world.

What is schooling about?

School is a process of first gaining basic abilities, and then providing challenging opportunities to develop the talents and abilities you want, or need, so you can live the life you choose. Learning opens up your choices in life.

What is potential?

Potential is something you can create. You have no special abilities locked away inside you. You can work daily to the maximum of your current abilities and potential, and seek to increase them. There is no limit to your potential, other than the opportunity to engage in the type of practice that creates it.

What does it mean to be good at something?

To be good at something means you've invested significant time and resources into developing talents and abilities. If you want to be good at something, you need to decide if you're prepared to invest your limited time and energy. Other than access to the resources that might help you develop those abilities, there's nothing about who you are that stops you from getting good at anything.

Indicators of a growth mindset

Now consider how these growth beliefs logically, sensibly and automatically influence the way learners engage in the learning process, but this time in a much more positive way. How the growth mindset autopilot works.

Embraces challenges

Someone with a growth mindset recognises challenges as the pathway to growth. Challenges drive improvement. They help you get better. So they are to be pursued and embraced.

People with a growth mindset understand you can do easy things all day. They'll keep you busy. But a day spent doing easy things doesn't help them achieve the growth that just one truly challenging thing will. Why would you choose to get busy when you can choose to get better?

Demonstrates persistence

Someone with a growth mindset expects their efforts to be rewarded with eventual mastery, so they are more persistent.

Unlike the person with a fixed mindset who sees challenges getting harder and harder, someone with a growth mindset understands that there is nothing inherently 'hard' about any challenge. Hard is a relative term. We only find something hard when we don't currently have the abilities to master it. The solution is to develop those abilities, and then the things that were hard will become easy.

NUDGE

IT'S ONLY EVER HARD. NEVER HARDER.

Values effort

Someone with a growth mindset understands that effort is the currency of growth. It's not the necessary evil that makes up for lack of ability, it is the essential element that, when invested correctly, leads to growth.

Someone with a growth mindset is more focused on effort and growth than standards. They recognise that effort increases their abilities. So their best is only their best if you measure by yesterday's standards. With further effort their best will become their second best. The effort is what allowed them to achieve their current standard, and what promises them further growth.

Rather than seeing 'effortless performance' as the goal, they understand it takes a lot of effort to make something look effortless.

Seeks feedback and learns from mistakes

For someone with a growth mindset, feedback and mistakes are valuable sources of information. They understand that 'what got them here won't get them there', so they are looking for the information they need to reach the next standard. They focus not just on what they are learning, but also on how they are learning. They critically reflect on their own learning behaviours to continuously improve and develop.

For someone with a growth mindset, mistakes are not judgement, they are information. Feedback isn't criticism, it's helpful. And they welcome offers of help as yet another source of information, a way to help them gain new abilities.

A growth mindset helps you understand that any failure you might experience when taking on a challenge is temporary. It only defines where you are up to, not who you are. It's an experience to draw information from to lead you forward, not an experience that defines you.

Celebrates the success of others

Someone with a growth mindset is quick to celebrate the success of others. When they see others succeed, they see evidence of effort and the growth it brings. They recognise that behind that momentary success was a backstory of growth. There has been a journey of creating new abilities. They value the other person's success as evidence that sustained effort can make what seems impossible now, possible in the future.

NUDGE

SPECIALISATION, NOT CATEGORISATION.

Other people's success illustrates what is possible. They might not want to do what the other person has achieved. They might be in an entirely different field.

But knowing that the other person started as a beginner, and could grow to achieve their goals, reinforces they can grow and achieve their own goals.

It is a growth mindset world

Seeing the world through the autopilot of a growth mindset means the behaviours above just make sense. They become your default setting. You don't have to tell yourself 'mistakes help me learn', because the thought that they reflect poorly on you doesn't occur to you in the first place. You don't have to prepare yourself to receive feedback constructively, because you automatically see it as potentially useful information. There's no need to feel less because of other people's successes – those successes naturally inspire you by reaffirming what can be achieved.

Of course the beauty of the growth mindset is that it isn't just a useful set of beliefs. It's a reflection of the way the world works. As humans our abilities aren't fixed. We are capable of growth.

Dweck refers to the growth mindset as the *belief* in your ability to change your most basic characteristics. I'd go further. I'd suggest that a growth mindset is better described as the *understanding* of your ability to develop your most basic characteristics. The difference between a belief and understanding is evidence.

The research underpinning all this work is our brain's capacity to rewire itself, referred to as 'neuroplasticity'. This capacity allows us to change our brain and create abilities that were not present before. We don't discover new abilities, we create them. In the words of psychologist Anders Ericsson, 'Learning is not a way of reaching your potential, it's a way of building it.' Without this capacity we really would live in a fixed mindset world.

Moreover, today we understand, better than ever, how learners must engage in the learning process to create these new abilities. We recognise the importance of identifying the right level of challenge to produce this change. We understand the behaviours and types of practice that produce this change. We know how to maximise this growth. The more students understand themselves as learners, the more they develop a growth mindset, and the more willingly and more effectively they can engage in the learning process.

A growth mindset forms the foundation of our learning community. It reflects every individual's understanding of themselves as a learner. A growth mindset makes productive learning behaviour everybody's default setting, and makes it easier to be an effective learner than to not be an effective learner.

> 66 A growth mindset makes productive learning behaviour everybody's default setting, and makes it easier to be an effective learner than to not be an effective learner.

The influence of a growth mindset extends well beyond effective learning. It impacts motivation, choice and agency too. Because it is a reflection of our human capacity to grow, when we act out of a growth mindset we tend to live more fulfilling lives, and move through life with less friction. In the next chapter we'll see how some of your toughest motivation issues are probably due to mindset, and how a growth mindset helps to raise the aspirations of all students.

Chapter 4
It's about having a choice

> There's a big difference between not getting
> better at something because you don't want to and
> not getting better at something because you
> don't believe you can.

As we seek to build a learning community that increases aspirations and opportunities for students, our work with mindsets takes on new importance. Yes, a growth mindset will help students to better engage in the learning process and reach their short-term learning outcomes, but even more importantly, it's critical for achieving our long-term educational goals.

Our mindsets impact so many elements of our lives: they affect our motivation, and how we see our choices in life and, therefore, our agency in the world. Let's take a moment to explore some of the surprising ways mindsets are influencing your learners every day.

UNMOTIVATED ... OR DEMOTIVATED?

Some students appear to just not want to learn. They seem stubbornly unmotivated and resistant to our attempts to make school interesting.

They have disengaged. As teachers, these students frustrate us, sapping our time and energy as we try – often unsuccessfully – to engage them. As leaders, we lament that these students are throwing away opportunities for growth and limiting their options in life.

While this disconnecting from learning can be the result of several factors, it is often another symptom of a fixed mindset. To determine if it's a mindset issue, the question we need to ask is, are students *unmotivated* or have they been *demotivated*?

Let me tell you a story to explain the difference.

My demotivating music experience

I had my first ever music lesson in year seven, and I didn't know what to expect. Within a few minutes of the class starting, I was blown away. The teacher had set up three drum kits in the middle of the room. There were bongos on the floor, and every table had a set of drumsticks. It was loud. It was fun. It only took a few minutes before the class had some basic rhythms going. I was engaged. I wanted to learn more. I even briefly considered a career as a drummer. I was certainly an interested and motivated learner!

Towards the end of the class, the teacher gathered us together and put a rhythm on the board. He said, 'I want to see who can do this'. Pay close attention to those words. Do you hear how they subtly imply our abilities were being tested? We'll come back to those words in a moment.

The rhythm involved doing something different with each hand. A 'Ta, Ta, TiTi' on one hand, and a 'TiTi, Ta, Ta' on the other. As a class, we all tried – and we all failed! It was a bit like trying to simultaneously rub your stomach and pat your head. We all got out of sync and it sounded awful. We had a bit of a laugh and left.

But I was still keen. I was still interested and motivated to learn to play the drums, so I went home and practised. It took several hours and many failures, but eventually I worked out a strategy to help me play that rhythm.

The next time I saw the music teacher was in the yard, and I went up to him and performed the rhythm – perfectly. I still remember his face.

His look of surprise, even a bit of wonder. With a smile he asked me how I'd done it. And I told him about the hours of practice, the mistakes and the work I'd put into it. And I watched his expression drop as he said, 'Oh … so you can't *really* do it then.'

My heart sank.

In his mind, there were two types of people. Those who could do it, easily and naturally. And those who had to work hard *instead*. I'd just been found out as the latter. I'd discovered my hard work was a sign of my lack of ability, and that my future as a drummer would be characterised by struggle and mistakes. It felt so unfair that, apparently, there were people who could do it effortlessly. I wanted to do it effortlessly.

So where do you think I sat in the next music lesson? The back of the room where I could hide. How many questions did I ask? None. They'd only highlight I didn't know something. How many times did I volunteer to try something? None. It would just prove I wasn't good at it. How much of the lesson did I listen to? Not much. Real drummers didn't need lots of instruction.

From that point, every attempt the teacher made to make the class more interesting, relevant or engaging didn't influence me. Every time he encouraged me to put in some more effort only served to discourage me. As far as I was concerned, if I wasn't musical, there was no point in doing music. It would be a waste of my time and effort.

And once I'd decided I wasn't musical, it became a self-fulfilling prophecy. My lack of engagement meant I didn't improve and my lack of improvement confirmed I wasn't musical.

There seemed to be nothing my teachers could do that would re-engage me in music – and they tried. I was hard work to have in a music classroom. To avoid showing that I couldn't do music, I did other things instead. I became disruptive. I didn't complete assignments or homework (why would I? I'd only fail anyway), so teachers needed to chase me up constantly to complete things. My mindset made teaching me hard work.

To be clear, it's not that I wasn't interested in drumming or music. I was. I loved the school musicals, and I actually admired the people who 'had musical abilities'. And although there were plenty of musical opportunities in the school – there was an environment to act – I never auditioned for the school play or asked to learn an instrument. I simply couldn't see a path that would lead me to becoming musical.

And it's not that I decided to be difficult because I didn't like music. It was that I knew I couldn't be good at music, so there was no point in trying.

On my report, the teacher wrote that I lacked interest and motivation in music. And I'm sure from his perspective I appeared unmotivated. But that wasn't accurate. I wasn't unmotivated. If I had simply lacked motivation, my teachers could have engaged me with interesting, relevant and enjoyable lessons. Actually, it felt like I left that first drumming lesson with enough motivation to last a lifetime!

The problem was that I had been demotivated. The experience had led me to believe my efforts to learn music would inevitably go unrewarded. I would struggle, and fail. I wasn't musical. I didn't really have the choice to learn music.

How many students in your school feel this way about music? Or maths? Or some other aspect of school? How often do you hear, 'I'm just not good at … ', or, 'I'm not smart enough to … '?

Today, my beliefs have changed, and I understand I could develop my musical abilities. And today I *choose* not to develop those abilities. Instead, I choose to work with educators to create true learning communities, and make the world a more thoughtful place. The difference is that today I know I have a choice. When I was in high school I didn't believe I had a choice.

The ability to recognise the choices we have in life matters more than motivation.

FIXED BELIEFS CREATE BOUNDARIES

And here we return to the issue I raised earlier. I wasn't *deciding* not to become a drummer. The issue is that I believed *I didn't have that choice*. Because I held the fixed belief that some people were simply 'musical' and I wasn't one of them, my choices and aspirations were limited. At its core, the fixed mindset is a set of self-limiting beliefs that tell us we can't change – at least, not much. For students with a fixed mindset, these beliefs create boundaries they believe they'll never be able to overcome. The impact extends well beyond the classroom, affecting the way students see their future.

Are you asking the right question?

I was coaching a principal recently who was telling me about how concerned she was that so many of her students were making what she considered to be poor choices. She'd worked hard to ensure there was a broad selection of traditional academic subjects and pathways into apprenticeships and work for her students to choose from. But her students didn't seem interested. They weren't taking advantage of the opportunities.

She felt many students had very limited aspirations in life. They were accepting the easy path, instead of challenging themselves to do better. Teachers were working hard to encourage students and provide support, but they just weren't responding.

Why were they making such poor choices?

I explained that from the perspective of the students' mindsets, asking why students were making poor choices might be the wrong question. I explained that students with a fixed mindset see themselves as limited by who they are today. *You are who you are. It's not your fault, there's no-one to blame, it's just the way you are. You can't ever expect to do better.*

The principal felt her students had many options to choose from – and on paper they did. But for many students, they weren't choices they believed they could make – like me with the drumming. They didn't 'have the required abilities', they weren't 'the right type of person', they weren't 'cut out for' those opportunities.

The moment of clarity for this principal came when she understood she had been asking the wrong question. Her students weren't making poor choices. In fact, they weren't making a choice at all. The problem she faced was that many of her students didn't believe they had the choice in the first place.

The question that needed to be asked was, why didn't these students see the choice? The problem to be solved wasn't how to create more choices, or how to make the choices more attractive. It was how to create a learning community that ensures students recognise they *can make those choices*.

Of course, once they understand they do have a choice, learners won't always make the choices we'd hope. However, we need to remember that in terms of our long-term educational goals, there is a big difference between students not getting better at something *because they don't want to* and not getting better at something because *they don't believe they can*. And that difference is the capacity to fully exercise their free will.

Free will is perhaps one of the greatest capacities we have as humans. The ability to fully exercise our free will is a fundamental part of leading a rich and fulfilling life. Without it, we become victims of our circumstances, frustrated by our inability to act in the world. Unfortunately, too many of our students see their choices in life, their capacity to exercise their free will, as limited.

As a leader seeking to maximise the aspirations and opportunities of learners, we must build our learning community on a foundation of a growth mindset. Without this, many students will believe there are some choices in life, some solutions to challenges and areas of growth or achievement, that simply aren't open to them.

Fully recognising our capacity to exercise our free will and choosing to become the person we want, or need, to be can also profoundly change the way we interact with the world. It allows us to step back from competition and conflict, to disengage from comparisons and become far more collaborative, altruistic and graceful in the way we participate in the world.

McENROE VS FEDERER – A BATTLE OF MINDSETS

Dweck uses the example of John McEnroe as someone with a fixed mindset. McEnroe was undoubtedly one of the greats of the game of tennis, but he exhibited many of the behaviours of someone with a fixed mindset.

McEnroe saw the need to practice, and the effort required, as a weakness. He would close courts so people couldn't see him practice. When he lost, he'd throw tantrums and assign blame to the ball boy, the umpire, the noise in the crowd – anyone but himself. He was the greatest, but when he lost and didn't appear to be the greatest, it wasn't his fault.

For McEnroe, tennis was a way of proving himself. His identity rested on him being the best. And despite his success on the court, these beliefs led to a degree of friction in his life that we wouldn't wish on our students.

Compare McEnroe's story to this quote from another tennis great, Roger Federer.

> I always question myself in the best of times. When I'm world number 1 for many months in a row, I'm asking, 'What can I improve. What do I need to do to change?'
>
> If you don't do anything, or you just do the same thing over and over, you stay the same. Staying the same means going backwards.
>
> It's important for me to actually hear criticism sometimes.
>
> That's what makes me a better player.

I love this quote. It reflects so much of what it means to have a growth mindset.

When Federer says 'staying the same means going backwards', he's recognising that everyone is getting better. If he doesn't improve, others will pass him. He understands being the world's best is a recognition of *where* he is, not *who* he is.

Federer is constantly asking what he can do to continue to improve. He recognises the need for practice and feedback to get the information he needs to grow.

But most of all, I love the way he says all of that is 'what makes me a better player'. He doesn't say 'that's what makes me the best player in the world'. He says that's what makes him a *better* player. That focus on growth, improvement, on pushing himself, on being a better player, might eventually make him the best, but it's being a better player that drives him.

That's what a growth mindset really looks like. It's not just about learning. It allows you to be a better person.

A growth mindset completely changes your view on competition and loss. Compare Federer's response to losing to McEnroe's. When Federer loses he is quick to congratulate the other player. To recognise and applaud the work they've put into their game. And if you watch closely, he'll often thank his opponent. Not for beating him, but for providing the challenge that highlighted areas of his game that need to be improved. Federer knows he can beat lesser players 6-0, 6-0, 6-0 every day of the week and learn nothing about how to become a better player. When someone pushes him to the limits or beats him, he can learn something about how to improve.

> " That's what a growth mindset really looks like. It's not just about learning. It allows you to be a better person.

Federer isn't interested in the fixed mindset idea of *proving* himself. He doesn't have the angst and behaviours associated with needing to 'be the best'. He's interested in *improving* himself. That comes from an understanding and appreciation of what it takes to get better. It allows Federer to be humble, gracious and respectful in his approach to competition.

This tweet to Rafael Nadal after Nadal's 2022 Australian Open win illustrates how Federer's growth mindset influences how he sees the world.

> What a match! To my friend and great rival Rafael Nadal. Heartfelt congratulations on becoming the first man to win 21 grand slam

singles titles. A few months ago we were joking about both being on crutches. Amazing. Never underestimate a great champion. Your incredible work ethic, dedication and fighting spirit are an inspiration to me and countless others around the world. I am proud to share this era with you and honored to play a role in pushing you to achieve more. As you have done for me the past 18 years. I am sure you have more achievements ahead of you but for now enjoy this one!

Notice how Federer's focus is on Nadal's backstory. It's on the dedication, improvement and work ethic that led to this outstanding achievement. And it's about how they have pushed each other to achieve more.

There's not a word of comparison. Not a note of needing to prove anything. Just recognition and admiration for the consistent growth that's led to being the first person to win 21 grand slams. The achievement of the moment, winning the Australian Open, is secondary to what the achievement represents.

This isn't simply being a good sportsman. It's genuine. The words in that tweet came as much from his growth mindset autopilot as McEnroe's racquet smashing came his fixed mindset autopilot.

This is why I believe people like Federer who truly embrace a growth mindset no longer compete, at least not in the sense that most of us think about competition. Sure, they are on the circuit, playing matches and winning. But I believe they are engaging in something I call 'coopertition'.

Coopertition is a word I've made up. It means to compete with someone to create a challenge that identifies areas for personal growth and improvement. It's a strategy that some of the most effective learners use to get into their learning zone (see chapter 9 for more) to achieve more growth.

Think of coopertition like a friendly argument. You're not doing it to win or to prove who's right or who's better. You're doing it so you can come to a better understanding and so you both improve. It's a type of collaborative competition focused on growth, not winning. The competition is against the previous version of yourself and not the other person. This is part of the growth culture that defines a strong learning community, and something we explore later.

For Federer and Nadal, competition isn't a way of proving themselves. It's a means of improving themselves.

GROWTH MINDSET – UNDERSTANDING YOURSELF AS A LEARNER

A growth mindset is not just a good thing to have to do well at school. It's a reflection of what it means to be human and to exercise your free will. It's an understanding of your capacity to change yourself. A recognition that you have the power to become whoever you want or need to be in the world. This insight enables you to take part in the world in a much more positive way. To free yourself of comparison and the need to prove yourself. It allows you to be much more humble and gracious, and to move through life with less friction.

> ❝ ... if the entire school community is operating with a growth mindset, it would be hard work not to achieve your long-term educational goals.

As a leader of a true learning community, you are seeking to ensure your students lead rich and fulfilling lives – not simply pass their exams. A growth mindset leads students not only to adopt the behaviours that help them pass their exams, it ensures they can exercise their free will, raising their aspirations and leading them to recognise choices that maximise their opportunities in life.

But it's not all about the students. When students have a growth mindset, teachers' lives are easier too. They can spend less time trying to engage and motivate the demotivated students. When students recognise their capacity to grow, they automatically engage in the behaviours that lead to growth.

In short, a growth mindset magnifies your impact as a school leader. When students and teachers are working from a default growth mindset it makes it easier to achieve your goals – in fact, if the entire school community is operating with a growth mindset, it would be hard work not to achieve your long-term educational goals.

The question is then, when it comes to developing a growth mindset, what works, and what doesn't? That's the topic of the next chapter.

Chapter 5
Changing mindsets: a nudge in the right direction

Nurturing a more growth-oriented mindset needs a nudge in the right direction.

The way your mindset guides your learning behaviours is critically important. In her book *Mindset: The new psychology of success*, Dweck documents several decades of research that illustrates the effects – both positive and negative – these beliefs can have on students' attitudes towards learning. There is now an overwhelming body of evidence to show the profound effect mindsets have on students' short- and long-term success.

But it turns out that *changing* mindsets isn't easy. In an interview with TES, Dweck acknowledges: 'There was evidence that growth mindset had been tested and shown to work in ways that were meaningful to students … but the evidence did not speak to how to implement it in the classroom … In the beginning we did not recognise the complexity of the implementation.'

The problem with implementation occurred when teachers took the idea of mindsets and started teaching *about* mindsets. Classroom walls were soon covered with 'grow your mindset' posters telling students what they should say and how to think. Teachers adopted numerous catchphrases. They indiscriminately 'praised effort', and choruses of 'not yet' filled classrooms. Essentially teachers told students what a growth mindset was and why it was important. They taught students what a person with a growth mindset thinks, says and does, and then essentially told students to 'do that'.

The results of these approaches were predictably underwhelming. Students developed what I refer to as a 'learned mindset'. They knew what someone with a growth mindset looked and sounded like. They could dutifully say 'not yet'. But like the pilot who steps in to override the plane's autopilot, there was a momentary change in behaviour but the underlying beliefs didn't change. Students quickly defaulted back to their autopilot.

Which is why, in most schools, growth mindsets became 'last year's initiative'. When there weren't quick and easy results and no other pathway presented itself, many schools moved on. But mindsets are too important to let become last year's initiative.

A better approach is needed.

It turns out that changing mindsets doesn't mean teaching *about* mindsets. It requires teaching *for* a growth mindset. We need an approach that changes students' underlying beliefs, their autopilot, and that means we need to look at mindsets in a completely new way.

The Mindset Continuum

The truth is that no-one really has a fixed mindset. Neither do they have a growth mindset. While thinking of mindsets as fixed or growth is useful for understanding their importance, it's not particularly helpful for the vital question of how to change mindsets. To understand how you go about changing a learner's mindset, you'll need a powerful new approach: the Mindset Continuum.

In the Mindset Continuum I've elaborated on Dweck's description of the fixed and growth mindset. I've taken the two extremes and filled in the gaps. It gives insight into the full spectrum between fixed and growth, describing both actions we observe and the underlying beliefs that drive them. In doing so, I add a richness to our understanding of mindsets, as well as offer a clear and practical route to nurturing a more growth-oriented mindset.

> 66 To understand how you go about changing a learner's mindset, you'll need a powerful new approach: the Mindset Continuum.

Take a moment now to review the Mindset Continuum, and ask yourself these questions:

- How accurately does the Mindset Continuum reflect your real-world observations of people's beliefs and actions?
- Where do you find yourself on the continuum? Are you at one extreme, or do you find your own mindset better described somewhere between the two extremes? What about your students?
- What are some of the experiences that might have left you with your current mindset?
- What are some of the questions you'd need answered to move you more towards the growth end of the continuum?

Download this infographic in full size from www.jamesanderson.com.au/mindset-continuum.

UNDERSTANDING MINDSET MOVERS

The world is not made up of people with fixed mindsets and others with growth mindsets. Nor do we have fixed mindset moments and growth mindset moments. Rather, we all fall somewhere between these two extremes. But why? Where do mindsets come from?

The Mindset Continuum

FIXED ⟵ ⟶ GROWTH

	FIXED	LOW GROWTH	MIXED	GROWTH	HIGH GROWTH
WORLD VIEW	Unchanging and unchangeable	Growth is very limited	Growth in a limited number of domains	Capable of significant growth	Understands they can change their most basic characteristics
CHALLENGES	Avoids challenges	Easy challenges	Prefers clear, immediate goals	Enjoys being challenged	Embraces challenges
DIFFICULTIES AND OBSTACLES	Gives up immediately	Tries for a while	Persists when seeing progress	Expects eventual mastery	Persists for long periods
EFFORT	Effort is associated with failure	Sustained effort is a bad thing	Effort is necessary	Effort is a good thing	Effort as path to mastery
FEEDBACK AND CRITICISM	Ignores useful negative feedback	Tends to focus on positive feedback	Formative feedback is seen as useful	Accepts and learns from feedback	Requests critical feedback
SUCCESS OF OTHERS	Feels threatened by comparisons to others	May mis-attribute success of others to luck or natural ability	Enjoys personal success	Finds lessons and inspiration in the success of others	Seeks out masters and experts in an effort to 'learn their secrets'
MAKING MISTAKES	Actively hides or ignores mistakes	Makes excuses for mistakes	Expects to make mistakes and understands mistakes can be corrected	Recognises mistakes are signposts for learning	Deliberately stretch themselves so errors have high learning potential
OFFERED HELP AND SUPPORT	Turns down help and support	Tolerates help when given	Accepts help and support when offered	Expects feedback and recognises it as desirable	Seeks out help and support

© James Anderson 2023

The short answer is our beliefs have built up slowly throughout our lives as we've experienced what I call 'mindset movers'. Mindset movers are the little messages we receive every day about our abilities, each one pushing us a little bit towards one end of the continuum or the other. Each message is either a growth mindset mover or a fixed mindset mover. Over time, these mindset movers write the program that becomes our autopilot. And because each person experiences different mindset movers, we end up with different mindsets.

> Mindset movers are the little messages we receive every day about our abilities, each one pushing us a little bit towards one end of the continuum or the other.

The story in chapter 4 about my experience learning the drums was a powerful fixed mindset mover. But it wasn't the first time I'd heard that fixed message. Rather, the impact of that experience was the culmination of many fixed mindset movers I'd experienced throughout my life.

For example, as a child, my parents encouraged me to try different activities. They took me to art classes, music classes, athletics, science activities and more. My parents would say things like, 'Go on. Give it a go. You never know, you might be good at it!'

When I heard that, some part of me registered I was being tested to see if I could do it. I was about to find out if I was the type of person who was naturally 'good at it' or not. They could have created a growth mindset mover by saying, 'Give it a go, you might enjoy it and decide it's something you want to invest your time in getting good at', but they didn't.

Throughout primary school, teachers grouped my classmates and me into 'ability groups'. I learned that part of the game of school was to find out what group you were in. Was I one of the kids who belonged in the top group? Or did I belong in a different group? Teachers could have explained that being placed in the high-ability group was a result of what each student had done prior to being placed in that group. They could have said that the high-ability group at this year level was roughly the same standard as the low-ability group the year above. But they didn't. They just told us what group we *belonged* to.

Some students apparently just naturally belonged in the 'high-ability' group. You know the ones I'm taking about. The smart kids. If you belonged to that group you could aspire to be a doctor, or to lead a business, or something else like that. Other students, like me, would have to set their sights a bit lower. So while I understood we were all learning, I also believed there were limits to *my* learning. There were some things that would always be too hard for me, but not for some of my classmates.

When some students appeared to be faster learners, there was no explanation given. They were 'just like that'. And I wasn't. I had to work harder for the same result. The teacher could have explained that learning was a skill. That my peers' ability to get more out of every learning situation was because they'd developed that skill. They could have shown me how to develop that skill, too. But they didn't.

I remember one day I was in a maths lesson and I got the answers really quickly. The teacher was so surprised, and so full of praise for how well I had done. I didn't want to tell her that the only reason I was good at it was because my older brother had taught me how to do it at home. It was much better to just be good at it. To appear as though I could do it easily was a prize, rather than to tell her I'd already done the work at home. Inside, I felt like learning it at home was cheating.

Later, as I began my career as a teacher, I fell victim to a personality test. A consultant came along with a questionnaire. I sat at the computer and answered a series of questions. They then identified me as a particular type. They labelled me as a red LMPT. As that type of person, I was 'suited to' or 'cut out for' certain roles. Those roles would be easy for me. But other roles would require extra struggle and effort – I wasn't suited to those roles and I was encouraged to follow a career path I was suited to. Apparently, my options in life were limited by my 'type'.

Our lives, and the lives of our students, are full of these types of experiences – the things we see, hear and share every day that form part of the culture of our community, each one carrying with it a brief message about our abilities, or supposed lack thereof. Most of the time we don't even notice them.

Where a person finds themselves on the Mindset Continuum is the total of all the mindset movers they have experienced in their life. Some have pushed them towards the growth end of the continuum, some towards the fixed end. Some have had large influences, others smaller influences. The overall impact of these mindset movers has left each member of your school community with the mindset you observe today.

Any one experience on its own may seem inconsequential, but cumulatively they are powerful. Mindset movers shape our mindset. This is why a more strategic and long-term approach to changing students' mindsets is needed. Our school environment is full of mindset movers. Some of them are growth mindset movers; some of them fixed mindset movers. To consistently create more growth-oriented mindsets in our community and make it easier to achieve the educational outcomes we seek, we need to fill our school environment with growth mindset movers.

Perhaps the greatest source of mindset movers in your school will be your teachers. Every day, teachers are creating mindset movers through what they say, what they do and how they do it. Unfortunately, not all of these are growth mindset movers. Even the most well-intentioned teacher can create fixed mindset movers. This is because of the influence of the false mindset.

THE FALSE MINDSET

Let me tell you a story that illustrates how and why well-meaning teachers unintentionally create fixed mindset movers, and why the Mindset Continuum is central to both addressing this problem and reshaping the way we work with mindsets.

I was recently giving a lively keynote to a large group of school leaders in Wellington. I took them on the same journey you experienced in chapter 3. I described the beliefs and symptoms of students with a fixed mindset. As I looked out across the audience, I saw many knowing nods of agreement. There was a recognition in the room that these leaders had plenty of students who behaved like that, which was working against them achieving their educational goals. Mindset was clearly a genuine issue for them.

I showed the stark contrast between the fixed mindset and the beliefs and behaviours of the student with a growth mindset. I explained that while someone with a fixed mindset will avoid challenges, someone with a growth mindset will embrace them. This generated a murmur of approval. I described how someone with a fixed mindset saw effort as a bad thing, associated with a lack of ability. But someone with a growth mindset saw it as the currency of growth. I illustrated why someone with a fixed mindset might avoid, or even hide, their mistakes, but someone with a growth mindset would try to learn from them. The murmurs rose to a buzz.

I asked these 300 school leaders if they'd rather have students with a fixed mindset or a growth mindset in their schools, and if it would help them reach their educational goals for their community if their students had a growth mindset. Unsurprisingly, I received a unanimous response. Every school leader in that room, and every school leader I've ever worked with, would rather see the behaviours associated with a growth mindset than those associated with a fixed mindset.

Pivoting slightly, I explained that it wasn't just students who had mindsets. We all have them. Every student. Every parent. Every teacher. Even every school leader, including everyone in the room that day, has a mindset – their autopilot guiding their actions, unconsciously, every day.

So I asked the room, 'Given how important mindsets are, I'm curious to know, how many of you have a fixed mindset?' The group went silent. As I looked out across the room, I saw people looking down. A few people were having a chuckle at everyone's discomfort. Two or three brave leaders tentatively put up their hands, but not very high.

The problem I'd set up reflected the way mindset is portrayed and communicated throughout our community, including our classrooms and staffrooms. You've got a choice of two. You either have a fixed mindset – which is awful. Or a growth mindset – which is wonderful! Given this choice, nearly everyone in the room accurately recognised that they didn't have a fixed mindset, and if that was the case, they must have a growth mindset! The problem this creates is that once you have a growth mindset, there's apparently no further work required. And that's exactly the logic that has led to the *false mindset*. (The false mindset was originally described by Dweck and her colleague Susan Mackie.)

We can see a false mindset in someone who intellectually understands fixed and growth mindsets. They may be the advocate for growth mindsets in your school and they'll adopt growth mindset strategies. But because they've *assumed* they have a growth mindset – and haven't deeply reflected on their own beliefs and how they act on autopilot – what they actually say and do in the classroom can fill it with fixed mindset movers.

For example, I worry about the number of teachers who, with good intention and in the belief they are nurturing a growth mindset, have adopted the strategy of 'praise effort'. Often, their good intentions are being driven by their own autopilot of their mindset. Instead of praising effort, they praise *struggling* students for effort. What children experience in the classroom is students who needed to put in more effort being praised and encouraged to do so. But the *real* rewards go to students who appear to achieve easily. Effort becomes the necessary evil that makes up for lack of ability, creating a fixed mindset mover.

The problem is that – like you and every other member of your school community – your teachers grew up with messages similar to the ones above. And so, as much as we might want them and advocate for them, we don't have growth mindsets ourselves. When we are unaware of that awkward fact, we end up with a false mindset. This leads well-intentioned teachers to create fixed mindset movers when they intend to create growth mindset movers.

Returning to the cognitive dissonance my audience was experiencing, I introduced them to the Mindset Continuum. I explained that none of them had a fixed mindset. There was a sigh of relief. Then I explained that none of them had a growth mindset either. They were a little less enthusiastic about this, but accepting nonetheless. Instead, they all fell somewhere along the Mindset Continuum.

I shared the continuum and invited them to reflect on the same questions I asked you above. I then asked those 300 school leaders from Wellington this question: 'How many of you would be prepared to admit you could be more growth-oriented in your views?'

Every. Hand. In. The. Room. Went. Up.

That's one of the greatest powers of the Mindset Continuum. It gives people permission to say, 'I don't have a fixed mindset. But I don't have a growth mindset either.' With that comes the recognition that there may be work to be done and that their current mindset, working quietly in the background, their autopilot, is likely to be generating fixed mindset movers in their school.

> ❝ As a school leader, the number one thing you can do to create more growth-oriented mindsets in your learners is to have the teachers and leaders in the school reflect on their own mindsets.

Recognising that nurturing a growth mindset is a process that takes time also helps our teachers reset their expectations for change. The Pinterest approach to growth mindset sets the expectation that our interventions would result in students 'having' a growth mindset. That was an impossible goal that set teachers up to fail and, when it wasn't achieved, led to schools dropping mindsets as 'last year's initiative'. The continuum helps us realise that our success with growth mindsets will be measured by how far students move along the continuum and how much more growth oriented they become.

As a school leader, the number one thing you can do to create more growth-oriented mindsets in your learners is to have the teachers and leaders in the school reflect on their own mindsets. The Mindset

Continuum helps leaders examine their own mindset, helps them recognise how their mindset is reflected in their actions towards others, and ask what they need to do to create a more growth-oriented mindset in themselves.

It's important to remember your teachers are well intentioned. They want to create growth mindset movers (just as you do). It's just that their default settings get in the way. So the strategy we adopt to help students, teachers and you overcome these default settings is to stop teaching *about* mindsets and instead teach *for* the development of more growth-oriented mindsets. To do this we need to give people's mindsets a nudge.

A NUDGE IN THE RIGHT DIRECTION

'Nudge' is a term that comes out of behavioural psychology. It's an intervention that gently steers individuals towards a desired action. Unlike catchphrases such as 'not yet' or rules like 'praise effort' that take a brute force approach to putting words into teachers' mouths and telling them what to do, nudges take a more subtle approach to gently guide you towards shaping a growth mindset mover.

The beauty of the nudges I've created for schools is they are short, simple and memorable – little reminders that help teachers overcome and gently reprogram their autopilots. A nudge helps you create a growth mindset mover when there's a risk you might unintentionally create a fixed mindset mover. It doesn't tell you what to say or do, rather it *shapes the message* that comes with that. It gently begins to rewrite the program that is your mindset.

For example, earlier I shared how my loving parents, who wanted the best for me, in an attempt to encourage me to try something new had said 'give it a go … you never know, you might be good at it'. Can you hear the discovery message contained in that? If I try, I might find out I'm good at it. There was a subtext behind the words that I didn't consciously recognise but it communicated the idea that learning was about discovering. Trying something new was a test to find out if I could do it. I'm sure that wasn't my parents' intention, but like our well-intentioned teachers, what they intend and what actually occurs are not always the same.

The nudge I've designed to help us create a growth mindset mover in this context is, 'Learning is about creating, not discovering'. This nudge helps us put a focus on growth and learning. Applying it to the words my parents used, we reframe the message to: 'Give it a go … you might enjoy it and decide it's something you want to get good at'.

The same nudge can be applied to my music teacher who said, 'I just want to see who can do this'. How many times are words like those repeated in your school every day? 'Who can do this?' Recognising the discovering message inherent in these words, the nudge of 'Learning is about creating, not discovering' might lead the teacher to rephrase this comment to, 'I want to see who's already learnt enough to be able to do this'.

The flexibility of the nudges means they can widely apply across your entire school community. They apply equally to the early, middle and senior years. They apply to different subject areas. They apply to the office staff. They apply to parents. They apply to teachers. And they apply to the leadership team. Importantly, they apply as much to the structures and policies you create as they do to the things you say. The way they'll be applied will be different in each context, but the result will be the same – the creation of a growth mindset mover that focuses on growth and learning, and a subtle rewriting of an autopilot for growth.

I've included examples of nudges throughout this book. The first time I mention a new nudge you'll find an image and QR code. If you'd like to know more about that nudge, just scan the code.

There is one nudge that rules them all, which we explore in the next chapter: 'All the value is in the backstory'.

Chapter 6
The value is in the backstory

Recognising that all the value is in the backstory is at the heart of developing a growth culture.

THE IMPORTANCE OF BACKSTORIES

There's one nudge, one key idea, that captures the essence of all the others. One nudge that, if you carry it with you and install it as part of your autopilot, will be more powerful than all the others. That nudge is the importance of backstories.

Let me tell you a story – possibly apocryphal – that beautifully illustrates the importance of the backstory. If you can carry the essence of this story with you and infuse it into your learning community, you will go a long way towards developing a culture of growth.

It was a warm day in Central Park, New York. Pablo Picasso was sitting quietly on a park bench enjoying the afternoon sun, sketchbook by his side.

A women recognised the famous artist and approached him. 'Picasso, I saw you sitting there and I just had to come over and speak to you. I've followed your work for many years. I've been to dozens of your exhibitions. Your art touches me in such a special way. You are an inspiration to me and so many others.

'I notice you have your sketchbook with you. I was wondering, if it's not too much trouble, if you could do a sketch for me?'

Picasso thanked the women for her kind words and graciously agreed to do a quick sketch. He took out his pencil, opened his sketchbook to a fresh page and began to draw. After about two minutes Picasso reviewed his work, and with a nod of satisfaction, carefully tore out the page and gave it to the women.

In awe, the women took the sketch from Picasso. 'Thank you. Thank you! This is incredible. I'll treasure this for the rest of my life.'

'You are most welcome,' Picasso responded. 'That will be twenty thousand dollars. Thank you very much.'

Shocked, it took the women a moment to respond. 'Twenty thousand dollars? Twenty *thousand*?!' Her mood changed and her voice rose. 'But, it only took you two minutes! How can you possibly charge twenty thousand dollars for two minutes of work?'

Picasso quietly and calmly responded, 'Ah ... I think you've misunderstood. You see, that sketch didn't take me two minutes. That sketch *took me a lifetime*.'

Picasso understood our key growth mindset message. He understood that the value was not in the two minutes spent sketching – the value was in the lifetime spent engaged in deliberate practice. A lifetime spent becoming the person who could do that sketch in two minutes. All the value is in the backstory.

When we deeply understand the idea that the value is in the backstory – the process of *becoming*, not the moment of *being* – and are able to communicate this in all we do, we will consistently fill our school environments with growth mindset movers.

Most people don't recognise the backstory. They only see the talent, the ability or the performance. They are unaware of the unseen journey of growth that preceded it. But there is always a backstory, the thousands of hours of practice that took place out of sight. The slow accumulation of skill. The development of ability. The investment of effort that created the growth. The improvement over time which led to that moment.

Picasso's backstory includes from age seven receiving training in figure drawing and oil painting from his father – also an artist, and a professor at the School of Fine Arts in A Coruna. Picasso studied at several art schools, accumulating years of practice, focus and dedication. Like many great artists his early works were not outstanding, and are only remarkable in that they illustrate the evolution of his work. He was never content to stay the same. He developed a rivalry with Henri Matisse that pushed both artists to new levels (something that in chapter 4 I referred to as 'coopertition'). His whole career was characterised by challenging himself, experimenting, improvement and refining.

Like all other cases, Picasso's talents were a lifetime in the making. He has a backstory of practise and development that most people aren't aware of. It's like entrepreneur Kent Clothier says, 'the overnight part of the overnight success is the sudden recognition of years of hard work'.

Understanding the journey of expertise

It's so much more insightful, interesting and rewarding to understand the journey of expertise. Once you get into the habit of looking for the backstory, you'll find it everywhere. Over the years I've been challenged numerous times by people with stories about supposed natural genius, but every time there is a backstory of a person who has slowly developed their skills.

> ❝ Once you get into the habit of looking for the backstory, you'll find it everywhere.

In his book *The Genius in All of Us*, David Shenk tells the backstory of the 'child genius' Mozart, whose story turns out to be very much like Picasso's. And Daniel Coyle beautifully describes the backstory of the Brontë sisters in his book *The Talent Code*. Malcom Gladwell's book *Outliers* essentially documents the backstories of many highly talented people, including Bill Gates, the Beatles and many more. In each case, circumstance and opportunity certainly played a role. But there's always the slow accumulation of ability through practice.

Professor Anders Ericsson – who made a career out of studying the acquisition of excellence – notes that the backstory behind the acquisition of any talent always includes these common elements:

- a supportive family
- access to a mentor, particularly in the early years
- the accumulation of around 10,000 hours of what he calls 'deliberate practice'.

We will consider Ericsson's work, and how to put it into action, in coming chapters.

The greatness gap

To nurture a growth mindset in our school community we need to maximise growth mindset movers and minimise fixed mindset movers.

Focusing on the backstory and using nudges will help us create growth mindset movers. But reducing the fixed mindset movers requires us to be alert to something else: the creation of the greatness gap.

Let me guide you through a process I regularly use in my workshops that highlights how easily we create the greatness gap. Take a moment to answer these two questions:

- Who do you consider successful?
- What is it that makes them successful?

I ask these questions of nearly every group I work with. The answers vary, but the reasons are always the same. It doesn't matter if I'm working with teachers, school leaders, corporates or students, the reasons people give for identifying someone as successful are always about the backstory. People are quick to say success is not about being the best, or the richest, or the most famous. It's about the struggles encountered and what people do to overcome them. And it's not simply overcoming one challenge – it's also about the person having the tendency to continually challenge themselves.

I find this consistency of how we identify success amazing. We all seem to have intuitively built the same idea of what success is. But what amazes me even more is that, nearly all the time, people name *others* as being successful, not themselves.

We have no trouble recognising the success of other people, but in the moment we recognise their success there can be a little voice in our minds telling us 'I'm not like you'. As soon as we attribute someone else's success to *who they are* rather than *what they have done*, we are creating the greatness gap.

NUDGE
CLOSE THE GREATNESS GAP.

The greatness gap is closely related to the fixed mindset and the idea that people are fundamentally and unchangeably different, that their successes are a part of *who they are*. This attitude will work against the creation of a culture of growth in your school. It is against this message you will need to be forever vigilant.

Dweck puts it like this: 'We like to think of our champions and idols as superheroes who were born different to us. We don't like to think of them as relatively ordinary people who have made themselves extraordinary.'

Why not?

When you think of successful people, you can think of them in one of two ways. You can either say, 'That's great for you. But I'm not like you.' When you do that you create the greatness gap and you absolve yourself not just of the responsibility but the mere possibility of ever being like them.

Or you can look at them and say, 'That's great for you, and I am just like you. In which case I'm currently underperforming.'

Which way do you think most people like to look at the world: *You could never expect that of me* or *I'm underperforming*?

Someone with a fixed mindset sees the greatness gap as an impassable chasm. Someone with a growth mindset sees the journey – the backstory that has developed the abilities.

We commonly hear echoes of the greatness gap in our schools. Every time a student says, 'Melissa is really good at writing – I'm not like Melissa', that's the greatness gap. Melissa's success is being attributed to who she is instead of what she's done. We hear it again when a parent tells their child who is struggling with maths that, 'It's okay. I wasn't very good at maths either'.

> 66 Someone with a fixed mindset sees the greatness gap as an impassable chasm. Someone with a growth mindset sees the journey – the backstory that has developed the abilities.

One of the skills you'll refine as you read this book is to become highly attuned to where the greatness gap is being created in your school. Every time you recognise it, the overriding nudge to remember is the story of Picasso and the importance of the backstory and the *journey of becoming* over the *moment of being*.

Imagine if my music teacher had carried this message with him. During my first music lesson, instead of saying, 'I want to see who can do this', he might have said, 'I want to see who's learnt enough by now to be able to do this'. The day I stopped him in the yard and performed the rhythm for him, he might have mentioned how everyone starts out as a beginner and highlighted the importance of practice in gaining mastery. If he'd carried the importance of the backstory with him every day, perhaps I'd have pursued my passion for music.

For our students, their journey is just beginning. They have yet to build their own backstory. As we fill our school environment with growth mindset movers, what we are giving students is an understanding of their ability to build their own backstory.

A GROWTH MINDSET IS AN INVITATION TO GROW, BUT IT'S NOT THE GROWTH

Moving your school community along the Mindset Continuum is just a starting point. It's the important foundation upon which you build your learning community, but it's not everything.

Carol Dweck lists in her book examples of world-class individuals who have achieved enormous amounts of growth with a growth mindset. And she lists world-class individuals who have achieved enormous amounts of growth with a fixed mindset.

That should give you pause.

That you can achieve growth with a fixed mindset or a growth mindset is significant. You don't *need* a growth mindset to grow, but it absolutely helps. And it's going to make your job, and the job of your classroom teachers, easier if students (and your wider community) have a growth mindset. If their autopilot creates growth-producing actions.

But at the end of the day, it's not your beliefs that matter. It's your actions.

A growth mindset is just the understanding that growth is possible. It tells you 'I can grow' but it does not tell you how. It gives you the choice to change but it's not the change.

Developing a growth mindset helps you understand yourself as a learner. Someone who is in charge of creating their own abilities. A person who can engage in becoming who they want or need to be. Once you understand yourself as a learner and your capacity to change, the next sensible question to ask is: how do I get really good at learning? If I can get better at anything, how do I get better at getting better? How do I become an expert learner?

That is the focus of the rest of this book.

PART II KEY TAKEAWAYS

- Your mindset works like your autopilot, quietly guiding your default learning behaviours.
- Your mindset is created from experiencing a mix of both growth and fixed mindset movers.
- Mindsets influence far more than just traditional learning behaviours. They influence our motivation, our ability to perceive and make choices in life, and through that, our agency in the world.
- 'Fixed' and 'growth' are useful for understanding, but to change mindsets you need to recognise mindset as part of a continuum.
- Where you find yourself on the Mindset Continuum is the result of all the fixed and growth mindset movers you've experienced.
- Changing mindsets means teaching **for** a growth mindset, not **about** a growth mindset.
- As a leader seeking to create a strong learning community, you can use 'nudges' to help fill the school environment with growth mindset movers, helping to sway learners towards the growth end of the continuum.
- The number one thing you can do as a leader to change students' mindsets is to change teachers' mindsets.
- The foundational nudge for changing mindsets is: focus on the backstory.

Use the space below to add some of your own part II key takeaways.

- _____
- _____
- _____
- _____
- _____

DISCUSSION AND ACTION

- Spend some time carefully observing your school environment. Watch and listen for the most common mindset movers. Are they fixed or growth movers? Listen carefully for the greatness gap.

- Go to www.jamesanderson.tv and watch the 'Growth Mindset All Your Questions Answered' video with your leadership group.

- Explore the Mindset Continuum with your leadership group. Where do you find your own beliefs, and those of your teachers and students, tending to fall along this continuum?

Use the space below to add some of your own discussion and action items.

- _____
- _____
- _____
- _____
- _____
- _____
- _____
- _____
- _____
- _____
- _____
- _____
- _____

WHERE TO FROM HERE?

A true learning community has a growth mindset as a foundation stone. Through our words, actions, policies and what we value, we can consistently nurture a growth mindset in all learners.

But at the end of the day, a growth mindset is not growth. It's just a belief that lives in our mind. An understanding that growth is possible. An invitation to grow. But it is not the act. It is not the growth.

We do not grow based on our beliefs – we grow based on our actions. In a learning community we align our actions with our beliefs. We create students who not only understand they are capable of growth but also understand how to go about achieving the growth.

Once students understand they're capable of growth, of changing their most basic characteristics and that they are learners, the next sensible question to ask is: if I can change myself and create my own abilities, how do I get really good at creating those abilities? That is the essence of Learnership.

Part III
What is Learnership?

As your community comes to understand themselves as learners, it's time to build an understanding of learning as a skill and introduce the concept of Learnership.

In this part I encourage you to change the way your community thinks about, talks about and celebrates learning. Instead of learning being a one-dimensional thing you 'do' to reach an outcome, in a learning community it becomes a multidimensional skill. Learning itself becomes something your community learns to do *well*.

I show you how understanding learning as a skill allows you to raise the status of learning in your school from an act to an art. I encourage you to take the paradigm of something that is skilful and apply it to learning. To imagine the master craftsperson, the elite sportsperson, the talented artist, the amazing author, the incredible dancer or the virtuoso musician. And to marvel at the expert learner in the same way.

Consider their journey to expertise. The time and dedication it took to master their craft, and their focus and attention to detail. Then think of the way you experience their skill. The wonder and awe. The recognition of witnessing something special. The culmination of years of growth.

Think of your students being incredible, amazing learners. Imagine walking through your school, witnessing their growth. Observing their dedication to developing the skill of learning. Imagine standing back, in awe, witnessing the beauty of expert learning in action.

This is what Learnership is about. The expertise we develop in the skill of learning.

Chapter 7
Transforming learning from an act to an art

> Skilful learning is a thing of beauty.

I was working with a teacher recently who was getting some of the best results in her state for her final year Business Management class, and had been for several years. Well, to be accurate, her students were getting the results, not her. But in the teaching culture that existed at the school, much of the credit was being attributed to the teacher, to the point where students wanted to be in her class because they knew they'd get excellent results.

She was an exemplary teacher, employing many of the most effective teaching strategies. In terms of the short-term measures currently valued by our system, she and her students were exceeding expected standards. Her students received some of the highest year 12 results in the state, and she received praise (and an eventual promotion) for being a highly effective teacher.

The problem wasn't the results – the problem was how the results were being obtained. Nearly all the focus was on the teaching side of the Learning Equation. This teacher did virtually *everything* for her students. She provided students with copious amounts of high-quality feedback, identifying their exact learning needs, and then telling them exactly what they needed to do and how to do it. This teacher was doing all the heavy lifting of learning for the students. All the students had to do was follow her lead and it virtually guaranteed they would receive great results.

As you've no doubt realised, the problems set in when these students left school and didn't know how to learn for themselves.

The teaching culture she'd established in her classroom had created what I describe in chapter 19 as Directed Learners. These are students who rely on the teacher to guide and manage the learning process. In a post-school environment, which doesn't manage the learning process for them, these students discovered they had achieved the learning outcomes but they were not learners. They had passed the test of school, but were not ready for the tests of life.

> ❝ ... these students discovered they had achieved the learning outcomes but they were not learners. They had passed the test of school, but were not ready for the tests of life.

This teacher is just one example of an entire system that has become focused on the skill of teaching. The problem is that this focus on teaching has often been at the cost of minimising or ignoring the skill of learning.

Take a moment to reflect on the following questions to see just how true this is.

Over the past 15 years, how much time have you and your staff spent talking about quality teaching practice? How many staff meetings have been devoted to exploring effective, high-impact teaching strategies (what teachers do in the classroom)? How much effort have you invested in helping teachers maximise the effect of their teaching on student learning outcomes? How much time and money has your school invested into describing and improving quality teaching and ensuring professional standards for teaching are being met?

Now ask yourself the same questions again, but this time about learning.

Over the past 15 years, how much time have you and your staff spent talking about quality learning practice? How many staff meetings have been devoted to exploring effective, high-impact learning strategies (what students do in the classroom)? How much effort have you invested in helping students maximise the effect on their own learning outcomes? How much time and money has your school invested into describing and improving quality learning and ensuring standards of learning are being improved?

It's quite remarkable, really. We call ourselves learning communities, but we spend nearly all our time focused on teaching. But it doesn't need to be this way. We can rebalance the equation. To do so, we need to start thinking of learning as a skill.

WHAT DOES IT MEAN TO BE A SKILFUL LEARNER?

I often reflect on an insightful conversation I had with emeritus professor of education Art Costa many years ago. We were discussing the nature of thinking and learning, and he pointed out that learning was kind of like moving:

> We can all move. It's innate. All children learn to roll over, crawl, stand up and eventually walk all on their own. No one has to teach us how to do it.
>
> The same is true for learning. Every child can learn. They don't have to be taught how to do it. As they experience the world, their brains re-wire and adapt. As a result, they've learnt something.
>
> Just like moving, learning is an innate part of being human.

Then with the great wisdom that has come from a lifetime invested in education, he said:

> But as we grow older, some of us become highly skilful at moving. We deliberately train our bodies to move in specific ways. We become dancers, acrobats, gymnasts or athletes. These people

learn to move with great co-ordination, stamina, power and grace. Over time, through practice, these people become highly skilled in the way they move. For the rest of us, it's a different story. Some of us continue to stumble through life with the proverbial two left feet, while others learn some basic moves. The quality of how we move as adults varies greatly.

The same is true for thinking, or learning. Some of us learn how to become highly effective, highly skilful learners. People who can learn with stamina, power and even grace. While others remain beginners.

Obviously, every child can learn. The question you are seeking to answer is: are you teaching them to be the most skilful and effective learners? How do we teach them to learn *well*?

VALUING THE SKILL OF LEARNING

In a learning community we value the skill of learning. It becomes a key driver and a measure for success across the school.

As we've already discussed, recent trends in education have seen a clear shift towards understanding what quality teaching looks like. Marzano's work aptly reflects this when he describes the 'Art and Science of Teaching'. We have moved beyond thinking merely about *what* we teach, to *how* we teach, to *how well* we teach. It's no longer enough to have an impact, we must *maximise* that impact.

> ❝ We expect to see learners shift from thinking about what they are learning, to how they are learning, to how well they are learning.

As teachers move through their careers, we expect them to develop expertise in teaching and become increasingly effective teachers. In a learning community we expect the same commitment to developing expertise in learning from our students. We expect to see learners shift from thinking about what they are learning, to how they are learning, *to how well* they are learning.

It is no longer enough that students simply learn, they must be seen to become skilful learners. In short, your role as a leader of a learning community is to shift the paradigm of learning from an act to an *art*.

To help you and your staff reframe learning from an act to an art, consider this question:

What comes to mind when you think of something done skilfully?

Perhaps, like Art Costa's story above, it's a sport and you are awed by how the athletes move. Or do you watch shows like *MasterChef* and marvel at how well they can prepare meals? Or maybe you think of a grand master chess campion? Or do you wonder at how Shakespeare weaves his stories together? Or do you think of how an outstanding leader can inspire and lead others? Perhaps you think of the expertise of your teachers?

As you think of this domain of expertise, what are some of the ideas it conjures up?

To begin with, there must be an understanding of what makes up quality in that particular domain. We can recognise and describe quality. There's a recognition that expertise does not come easily. It often takes many years of dedicated practice for the expert to gain their skills. There has been a journey of slow, incremental improvement that defines the path from beginner to expert. There's great effort spent in developing the expertise, but at the end the expert can make the performance appear effortless. And there's often an entire language associated with the domain that allows experts to describe and reflect on the performance. Experts perform with intentionality and a degree of nuance and detail that beginners simply don't have.

Each member of your school community will have a unique example of a domain they consider skilful. It will be a field they know a bit about, and a field where it's possible to recognise mastery. Something they understand takes time, focus, dedication and the intention to improve. Something that leads to the development of what we recognise as expertise.

To raise the status of learning from an act to an art, you will need to take that paradigm of developing expertise, with all that entails, and apply it to the way each member of your school community thinks about learning.

There's something very special about recognising learning as an art, as something that can be performed with skill and fidelity. When we do that, we recognise learning, when done well, is a thing of beauty. Just as we can respond with wonderment to the expert craftsperson, the exceptional dancer or the virtuoso singer, we can also respond with wonderment to the expert learner.

> ❝ ... learning, when done well, is a thing of beauty.

I imagine a time when a teacher, steeped in a deep understanding of what skilful learning looks like, can observe her students learning. Independent of what they are learning about, she can observe how they are learning and how skilfully they are going about achieving growth. That recognition elicits a deep acknowledgement that she's witnessing something special, and the same sense of awe as seeing an expert in another field at work. With that realisation she turns to her students, pauses, and with wonderment in her heart and joy on her face, tells them the way they are learning is ... beautiful.

Moreover, as a school leader you'll walk past a classroom in your school and observe the skill of the teacher being matched by the skill of the learner, the two engaged in a magical dance of learning, like the example of figure skaters Torvill and Dean from chapter 2. At that moment you will have raised the status of learning in your school from an act to an art, and you'll know you have created a true learning community.

Chapter 8
Learnership: the skill of learning

Learning + Craftsmanship.

Language is powerful. Words allow us to capture ideas and focus on concepts, and communicate them quickly and more effectively. Each year we add around 1000 new words to the English language to help us communicate new ideas.

When psychologist Daniel Goleman popularised the term 'emotional intelligence', the idea that emotions and intelligence could go together seemed crazy. In fact, most people considered emotions and intelligence as opposite – or at least separate – attributes. Today, we consider the idea of developing emotional intelligence an essential skill for life and work.

Similarly, when Edward de Bono coined the term 'lateral thinking', it created shockwaves. The dominant paradigm was about deep thinking. Why would anyone think sideways, and what did that even *mean*? But de Bono changed all that, and unless you're stretching out well towards the end of your career, you've probably just always assumed lateral thinking was a thing. It wasn't. Edward de Bono made it up, and the term 'lateral thinking' is now part of our vernacular.

You are going to need a word to describe the skill of learning. A word to use with your leadership team, your teachers, your students and your wider community. A word that allows your school community to bring the skill of learning into focus. That word is 'Learnership'.

Learnership brings together the idea of craftsmanship – and its association with expertise – with the idea of learning. Craftsmanship is the expertise of a craft. Learnership is the expertise of learning.

The more you use the term, the more Learnership will become part of the way your school community talks about learning. Using the term 'Learnership' amplifies the vision you have for your school culture. And your school community will thank you for it. The term alone will have a subtle but powerful effect on how your community thinks about learning. It opens up a whole new conversation that teachers and parents have long wanted to have but didn't have the words to describe. It invites a new way of thinking about learning, shifting the conversation from what you are learning to how you are learning to how well you are learning.

> ❝ Craftsmanship is the expertise of a craft. Learnership is the expertise of learning.

Just as emotional intelligence is how we now think about emotions, and lateral thinking is how we think about creativity, schools and parents will talk about *how well* their child is learning rather than just *what* they are learning. Parents will ask to be informed about how their child is developing as a skilful learner. Schools will differentiate between students achieving a learning outcome and the strategies they used to achieve it, recognising that how students are achieving curriculum outcomes is a better indicator of future success than the outcomes themselves. Schools will shift from being places where 'learning happens' to places where children learn to become skilful learners. We'll look back and wonder how we ever did without the concept.

EXPERTISE IN LEARNING

So, you get it. But what does Learnership mean, exactly? New words need to be defined. I define Learnership like this:

> Learnership is the expertise a person develops in learning. Like all skills, it is acquired over time, through the deliberate use of practice and dedicated strategies. It is an improvement in the ability to learn, and results in the learner gaining more from every learning opportunity.

There's a bit to unpack in this definition, all of which plays into how we build a learning community. So let's go through it one part at a time.

Learnership is the expertise a person develops in learning.

Learning communities recognise that learning is a domain in which we must develop expertise. To simply say 'we learn' makes about as much sense as saying 'we move' or 'we write'. It's not simply an action. Like moving or writing, learning becomes the focus of improvement. Every lesson provides an opportunity to exercise and develop Learnership.

Imagine your students coming home after school, and instead of being asked, 'What did you learn at school today?', they are asked, 'How well were you learning today?'

Like all skills, it is acquired over time, through the deliberate use of practice and dedicated strategies.

A learning community recognises that learners gain expertise in learning over time. It's not a 'learning how to learn' program that is covered at the beginning of the year and then 'applied'. It's never fully mastered. Our focus on getting better at the process of learning is a constant in the life of the school. We recognise and celebrate the growth in Learnership, not the attainment of Learnership.

Of course, that raises the question of how we do that. Be patient. We explore this in chapter 27.

To facilitate this growth, learning has its own language and vocabulary. Like other areas of expertise, this language gives a depth and richness to the domain and allows us to talk about and better understand the skill of learning, so the entire school community can discuss it in a meaningful and nuanced way.

Learning communities understand that learning is not a collection of independent skills, grouped together a bit like a jigsaw puzzle. Instead, like other areas of expertise, Learnership represents growth in a specific set of sub-domains. There are areas we must master and understand in sequence before moving on, allowing the student to grow in their ability to learn. So in learning communities, there is an understanding of the scope and sequence for developing Learnership (see chapter 27).

Imagine sitting in on a parent–teacher conference where the conversation weaves in and out of what the student is trying to learn, and how they are learning. There are discussions about both what the child is trying to master and how they are going about leveraging that learning to become better at achieving that mastery.

It is an improvement in the ability to learn, and results in the learner gaining more from every learning opportunity.

Like all other areas of expertise, Learnership has a purpose. To play a better game of chess, the Grand Master chess player develops their skills. To create a more appetising meal, the master chef develops their skills in cooking. To get more out of every learning situation the expert learner develops Learnership.

Consider this situation. Two students, in the same class. They experience the same lesson. They hear the same words from the teacher, take part in the same activities. But one walks away having gained more from the lesson than the other because they engaged in the learning process differently. (Recall Holt's words about the activity of learners.) That's what Learnership does. It helps the student get more out of every learning opportunity, whether that learning opportunity is inside a classroom, at work or anywhere else in life.

> That's what Learnership does. It helps the student get more out of every learning opportunity.

Of course, the benefits of being able to get more out of every learning opportunity extend well beyond the classroom. As we will discuss in the coming chapters, being an expert learner allows students to thrive, not just survive, in the world. It allows them to futureproof themselves and go beyond resilient to become anti-fragile – but more on that later.

ELEMENTS OF LEARNERSHIP

When you look closely, you can understand any area of expertise by analysing the distinct elements that make up the domain. For example, when we think about expertise in languages, we often refer to the domains of reading, writing, listening and speaking. They are developed alongside each other, not in sequence.

Similarly, I define five distinct elements that make up Learnership. These are the elements we consider and develop as we build our expertise as learners. They are:

- **Challenge.** Challenge provides the stretch that drives growth upwards, towards improvement and eventual expertise. Our attitude towards challenge can hold us back or accelerate our learning. Skilful learners develop a positive and productive relationship with challenge.

- **Habits of Mind.** Our Habits of Mind are the dispositions we bring to a challenge. They are our patterns of behaviour that allow us to succeed at increasingly difficult challenges. How we go about developing and improving these behaviours determines how well equipped we will be to meet increasingly demanding challenges, and ultimately succeed at them.

- **Mistakes.** Mistakes can provide important information for learning (although not all of them do). This information helps fill the gap between where we are now and where we want to be. We can use our mistakes to find or generate information and leverage it to drive our learning forward.

- **Feedback.** Feedback is another important source of information that fills the gap between where we are now and where we want to be. We often think of feedback in terms of the quality of the information provided to the learner. In the context of Learnership, feedback is more about what the learner does with the information provided.

- **Effort.** Ultimately, it is our effort that drives our growth. Understanding that not all effort is equal, choosing to engage in the most effective types of effort, and understanding the value of effort we must expend to achieve our growth is a critical aspect of being an effective learner. Skilful learners understand it is how they spend, invest or waste their effort that drives growth.

Drawing on these five elements, and how our relationship to them changes, allows us to describe what skilful learning looks like. We will explore each of them in more detail over the next five chapters. Doing so also helps us develop our language for learning, allowing us to engage in a more nuanced and detailed description of the learning process.

PART III KEY TAKEAWAYS

- Teaching is a craft. With appropriate practice, teachers can develop the skill of teaching and become experts in the domain of teaching.
- Learning is also a craft. With appropriate practice, learners develop the skill of learning and become experts in the domain of learning.
- Teaching and learning are separate, but related, areas of expertise.
- Learnership is the skill of learning. It brings the concepts of learning and craftsmanship together.
- As a leader of a learning community, you should seek to raise the status of learning from an act to an art.
- There are five elements that help us describe and understand Learnership:
  - challenge
  - Habits of Mind
  - mistakes
  - feedback
  - effort.

Use the space below to add some of your own part III key takeaways.

- _____
- _____
- _____
- _____
- _____
- _____
- _____

DISCUSSION AND ACTION

- Bring to mind a domain you are familiar with and consider skilful. It will be something where you can recognise the journey from beginner to expert. What ideas, language and concepts do you associate with this journey? Now, apply that paradigm to the concept of learning to consider what it takes to become a skilful learner.

- With your leadership team, debate the idea that schools today have become more focused on skilful teaching than on skilful learning.

- With your leadership team, discuss what 'beautiful learning' might look like, or when you might have experienced it.

Use the space below to add some of your own discussion and action items.

- _____
- _____
- _____
- _____
- _____
- _____
- _____
- _____
- _____
- _____
- _____

WHERE TO FROM HERE?

Expertise in learning can be described in terms of how a learner develops their relationship with five key elements: challenge, Habits of Mind, mistakes, feedback and effort. In the next part we take a deep dive into each of these elements, building our understanding of what this development looks like, why each is important and how a learner's relationship with each element develops over time.

Part IV
The five essential elements of Learnership

Learning communities are places where people build expertise in learning. But what does that look like?

Think about an expert you've met, or an area in which you've developed your own expertise. You'll find that experts have a deep, rich understanding of their field. They view their expertise through different elements of their domain. They share a specialist language that allows them to reflect on their expertise in a highly nuanced and meaningful way. The same is true of expertise in learning.

When we think about Learnership, it too has a deep structure. These are the five essential elements you need to focus on to become an increasingly skilful learner. In this part we examine each of these elements in detail, and in doing so build a rich language for learning in your school community.

Think of the way your learners respond to challenge. Do they embrace it, or avoid it? Challenge is the foundation of all progress. Without it there can be no true growth. So our relationship with challenge is central to becoming a skilful and effective learner. I tease apart the idea of challenge and introduce you to the four different zones of learning. I show you how skilful learners become 'comfortably uncomfortable' with challenge.

The 16 Habits of Mind are the actions we employ to achieve growth. I show you how these are not simply demanded and applied, but rather are dispositions to be nurtured and developed. You'll see how skilful learners come to cultivate their Habits of Mind as their greatest asset. And I introduce you to a unique and powerful tool for assessing and guiding the development of learners' Habits of Mind.

An essential part of growth is information. How learners gather this information – from mistakes and feedback – is another crucial part of Learnership. I show you how to break away from unhelpfully broad concepts like 'mistakes help me learn' and deepen both your understanding of mistakes and enrich your language for learning by introducing six different types of mistakes. I show you how skilful learners proactively 'design' mistakes and cultivate feedback.

Rounding out our discussion of the elements of Learnership, I give you a powerful new construct for effort: the Effective Effort Matrix. Instead of thinking of effort as the amount of time and energy a learner spends on a task, we frame it clearly as being about *how* that time and energy are spent. You will learn to appreciate effort as the currency of growth, and to recognise how it's wasted, spent or invested in learning.

Remember also that someone with a fixed mindset doesn't understand the process of learning. For them, learning is about *discovering* their abilities, not *creating* them. Every time we help our learners understand more about how the elements above help them become better learners, we are creating growth mindset movers. So keep an eye out for nudges throughout these chapters.

Learning communities understand, value and develop expertise in learning. So let's build our understanding of each of these five key elements now. In section VIII we look at how we develop each in classrooms.

Chapter 9
Challenge: the pathway to growth

Are you getting better? Or just keeping busy?

IMPROVING YOUR LEARNERS' RELATIONSHIP WITH CHALLENGE

The first time you hear the phrase 'a learner's *relationship* with challenge', it can sound a bit odd. But it's accurate. We can think of having a relationship with challenge – not a specific challenge, but the *idea* of challenge.

You're probably familiar with the idea of someone loving a challenge or hating it. A learner's relationship with challenge drives their growth over time and fuels their long-term success. So, developing a productive relationship with challenge is a key component of Learnership.

As you reflect on your students, what type of relationships do they typically have with challenges?

Do you have learners who avoid challenges altogether? Or learners who constantly seek the easiest option, choosing their path of least resistance, not truly challenging themselves at all? Like most schools, I'm sure you have some students who are always wanting to do their confident best, without ever pushing themselves to do better.

Perhaps you have learners who take on challenges only because they are told to, dutifully and compliantly following instructions, their growth controlled and directed by the teacher. For these learners their growth is dependent on them being given goals to pursue. Do you wish more of your learners set their own goals and willingly tackled challenges to reach them?

An expert learner has a rich and productive relationship with challenge. They value challenges because they represent an opportunity to grow, to improve themselves. These learners get into the habit of challenging themselves. They understand challenges change them. They don't need to be told to take on challenges. They don't take on challenges solely because they are an obstacle on the path to reaching a goal. They take them on because they want to achieve growth and they recognise there can be no growth without challenge. Perhaps most importantly, they recognise the long-term benefits that arise when they adopt the attitude of embracing challenges.

> ❝❝ An expert learner has a rich and productive relationship with challenge.

Of course, a learner's relationship with challenge is strongly influenced by their mindset. So as we help learners develop a deeper understanding of challenge, we are also creating many growth mindset movers.

In a learning community, the entire community of students, teachers, leaders and parents develops a deep understanding of challenge. They understand the value and benefit of challenges. They have a shared language to describe challenges and how they interact with them, and they intentionally move in and out of challenge.

So what does it mean to understand challenge? What will it sound like when your school community has a language to understand and describe challenge? And how do we go about building a healthy relationship with challenge? To answer those questions, we need to get into our zones of learning.

THE ZONES OF LEARNING

What makes something *challenging*?

We tend to use the word challenge, and the concept of taking on a challenge, fairly loosely, both in schools and in the wider community. In a learning community that is focused on building expertise in learning, we develop a more nuanced understanding of challenge. We recognise that not all challenges are the same.

Recall the work of Anders Ericsson, the internationally renowned expert on expertise, mentioned in chapter 3. Ericsson noted we often see that the development of skills follows a predictable pattern (see the following figure). Initially, progress is relatively rapid. Then progress slows, and eventually we reach what he calls a performance plateau – something you might have heard colloquially referred to as 'the bar'.

This performance plateau represents your current best. From the perspective of someone with the fixed mindset we discussed in part II, this bar is a fixed point. It is their unique potential. A point to be reached. But from our growth mindset understanding, the goal is to raise the bar.

Take a moment to study this diagram. I'm sure you can relate to this pattern of growth. It's a perfectly normal process of learning that we have all experienced. Understanding this pattern will help you define and understand the three different zones of learning. It is a key diagram that we will refer back to often.

The zones of learning

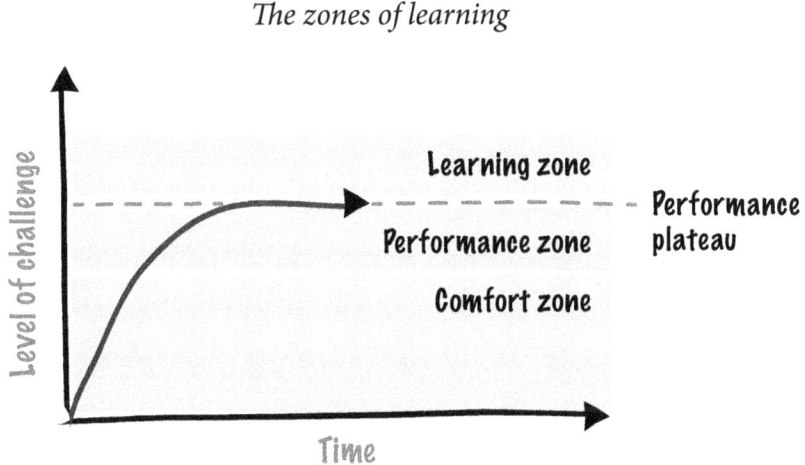

Let's consider each of the zones.

The comfort zone

The early part of skill development, where growth is rapid, occurs in what we refer to as our 'comfort zone'. Our comfort zone is full of those things we've mastered long ago. These are things we know how to do, and can do them easily.

But that's not all. Your comfort zone isn't just full of what you can already do. It's also full of what I call 'easy things you haven't done yet'. These are things you don't know how to do yet, but could still do easily if the need arose. Stop for a moment and think about the concept of 'easy things you haven't done yet'. The world is full of these types of easy challenges.

> ❝ Your comfort zone isn't just full of what you can already do. It's also full of what I call 'easy things you haven't done yet'.

In many environments – home, school, the workplace – we talk about the importance of getting out of our comfort zone and doing something *new*. You've probably stood in front of your staff and talked about the importance, even the necessity, of teachers and students doing this.

The problem with doing something new is that the world is full of things that are *new* that are also *easy* things you haven't done yet. These activities, although new, are well within your current abilities. As we spoke about in chapter 1, you already have agency over easy things you haven't done yet. These types of challenges do not help you achieve a higher standard; they don't change you, and do not represent true growth.

In your comfort zone, the solution to a problem or the path to achieving a goal is immediately apparent. There is little chance of significant errors being made, and very little risk of not achieving the goal. These activities feel like tasks that simply need to be ticked off a to-do list. They are activities that take little effort but they keep you busy. You approach them with a high degree of confidence and certainty that you'll be successful.

For example, consider the 13 times table. If you're like most adults, you've never needed to learn your 13 times table. But mastering it is well within your abilities. If the need ever arose, you'd simply allocate the time and get it done. There would be little effort involved, and you'd approach the task with high confidence. That's what an easy thing you haven't done yet – something that's in your comfort zone – feels like.

Life frequently presents us with 'easy things we haven't done yet'. Although we might refer to these as challenges, they don't *really* challenge us. They require effort, but the type of effort required leads only to the completion of the task, not personal growth. It is time spent, not time invested.

How many times have students in your school been asked to get outside their comfort zone and try something new? Perhaps when they've been given the opportunity to choose a passion project or something similar. But the goal they set themselves was actually *inside* their comfort zone? How often do students in your school do this habitually?

The performance zone

Your performance zone is the part of the graph where your progress slows, and eventually levels off.

Your performance zone is where you bring all your current abilities to bear on a task. You produce your current peak performance. Compared to our comfort zone, we approach our performance zone with increased concentration, but still with a high level of confidence that we will succeed. We often find our performance zone enjoyable and rewarding.

Our performance zone can be seductive. We look good when we do our best. Completing goals in our performance zone brings with it a sense of satisfaction and pride. We feel like we've got value for our effort.

Students are very aware of their performance zone. It's the point where they get the greatest return (grade or standard) for minimum effort – something that is referred to as the 'minimax principle'. This is also why, according to Hattie, self-reported grades are one of the best predictors of student success. Students are both attracted to, and excellent judges of, their performance zone.

Many significant tasks can fall within our comfort and performance zones. In chapter 17, I'll share a story of a long-term principal who spent nearly his whole principalship in his comfort and performance zones. The goals he achieved required only the allocation of significant resources and time, and he achieved some great outcomes for his school. But there were both personal and long-term costs to staying in his comfort and performance zones.

The comfort and performance zones have their purposes. It's not that they should be entirely avoided. As a school leader you want your teachers to be in their performance zone, doing a good job, much – but not all – of the time. And many of those 'easy things you haven't done yet' actually need to get done.

The problem with staying constantly below the bar, in our comfort and performance zones, is that we don't get better by doing our best, we only get things done. We only get better, and achieve personal growth, by stretching and challenging ourselves to do a little better than our best.

That means going into our learning zone.

The learning zone

It's the standard just beyond our current best which is truly challenging. To attempt this type of challenge we need to go into what I call the 'learning zone'. Learning to recognise, understand and eventually embrace your learning zone is one of the foundation stones of Learnership.

The concept of a learning zone is not new. Psychologist Lev Vygotsky referred to this level just beyond your current abilities as the 'zone of proximal development'. Hattie describes this level of challenge as being '+1', and notes it is one of the critical ingredients of learning. In his book *The Talent Code*, Daniel Coyle refers to it as the 'sweet spot' for learning. In my book *The Agile Learner*, I refer to it as the Goldilocks zone because it represents a level of challenge that is not too easy, not too hard, but just right! I've heard others refer to it as 'the growing edge'.

Today, I prefer the term 'learning zone' because it is more accessible and meaningful to our school community. It seems odd to tell a five-year-old to get into their zone of proximal development, or to describe a challenge as being in a student's Goldilocks zone. The term 'learning zone' is more easily integrated into our language of learning.

As you lead your school towards becoming a learning community, it's not simply understanding the learning zone that's important – as educators we've understood it for a long time. The key to becoming a skilful learner is having the ability to understand the learning zone in relation to the comfort and performance zones, and to be able to distinguish between challenges in each zone and be intentional about how our behaviour and expectations change when we are in each zone.

> Learning to recognise, understand and eventually embrace your learning zone is one of the foundation stones of Learnership.

In your learning zone, the solution to the problem you are facing is not immediately apparent. You feel stretched. The task is 'hard' and not solved simply by allocating more time. While your comfort and performance zones are full of confidence and certainty, the learning zone feels uncomfortable. There is struggle, effort and uncertainty.

Our learning zone is also where we experience adversity, the only difference between challenge and adversity being its source. A challenge is something we decide to take on. Adversity is something that is thrust upon us, without choice. Circumstance forces us beyond our current abilities. This realisation is important for our developing understanding of agency.

Research has consistently shown that in many professions, including teaching, most people reach a level of proficiency – they become adequate at their job – and then remain there. They stay in their comfort and performance zones for most of their career, never truly growing. As one insightful principal put it, these teachers don't have 20 years' teaching experience. They have one year's experience 20 times over.

Significant growth occurs only when we regularly take on challenges in our learning zone. Constantly stepping into our learning zone increases our abilities and raises the bar. This is why a learner's relationship with challenge and their learning zone is so important. If a learner's relationship with challenge does not bring them regularly into their learning zone, growth slows or stalls completely.

Beyond our learning zone is our aspirational zone. This is where the stretch becomes a strain. It is too far beyond our current abilities to achieve right now. We can aspire to this level of achievement, but we must first grow to bring it into our learning zone.

As we'll explore in a moment, the amount of effort required to achieve a goal in your learning zone is much higher, and the rewards are less certain. Errors are far more likely (and as we'll see later, useful) in our learning zone. Our learning zone holds the real prospect of failure – and it also holds the potential reward of growth.

Once you've grasped the idea of these zones, ask yourself this question: as you reflect on your own goals over recent years, have you been getting better in your learning zone, or have you just been keeping busy in your comfort and performance zones?

HELPING YOUR STUDENTS GET COMFORTABLE IN THE LEARNING ZONE

In learning communities the language of the zones becomes part of the language of learning. Teachers intentionally stretch and guide students into their learning zone by setting appropriately challenging tasks. This is what we hope is happening in every school. But in a learning community we take this one step further and seize this opportunity to help students recognise, understand and value their learning zone.

Being a skilful learner means they understand what their learning zone feels like and when they are expected to be in their learning zone. They come to understand that struggle and effort are the cost of growth, and that being in their learning zone should feel 7/10 uncomfortable – a stretch, but not a strain. When they are working in the learning zone there is an expectation they will make stretch mistakes and need to ask questions. They will also understand that the feeling of struggle passes, and that the investment of effort develops new abilities, raises the bar and makes hard things easy.

To help students recognise, understand and value the learning zone, one teacher I worked with formed the habit of signalling when students were expected to go into their learning zone by welcoming his students as they came into the classroom by saying, 'Come in. Sit down. Make yourself uncomfortable!' Another group of schools developed the classroom expectations poster shown below, which is displayed in classrooms throughout the school.

LEARNING EXPECTATIONS

Expect to be challenged

Expect to not immediately know the answer

Expect to feel uncomfortable while in your Learning Zone

Expect to make mistakes

Expect learning to involve struggle.
Effort is the cost of growth.

This is all a normal part of learning...

Expect these feelings to pass

Expect to create new abilities, to make possible what was not possible before

Expect what you find difficult today, will become easy tomorrow

Expect to gain success and mastery in learning.

Pause to celebrate your growth.
Appreciate what you did to achieve it.

Expect to repeat this process and continue to grow!

Most students feel uncomfortable in their learning zone. They need to be taught to recognise and appreciate that this is an expected part of learning. And they need to taught the long-term value of taking on challenges. And let's face it, it's easier being in your comfort zone and more enjoyable to be in your performance zone. So given the choice, most students choose not to go into their learning zone. As they become more skilful learners, they become comfortably uncomfortable with the struggle inherent in challenge. To know it, recognise it and value it.

Teachers should normalise and celebrate the struggle inherent in doing difficult things. To call out students when they are cruising, and tell them that's what 4/10 uncomfortable looks like and that it's not what is expected at that moment. To reward and praise students for struggle, and *not* for the quick and easy completion of work when students are meant to be in their learning zone.

The good news is that as we work with the importance of backstories and an understanding of the zones, we can change a learner's attitude to challenge. Another teacher I worked with recently was telling me the story of one of her year 10 students. After being identified as gifted, this student habitually avoided challenges. He would say things like, 'Of course I can do that. That's too easy for me.' But he wouldn't actually attempt the task. He spent his time in his comfort zone, afraid that if he went into his learning zone he would struggle, and that struggle might mean his identity as being gifted was threatened.

The teacher spent time explaining the zones of learning to her class. She made a point of overtly identifying and valuing students for venturing into their learning zone, describing what it looked like and felt like to be in their learning zone. She told stories of experts who struggled, highlighting their backstories. She focused on the growth being achieved as a result of going into the learning zone, each lesson creating little growth mindset movers that emphasise the importance of the learning zone.

This teacher was excited to tell me that this student had stopped her on the way to class to tell her, 'I hope we are going to do something challenging today, or I'm going to be really annoyed!' The student had finally realised that challenge was the pathway to growth, and time spent in his comfort zone wasn't helping him get better.

At Asquith Girls High School, a school in Sydney that I have been working with for several years, they used the 'Tell Them From Me' survey (a wellbeing and learning tool used widely in NSW public schools) to measure students' responses to challenges. They saw their work with Learnership result in the number of students setting challenging goals increase by 12.5% in just two years.

Not that the goal is for students to be in the learning zone all the time. They should spend time in their comfort and performance zones. The performance zone defines their current best. We aim performance measures and assessment at this zone. Students also spend time consolidating skills in their performance zone. Similarly, we should expect them to spend time in their comfort zone. There are some tasks that just need to get done. The comfort zone can also be where they begin learning a new skill, or where we can cover breadth in a domain.

One of the benefits of teaching students about their zones of learning is they can intentionally move in and out of them, and begin to understand the different expectations and behaviours required in each. This ability to switch between zones helps students bring increasing intentionality and deliberateness to their learning. As we will see later it also helps manage expectations around mistakes, and more accurately judge the cost of growth.

In any given day we regularly move in and out of each of these zones. Skilful learners learn how to do this intentionally, and to differentiate when they should be in each zone. We should not expect students to be in their learning zone all day. According to Ericsson's research, the maximum we can spend in our learning zone, deeply focused on improving our best, is about three hours a day. And people who are engaged regularly in this type of practice need to sleep more, because it's exhausting!

BUILDING A BACKSTORY

Of course, the performance plateau is not a fixed point. One of the key goals in a learning community is to 'raise the bar'. To do this, we design our curriculum to challenge students progressively with increasingly difficult tasks. We are not trying to find where each student's bar is set (as someone with a fixed mindset would believe). Rather, we recognise that every student, teacher and principal is achieving to their *current* best, and the goal is to set a higher standard and make their best better.

There's another important nudge here. Did you notice the way I used the term *current* best. Through the eyes of someone with a fixed mindset the performance plateau is a fixed point. Their best. By attaching a time stamp to our discussion of performance we remind students that their best is a point in time, something that changes, not the limit of their abilities.

Many schools, and most parents, focus on the level of the bar – the standard being achieved. And this is important. However, by focusing only on the standard being achieved, the immediate challenge and learning outcomes, we overlook and undervalue one of the most important reasons for raising the bar. Learning to do *better*, not simply learning *more*, has a much greater benefit than simply reaching the short-term learning goal. It has long-range benefits as well.

Look at the following figures showing the consequences when we invest our effort in raising the bar. Obviously, we reach new and higher standards. But look closely; what else is happening?

Note that the learning zone is always *just beyond* our current best. This highlights a point that we'll explore later. Challenge and the concept of something being 'hard' are relative terms, not absolute terms. Nothing is inherently 'hard' or challenging. We experience challenge and 'hard' problems as we move beyond our current abilities into our learning zone – but our learning zone moves.

The important part to note in the figures is that as you raise the bar, your comfort zone gets bigger and bigger. You've not simply succeeded at the immediate challenge and achieved the short-term learning goal. Being beyond your current best has forced you to focus not only on what you were learning but also on how you were learning. As we see in the next chapter, you've developed your Habits of Mind. Your comfort zone gets bigger. And as your comfort zone grows, you fill your world with easy things you haven't done yet.

Raising the bar – growing your comfort zone

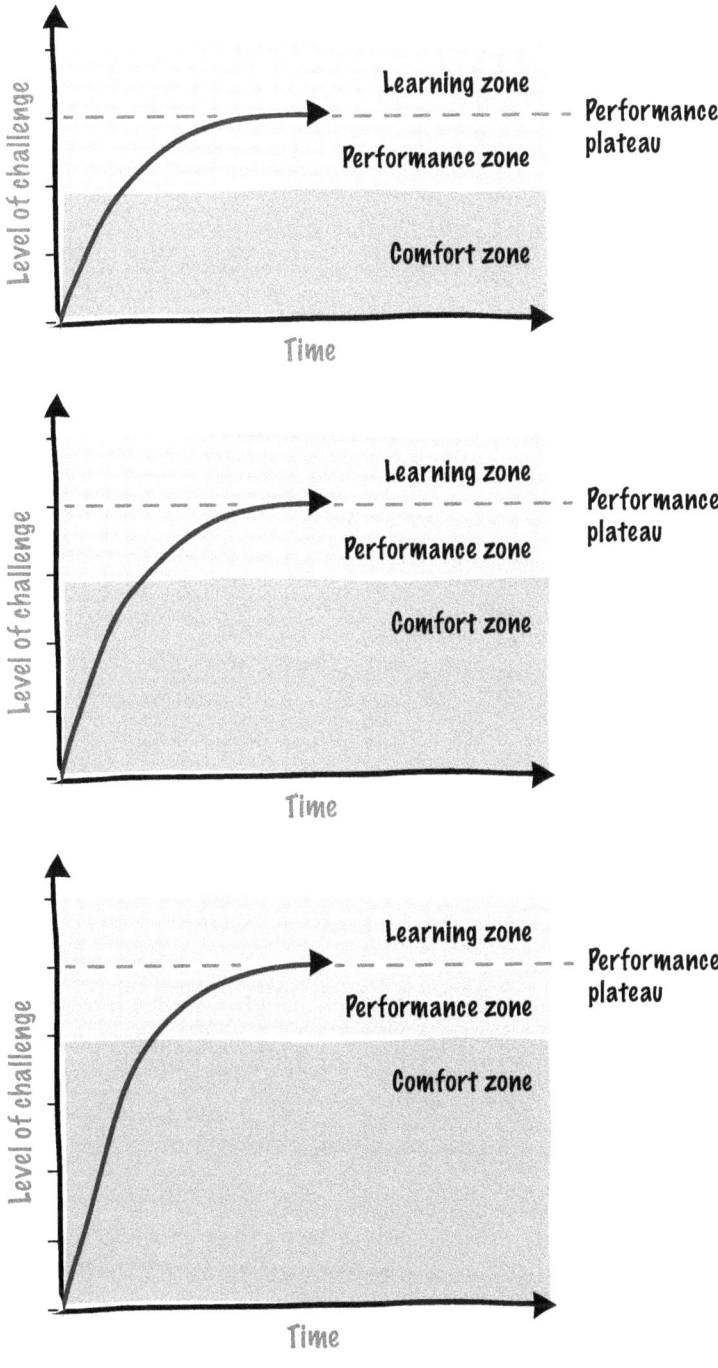

The long-term benefit of growth goes well beyond success at the immediate challenge. It prepares you for the challenges of the future as well.

You've almost certainly recognised this effect yourself. Take a moment to bring to mind someone you know who's invested considerable effort in developing expertise in a particular domain. Perhaps they are a mentor, or another principal you aspire to be like. Have you ever noticed they are often pretty good at lots of things? They can easily 'turn their hand to' new challenges. They aren't experts in other domains, but the effort invested in their own growth, by regularly taking on challenges and consistently raising the bar, has filled their world with easy things they haven't done yet.

> " The long-term benefit of growth goes well beyond success at the immediate challenge. It prepares you for the challenges of the future as well.

When we complete tasks below the bar, in our comfort and performance zones, there is an immediate short-term benefit: we achieve our goal. Our relatively low investment produces an immediate return. However, tasks completed in our comfort and performance zones have little or no long-term value. We complete them and we move on. But the task hasn't changed us.

Investing effort in your learning zone has a very different effect. The cost of this achievement is significantly more effort than achieving a task in your comfort or performance zones. However, the long-term benefit of investing effort in your learning zone is that your comfort zone gets bigger. It fills your future with easy things you haven't done yet. This is the long-term, future-focused benefit of growth.

Completing a thousand easy tasks does not reap the rewards that completing just one truly challenging task does. In fact, it is consistently challenging yourself to go beyond your current best that builds the backstories we examined in chapter 6. That's why it's critical our learners build a healthy relationship with challenge.

Chapter 10
Habits of Mind: actions for growth

> If challenge is the pathway to growth, the
> Habits of Mind are actions that take students
> down that path.

WHAT ARE THE HABITS OF MIND?

Challenging students is one thing. Having them succeed at a challenge is something else entirely. As we saw in previous chapters, a growth mindset tells students they are capable of growth. It encourages them to go into their learning zone, knowing that the struggle will be temporary and eventually result in growth. It gives them the will to act. But the growth mindset does not tell students how *to act* to succeed at those challenges.

If challenge is the pathway to growth, the Habits of Mind are actions that take students down that path. When students enter their learning zone and take on a challenge or face adversity, it's effective use of their Habits of Mind that will allow them to succeed at that challenge and ultimately raise the bar. Students who become skilful learners value and cultivate their Habits of Mind as their greatest asset.

You've probably come across Habits of Mind. They are one of the true classics in education. They have had a huge impact on teaching and learning in many schools around the world. In the context of Learnership, they offer us both a rich language for learning as well as a way to help students learn how to succeed at increasingly difficult tasks.

Art Costa and Bena Kallick identified the 16 Habits of Mind based on studies of characteristically successful people in many walks of life. These were people who, like the students we aspire to create in our learning community, had agency in the world, people who regularly succeeded at challenges and achieved growth. Many were skilful learners and masters in their domains.

From artists to athletes, entrepreneurs to doctors and many others, Costa and Kallick drew on research to identify the common patterns of behaviours that these people employed as they took on challenges and strove towards ever-increasing standards.

Based on this work, Costa and Kallick define the Habits of Mind as the dispositions that are skilfully and mindfully employed by characteristically successful people when they are confronted by problems, the solutions to which are not immediately apparent.

And where do you find problems, the solutions to which are not immediately apparent? In your learning zone, of course. The Habits of Mind form a critical part of Learnership because they describe how students need to behave when they are in their learning zone.

A list of these Habits of Mind is provided on the next page. A more detailed version can be downloaded by scanning the QR code.

HABITS OF MIND

PERSISTING
Stick to it! Persevering in task through to completion; remaining focused. Looking for ways to reach your goal when stuck. Not giving up.

LISTENING WITH UNDERSTANDING AND EMPATHY
Understand others! Devoting mental energy to another person's thoughts and ideas. Make an effort to perceive another's point of view and emotions.

THINKING ABOUT YOUR THINKING (METACOGNITION)
Know your knowing! Being aware of your own thoughts, strategies, feelings and actions and their effects on others.

QUESTIONING AND PROBLEM POSING
How do you know? Having a questioning attitude; knowing what data are needed and developing questioning strategies to produce those data. Finding problems to solve.

THINKING AND COMMUNICATING WITH CLARITY AND PRECISION
Be clear! Striving for accurate communication in both written and oral form; avoiding over-generalisations, distortions, deletions and exaggerations.

CREATING, IMAGINING AND INNOVATING
Try a different way! Generating new and novel ideas, fluency, originality.

TAKING RESPONSIBLE RISKS
Venture out! Being adventuresome; living on the edge of one's competence. Try new things constantly.

THINKING INTERDEPENDENTLY
Work together! Being able to work in and learn from others in reciprocal situations. Team work.

MANAGING IMPULSIVITY
Take your time! Thinking before acting; remaining calm, thoughtful and deliberative.

THINKING FLEXIBLY
Look at it another way! Being able to change perspectives, generate alternatives, consider options.

STRIVING FOR ACCURACY
Check it again! Always doing your best. Setting high standards. Checking and finding ways to improve constantly.

APPLYING PAST KNOWLEDGE TO NEW SITUATIONS
Use what you learn! Accessing prior knowledge; transferring knowledge beyond the situation in which it was learned.

GATHERING DATA THROUGH ALL SENSES
Use your natural pathways! Pay attention to the world around you. Gather data through all the senses; taste, touch, smell, hearing and sight.

RESPONDING WITH WONDERMENT AND AWE
Have fun figuring it out! Finding the world awesome, mysterious and being intrigued with phenomena and beauty.

FINDING HUMOUR
Laugh a little! Finding the whimsical, incongruous and unexpected. Being able to laugh at oneself.

REMAIN OPEN TO CONTINUOUS LEARNING
I have so much more to learn! Having humility and pride when admitting we don't know; resisting complacency.

Source: www.habitsofmindinstitute.org, reproduced with permission.

The Habits of Mind can be learned and developed

As you review the 16 Habits of Mind, there is one aspect you should pay particularly close attention to: they are all verbs. The Habits of Mind are not traits or qualities that some people have and others lack. They are ways of acting that can be learned and developed. Each of the Habits of Mind is something you *do*, and can learn to do *well*.

You will recognise growth in your students as they develop their Habits of Mind. The way your students persisted last year won't meet the demands of this year; they'll need to get better at persisting. To raise standards, overcome challenges and achieve more highly, learners need to change the way they behave. They need to develop their Habits of Mind.

This matches the way Carol Dweck describes intelligence. It is a malleable construct, something to be developed. In fact, early in Costa and Kallick's work they referred to the Habits of Mind as 'intelligent behaviours' – a term I personally find very powerful. For me it highlights that as students develop their Habits of Mind, they become capable of succeeding at increasingly difficult tasks, and in every practical sense become more intelligent.

Think about that for a moment. In a learning community, Habits of Mind allow us to recognise intelligence as something students learn to *do*, not something they *have*. For many of us this way of thinking about intelligence bumps up against some of those fixed mindset beliefs we discussed in part II. We've been raised in a society that has long held the belief that intelligence is a fixed, innate characteristic. The Habits of Mind help us address this, and in doing so create a powerful growth mindset mover.

Let me tell you a story to illustrate. When I heard Dweck warn of the dangers of labelling students as 'being' intelligent, and the fixed mindset messages this carries, I began to reflect on how I'd heard these words used in my own childhood. Growing up, I regularly heard the words 'smart' and 'clever' being used by my parents.

As I reflected on how my parents used the terms, I realised I never heard the phrases 'James is so smart' or 'James, you are so clever'. What I heard was 'James, *what you just did* was very clever'. Or, 'That was a very smart *way of doing that*'. I was encouraged to work at being smart*er*. By making ideas like clever, smart and intelligent something I did, not something I was, my parents were creating growth mindset movers.

What my parents lacked, which you now have, was clear and concise language to describe what behaving intelligently looks like. This is one of the gifts Costa and Kallick have given us with the Habits of Mind. They have identified the behaviours your learners need to develop to behave more intelligently. As you create a learning community and build a culture of learning and growth, the Habits of Mind will become the language of learning in your school. They'll allow you to talk to students about how to learn to behave more intelligently.

HABITS OF MIND, INTELLIGENCE AND THE PERFORMANCE PLATEAU

There is an important relationship to be understood between the performance plateau and the Habits of Mind. Consider the learning zone diagram from the previous chapter again. Pay attention to the position of the performance plateau. Why is the bar there, and not higher or lower? What sets the height of the bar? What makes a student struggle as they go into their learning zone?

Now, brace yourself. As I answer these questions, I'm likely to push one of your fixed mindset triggers again. You might feel a bit uncomfortable for a moment. Stay with me. Here we go ...

When you see a student moving into their learning zone and you see them struggle and make mistakes, progress is difficult and they are unable to immediately succeed, and they are spending time and energy but progress has stopped – this is a sign they *aren't smart enough* to do better.

In fact, we can think of the performance plateau as the limit of their intelligence.

Okay. Deep breath ... I know. I just said your students weren't smart enough. And if you're like 95% of the leaders I work with, you probably just drew a sharp breath, winced, and your opinion of me just dropped several notches. I said your students had reached the limit of their intelligence. Something deep inside you was triggered. Was I calling your students stupid? Part of you is saying, 'Oh James, you can't do that.'

The reason most people react when I say that is it hits one of your fixed mindset triggers. All your life a person's intelligence, how smart they are, has been seen as a fixed quantity.

So let me rephrase that ...

When you see a student moving into their learning zone and you see them struggle and make mistakes, progress is difficult and they are unable to immediately succeed, and they are spending time and energy but progress has stopped – this is a sign that their Habits of Mind aren't *currently* well enough developed to do better.

In fact, we can think of the performance plateau as the limit of the learner's current level of development of their Habits of Mind. (Notice again the use of the nudge to attach time stamps.)

This way of viewing struggle and the limit of a student's current abilities powerfully changes our response. For the learner to improve, you need to guide them to develop their Habits of Mind. You need to recognise that the behaviours that got them to their current level of achievement won't get them to a higher level of achievement. As a teacher you need to help them develop their Habits of Mind and teach them to behave more intelligently.

In a learning community, teachers are thinking not just about what needs to be learned. They are also thinking about how they can leverage each learning experience to help develop students' Habits of Mind. They are considering how the challenges they create both demand and develop students' mature application of their Habits of Mind. They are focused not just on what is being learned, but how the learning drives growth.

This highlights an important relationship between challenge and Habits of Mind. Challenge drives the development of your Habits of Mind. If a learner consistently avoids challenges, avoids their learning zone, they have little or no opportunity to develop their Habits of Mind. But the learner who is constantly seeking out challenges is continually developing their Habits of Mind.

> ❝ Challenge drives the development of your Habits of Mind.

Habits of Mind and Learnership

The Habits of Mind play a critical role in developing Learnership and building a learning community. They give us the language of learning in the school – shared by students, teachers and the wider community – that describes how learners engage in the learning process.

Recognising the Habits of Mind as dispositions that can be developed creates a powerful growth mindset mover. The entire learning community understand that the pathway to greater learning and higher standards is through developing learners' Habits of Mind. This strongly impacts learner agency.

The Habits of Mind also give teachers clarity around the learning behaviours they seek to develop, allowing them to focus not just on what students need to learn but also on how they are learning. Teachers can identify and target specific Habits of Mind for development to support students with specific goals and challenges.

It's not simply that students are developing their Habits of Mind that matters. From the perspective of Learnership, it's the relationship students have with the Habits of Mind and how they go about developing them that matters. Learnership is about deepening and enriching the relationship learners have with the Habits of Mind.

Consider the different ways learners might go about developing the habits.

Some learners spend their time in their comfort and performance zones, avoiding challenges. They fill their time with 'easy things they haven't done yet'. For these learners, the Habits of Mind are at best a simple description of what they do, not something they are learning to do better. In the absence of challenge they cannot develop their Habits of Mind at all.

Other learners develop their Habits of Mind only because they are *told to*. The teacher is in charge, will identify when development is needed, and provides instruction, scaffolds and processes to ensure the development takes place.

Some develop their Habits of Mind in response to the demands of a goal they have set. They develop their Habits of Mind because they *need to*. For these learners the development is in response to an immediate need.

Others recognise and value the Habits of Mind as their greatest asset. They seek to leverage every learning opportunity, embracing challenges because they give them the opportunity to cultivate their Habits of Mind. They develop the Habits of Mind because they *want to*. They recognise the Habits of Mind they develop in response to the current challenge are largely transferable and will serve them into the future.

At the core of enriching that relationship is helping students recognise, understand and value the intimate connection between challenge and the Habits of Mind. It's a shift from being reactive and allowing the problems they encounter to drive the development of their Habits of Mind, to becoming proactive and selecting challenges that allow them to target and cultivate specific Habits of Mind.

THE HABITS OF MIND LEARNER PROFILE

About now, you've probably got some questions about the Habits of Mind. How do you introduce Habits of Mind to students? What do the Habits of Mind look like in a classroom? How do teachers make use of them? Where can I find examples of schools that have successfully adopted the Habits of Mind? These are all relevant questions, and I've included some links and resources at the end of the chapter that will help you find the answers.

One question in particular I'm often asked is: 'How do we assess a student's Habits of Mind?'

The question of assessment is an important one. If one of your goals is to develop students' Habits of Mind, you are going to need a tool that will meaningfully assess them – a way to guide and track the development of students' Habits of Mind over time. This is what The Habits of Mind Learner Profile that I've developed does.*

The unique aspect of the tool is that at its heart it respects the relationship between the Habits of Mind and the problems a learner is trying to solve. Most common assessment mechanisms (like rubrics and checklists) try to assess the Habits of Mind directly against an external standard. They try to place the level of development on a scale, often in a summative way, from beginner to expert, or low to high. In short, they attempt to answer the question 'how well developed' are a learner's Habits of Mind?

But you can't meaningfully separate the Habits of Mind from the problems they solve. It makes no sense to talk about how well developed a learner's Habits of Mind are without asking if that level of development is sufficient to solve the problems the student regularly encounters.

It doesn't matter *how well* developed your Habits of Mind are. All that matters is that they are *well enough* developed to succeed at the problems you regularly encounter, or as we'll see later, that they are well enough developed to succeed at the problems you anticipate you'll encounter in the future. We only need to develop our Habits of Mind because we are going beyond our current abilities, into our learning zone. And going into the learning zone drives the development.

The Habits of Mind Learner Profile embraces this relationship. The assessment it provides tells the learner if the problems they are encountering, that demand a particular Habit of Mind, are in their comfort zone, performance zone or learning zone.

---

* It's beyond the scope of this book to give a full account of how the Habits of Mind Learner Profile can be used to assess students' Habits of Mind and to help improve Learnership. I'd love you to make use of the Habits of Mind Profile for yourself too.

Knowing this guides the learner to take appropriate actions for further development, including seeking out more difficult problems to stimulate further growth. In this way the Habits of Mind Learner Profile is a formative assessment tool.

The Learner Profile allows you to take a snapshot of the current level of development of a learner's Habits of Mind. Interpreting that snapshot provides unique insights that guide the actions students must take to continually develop their Habits of Mind and increase Learnership. Take a moment now to have a look at the following example.

The Habits of Mind Learner Profile

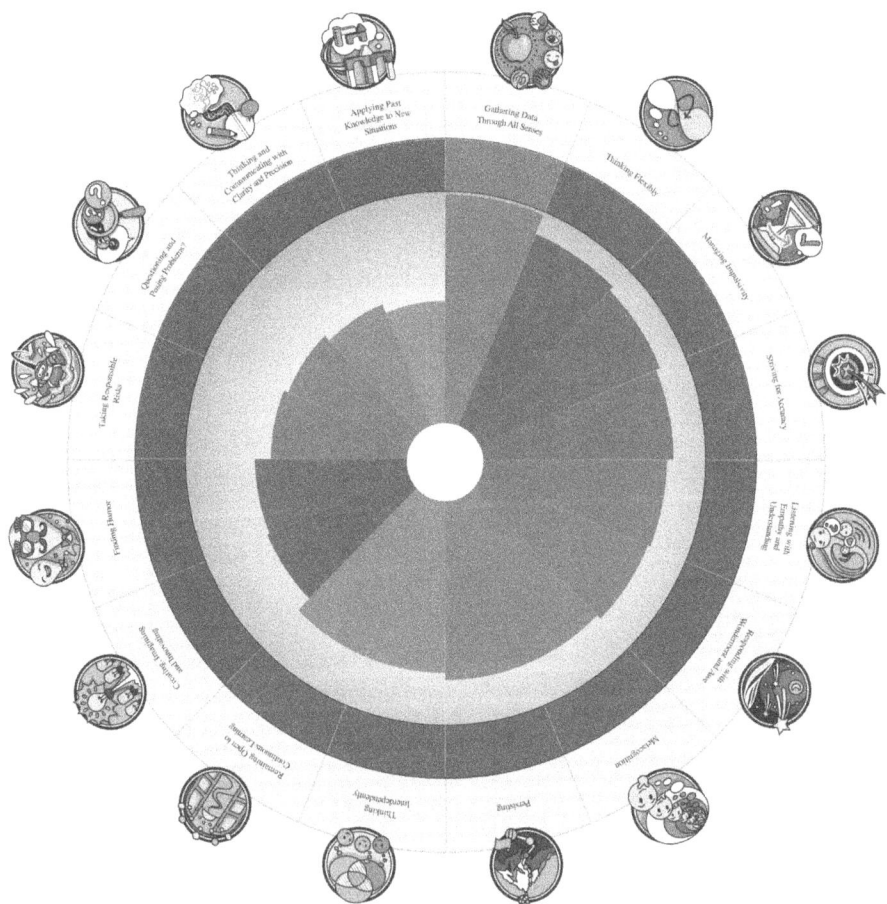

The Learner Profile mediates the learner's constant reflection on their Habits of Mind, and the types of challenges the learner is using to create growth. It helps them gain a clear picture of how Habits of Mind are helping them succeed at the problems they are encountering. It both guides and monitors what they need to do to further develop their Habits of Mind. It helps to nurture a deeper understanding of themselves as a learner, and creates a greater valuing of the Habits of Mind.

> 66 In a learning community ... we seek to help students develop a deep understanding of the relationship between challenge, Habits of Mind and growth. The Habits of Mind Learner Profile helps us achieve this.

In a learning community, the development of the Habits of Mind goes beyond being a requirement to help students meet particular learning goals. We seek to help students develop a deep understanding of the relationship between challenge, Habits of Mind and growth. The Habits of Mind Learner Profile helps us achieve this. Students become more skilful learners as they recognise their Habits of Mind as their greatest asset, cultivating in them a means to futureproof themselves and – as we'll see in chapter 22 – become antifragile.

To find out more about how you can use the Habits of Mind Learner Profile at your school please visit www.jamesanderson.com.au/learnerprofile where you can access a free trial.

For more general information about the Habits of Mind please visit the Institute for Habits of Mind www.habitsofmindinstitute.org or www.jamesanderson.com.au/habits-of-mind.

Chapter 11
Mistakes: finding information for growth

*Mistakes are not good, or bad.
They are merely signposts to tell you what
you have yet to learn.*

A DIFFERENT VIEW OF MISTAKES

As learners move into their learning zone, they are moving beyond their current abilities. The level of development of their Habits of Mind is insufficient to bring about immediate success. There is a period of struggle. It's during this struggle that learners make mistakes. Skilful learners understand that these mistakes are important sources of information and use them to guide their actions.

Unfortunately, the way our education system has misunderstood mistakes gets in the way of learners developing a healthy and productive relationship with mistakes and becoming more skilful learners. If you've been in education long enough you will remember when mistakes were 'bad'. There were negative consequences for making mistakes. The red crosses we put on a page were signs students had got something wrong. For students, mistakes were to be avoided if possible, and corrected if necessary. Mistakes were a source of judgement.

The current educational thinking takes a different view of mistakes. Mistakes are to be encouraged and celebrated. Today, we are told that mistakes help us learn. To address some of the negative associations of mistakes, teachers now tell students that mistakes are good. They encourage mistakes. One teacher told me he has an enormous banner above the board that reads, 'In this classroom we make magnificent mistakes!'

Saying mistakes were bad discouraged students from going into their learning zone. It even led them to fear their learning zone, instilling a sense of risk and fear of negative consequences. As a result, students remained in the relative safety of their comfort and performance zones, where the chance of mistakes, and the consequences associated with them, was low. The problem of course was that staying in their comfort and performance zones got in the way of their growth.

Skilful learners understand that mistakes are not bad. And they are not good either. They understand that mistakes are merely signposts to tell them what they have yet to learn. Their value is in how they help fill the gap between where they are now and where they want to be – how they help raise the bar. And if a mistake does not provide that information, it has little value. In Learnership, mistakes are not sources of judgement or sources of encouragement, they are potential sources of information.

> In Learnership, mistakes are not sources of judgement or sources of encouragement, they are potential sources of information.

As learners come to recognise mistakes (and as you'll see in the next chapter, feedback as well) as sources of information, it creates an important shift. It no longer makes sense to talk about the mistake, instead you can talk about the information the mistake provides. That leads you to focus on the actions the learner can take to either gather or act on that information. After all, mistakes don't help us learn. It's the actions we take to correct mistakes that helps us learn.

The power of recognising mistakes as potential sources of information is that it shifts our focus from the mistake to what the learner does to generate and act on that information. The mistake simply exists. From a Learnership perspective we put the focus clearly on the student's actions, and how those actions help them learn and get them from where they are now to where they want to be.

NOT ALL MISTAKES ARE CREATED EQUAL

As learners develop Learnership they develop a much more nuanced understanding of mistakes. They recognise not all mistakes are created equal. It's not that mistakes are good or bad. It's a matter of them being helpful or unhelpful to learning. Some mistakes provide us with useful information that pushes us forward and helps us raise the bar. Others are less helpful, or even detrimental to our learning.

Skilful learners recognise six different types of mistakes:

- **Confusion mistakes:** These mistakes don't help us learn much at all. They leave us without any new information and without any path forward.
- **Sloppy mistakes:** These mistakes happen when we aren't paying enough attention. We don't learn anything new from them. They don't help us learn.
- **Performance mistakes:** These mistakes can happen when we are trying to do our best. We can learn from them, but we try to avoid them because they have negative consequences.
- **Aha mistakes:** These mistakes happen unexpectedly! Sometimes they can show you things you weren't even expecting to learn. They can be rare, and special.
- **Stretch mistakes:** These mistakes happen when we go into our learning zone. We have to work out why they happened so we can learn from them. Very good for learning.
- **Design mistakes:** We think about these mistakes before we make them so they will tell us what we want to know. They are great for learning!

It is worth noting the key differences between the types of mistakes. Understanding these mistakes helps students increase their intentionality in learning and further enhances the language of learning you are creating in your school. So it's worth taking a moment to explore the important differences between these six types of mistakes.

Confusion mistakes

Confusion mistakes occur because the learner goes too far beyond their current best. Instead of being in their learning zone – where they feel stretched – they have entered what I refer to as the 'aspirational zone' – where they feel strained. As the name suggests, these mistakes leave the learner confused. They are no better off than they were before they made the mistake, and they may be worse off because of the confusion they generate. While there may be information in these mistakes, it's not accessible by the learner, so they aren't useful for learning.

Sloppy mistakes

We've all made careless mistakes. These are mistakes we shouldn't make. They occur in our comfort zone, not because we were attempting something beyond our current abilities but because we weren't paying adequate attention. We weren't applying our existing abilities to their fullest extent. These types of mistakes aren't useful to learning because they don't provide the learner with any *new* information. Skilful learners seek to minimise or eliminate these types of mistakes.

Performance mistakes

Let's be honest – sometimes we don't want to make mistakes! Some mistakes really are bad. These mistakes are called performance mistakes and can have significant negative consequences. They occur in a learner's performance zone during real-world performance situations. While it is possible to learn from these mistakes, the consequences of the mistake are usually something best avoided.

Some learners behave as if *all* mistakes are performance mistakes. The performance cultures that have been created in our schools mean students feel they are being constantly measured and judged. That any mistake they make will have a negative consequence.

Telling students who feel like all mistakes are performance mistakes that 'it's okay, we all make mistakes' or 'mistakes are part of learning' is another reflection of the vague way we talk about mistakes in our classrooms. For these students mistakes are not okay, and are part of being judged. Because some mistakes really are like that.

I find it contradictory that many teachers simultaneously tell students that mistakes are okay, but at the same time encourage their students to 'take risks' with their learning. There is the mixed message that students should be okay with mistakes, but there is still the 'risk' of negative consequences. This is a reflection of an incomplete understanding of mistakes and their role in learning.

> ❝❝ The path to becoming a better learner involves understanding that not all mistakes are equal.

Students don't fear mistakes. They fear a negative consequence of mistakes. The path to becoming a better learner involves understanding that not all mistakes are equal. With an understanding of the different types of mistakes, a student's aversion to making mistakes can be recognised as valuable, in the right context. Teachers can then help students recognise the different contexts in which their avoidance strategies are, and aren't, helpful. Students can become more intentional in the way they use, or avoid, mistakes, and recognise that not all mistakes have negative consequences – just some. They can learn that other types of mistakes, like those that happen in your learning zone described on the next page, are different. They have *positive* consequences.

Stretch mistakes

Stretch mistakes are the mistakes meant when talking about encouraging students to make mistakes. These mistakes happen in the learning zone. Because they occur just beyond a learner's current abilities, they can shine a light on what they are yet to learn. They provide information that helps to close the gap between where they are now and where they want to be.

Skilful learners understand the purpose of stretch mistakes and skilful teachers ensure the consequences of these types of mistakes are low or non-existent. We learn to recognise them as a natural, and desirable, part of being in our learning zone.

Our response to stretch mistakes is reactive. We interrogate the mistake for the information it can provide, but only after we have made it.

Aha mistakes

What I refer to as aha mistakes are the mistakes that can provide us with unexpected, but sometimes very valuable, information. Like stretch mistakes, they occur in the learning zone. But unlike stretch mistakes where the learner deliberately goes into their learning zone, with aha moments you arrive by chance. And aha moment mistakes don't need to be 'corrected'. We don't need to find or tease out the information. It's immediately revealed by the mistake.

Teachers sometimes manufacture circumstances for students to create aha moment mistakes during discovery learning, play-based learning or constructivist learning. These mistakes sometimes result in unexpected but highly valuable discoveries. An example is Alexander Fleming's discovery of penicillin.

Design mistakes

Design mistakes are the mistakes that we make proactively. We think like a scientist and deliberately create the circumstances that will generate the information we need.

Think of the often-quoted reference to Thomas Edison that he found '10,000 ways a light globe didn't work'. Edison wasn't randomly creating different light globes, discarding the 'mistakes' that didn't work in the hope of finding one that did. He maximised the information from every test by planning, controlling the variables, and knowing specifically what information he was looking for.

Design mistakes are the most valuable mistakes because they provide the most targeted information.

LEARNERSHIP AND MISTAKES

Learnership is not simply about taking on challenges, it's about our understanding of challenges and our relationship to them. And Learnership is not only about the need to develop our Habits of Mind, it's about understanding and valuing the Habits of Mind and the way we go about achieving that development. Similarly, Learnership is not about mistakes. It's about understanding mistakes as a source of information, and how learners get better at acquiring that information.

The common approaches to mistakes widely adopted by schools are actually hindering the development of students' Learnership. Catchall phrases like 'mistakes help me learn' don't hold up to close inspection. Not all mistakes help you learn. The more nuanced understanding of mistakes we develop as part of Learnership helps learners better understand how to use mistakes to find or create the information they need for learning.

Recognising mistakes as sources of information changes the way teachers respond to a learner's mistake. Instead of celebrating mistakes and encouraging learners to take risks with their learning, teachers praise students for going into their learning zone – where they are expected to make mistakes and the consequences of those mistakes are low. Teachers praise students for the way they respond to and correct those mistakes. They might even be praised for the actions they take to avoid mistakes in a performance situation. Praise shifts from being about the mistake to instead being focused on the actions of the student, how the student generated information from the mistake, and what they are doing with that information to achieve growth.

As students move through school and develop Learnership, this understanding of mistakes helps guide them to make more effective use of mistakes for learning. Initially, teachers might help students get over their fear and avoidance of mistakes by recognising when mistakes have negative consequences and when they have positive consequences. They can help students distinguish between helpful and unhelpful mistakes by recognising when they are in their learning zone or their performance zone. Students might then need to be guided through the process of learning to follow a teacher's instructions to correct mistakes. Then they learn how to interrogate mistakes for themselves, prying the information from the error they have made. Eventually, comfortable knowing that the right mistakes are useful tools to help them grow, they deliberately set out to design circumstances where mistakes generate the information they need.

Chapter 12
Feedback: seeking information for growth

The skill of feedback lies in the receiving.

As learners venture into their learning zone they must seek out the information they need to help them progress. While mistakes can provide that information, they don't always provide all the information learners need, or provide it in the most efficient and effective ways. So learners may need to find other sources of information. This is where feedback plays an important role in Learnership.

After Hattie's analysis showed that the effect size of feedback on student performance is around 0.73 – almost twice his hinge point of 0.4 – teachers have become almost obsessed with feedback. In the past few years, how many days of professional learning have your teachers attended to learn how to give quality feedback? And have you noticed that almost all the professional learning has been from the perspective of the teacher? It's been about the skill of teaching, and the teachers' responsibility to *provide* quality feedback to students. Students have been viewed largely as simply receivers of that information.

The problem with this view of teachers providing feedback is it ignores the role of the learner, and the skill of learning. After all, a teacher might craft the most beautiful feedback, that is specific, timely, actionable, accurate, non-judgemental and concrete. But if the learner ignores that feedback, or if they do not act on it, it will have no impact on learning and growth so has zero value.

From our Learnership perspective we shift the focus from the skill of the teacher to the skill of the learner. We can think of the learner's relationship with feedback in three parts:

- how the learner goes about acquiring the information they need
- how the learner ensures the information meets their needs
- how the learner acts on that information.

HOW LEARNERS RECEIVE FEEDBACK

How do your learners typically relate to feedback? Chances are you have some learners who habitually disregard feedback – even though your teachers are doing a great job of providing it, and the information may be highly valuable, you have learners who don't take advantage of that information. A comment on an assignment isn't even read. If learners don't pay attention to the information provided, there's no way it can change their behaviour. Consequently they gain no value from it.

You also are likely to have learners who will simply acknowledge that feedback has been given – listening to or reading the comments – but they don't action it. At best they see the purpose of feedback as a means of assessing their learning, at worst a simple commentary on their work. They don't see it as a source of information to be acted on. So in practice the feedback does little to improve their outcomes.

Other learners can be highly selective about feedback. These are the ones who would frustrate me the most in my classroom. They would pay attention to only some of the feedback: typically the positive feedback, the affirmations and the information that confirms what they can already do. But the rest of the feedback – anything constructive or formative which they may view as critical – they ignore. Again, although they paid attention to (some of) the information, it didn't change their actions, only affirmed some of them, so ultimately was of little value.

In all three cases above the learners are not taking any action to gather the information they need. They are, at best, passive receivers of information. Neither are they playing any role in ensuring the information they are being provided meets their needs. Nor are they using the information to improve performance. None of these responses results in any significant action on behalf of the learner.

The ways of relating to feedback I just described are often a reflection of a student's mindset. Students at the low-growth end of the Mindset Continuum believe their abilities cannot be changed. From their perspective, feedback can at best only be conformational, at worst critical. It only identifies what they can and can't do – their perceived limits. From their perspective it can't be helpful in changing their abilities, so it is largely ignored.

This underscores the importance of continually focusing on moving students towards the growth end of the Mindset Continuum. While students continue to hold on to fixed beliefs, our efforts to help them become better learners, including developing a better relationship with feedback, will be undermined.

> 66 Skilful learners ensure that feedback is tailored to their needs.

As learners become more skilful they take action to seek out feedback. They ask for help. Although the degree to which they are able to identify what type of help they need varies. They take charge only of the acquisition stage of feedback. They seek out a source of information – often the teacher – and ask for the information they require and what steps they need to take to achieve mastery.

Whether the learner is passively waiting for feedback to be given to them, or actively seeking it out by asking for it, they still rely on the teacher to determine what information they need. But we have all experienced times when the feedback provided doesn't 'fit'. It might have been accurate, but not exactly what we were focusing on.

Skilful learners do better. A more skilful approach that maximises the value they receive from feedback is for the learner to take charge of acquiring it, and ensuring it meets their specific quality needs as well. Skilful learners ensure that feedback is tailored to their needs.

TAILORING FEEDBACK

Tailoring feedback involves the learner first knowing what their learning goals are. They identify a goal, and develop a clear idea of the type of information they'll need to measure progress towards that goal. They then identify a way to capture that information, and ensure the way it is captured and communicated to them will provide them with the most value. In this way the learner takes charge of all aspects of feedback, from its acquisition to its quality and how to act on it. This is called 'tailoring feedback'. This puts the learner in charge of the feedback, ensuring they get maximum value and maximum growth from the feedback they receive.

A missed opportunity

Several years ago I was asked to give a keynote to a group of school leaders in New Zealand. I'd just achieved recognition as a Certified Speaking Professional (CSP) from the Professional Speakers Association (PSA) of Australia. I was feeling pretty chuffed – being a CSP put me among the top non-celebrity speakers in Australia.

Naturally, I was feeling pretty confident about the keynote. After all I was a CSP now. This was my performance zone. I was going to confidently walk on stage. I was going to knock the keynote out of the park. The audience were going to laugh. They were going to be challenged. They were going to learn. And at the end of the hour they were going to give me a huge round of applause.

The morning I arrived at the venue, I immediately recognised the MC for the event as a past president of the PSA – let's just call him Glen. For him, being a CSP was certainly an achievement, but it was the start of the journey of being a professional speaker, not, as I felt, the pinnacle.

At the time I was working on an aspect of my speaking related to 'placing' particular ideas on different parts of the stage. I was trying to help the audience see the Mindset Continuum by deliberately 'placing' fixed mindset ideas on one side of the stage and growth mindset ideas on the other. I'd then walk between these two points, stepping out the changes in behaviour associated with developing an increasingly growth-oriented mindset.

The sensible thing to have done would have been to introduce myself, tell Glen my learning goal, and ask him to pay attention to how well I was achieving it. I would have been proactively taking charge of acquiring the information I needed, tailoring my feedback to ensure it was going to fit my learning needs. That is what a skilful learner would do: prime the person who is going to give the feedback to make sure it best meets their learning needs.

But I didn't. In the moment, the fixed mindset messages of being judged or being called out for being a fraud all came crashing in on me. I avoided any interactions with Glen and basically hid until it was my turn to speak.

The keynote went very well. People laughed in the appropriate places, nodded meaningfully when I challenged certain ideas, and there was a rousing round of applause at the end, followed by many school leaders wanting to know more about my work.

Feeling like I'd 'proved' myself, I now felt confident to approach Glen and ask for some feedback. After all, he was probably the only person in the room who understood what I was trying to do, and had the skills, experience and expertise to provide the feedback I needed.

What a great opportunity for me to learn from the master!

So I approached Glen full of confidence and asked him about how effectively he thought I'd placed the ideas in different locations on the stage, and if he had any advice about how I might improve. His response was, 'Oh, James. I'm sorry. I would have loved to have given you some feedback, but I didn't know you were going to ask. I was actually paying attention to something else. I'm happy to give you some notes on a few things I noticed about your slides if that's helpful.'

I'd missed my opportunity.

He hadn't captured the information *because I hadn't asked him to*. Glen was gracious and helpful, but because I hadn't primed him to capture the information I needed, the information he could give me didn't match my learning goals. That was a lesson learned for me. That day I became a more skilful learner. I learned to make sure I maximised the value of the feedback I received by first identifying the information I would need (by being clear about my learning goals) and then ensuring that information is being gathered. In that way the feedback is tailored, an exact match to my learning needs, so it has maximum value.

Identifying goals

At several of the schools I work with, teachers have been helping students understand how to tailor feedback. I'll describe how a year 11 English teacher made tailoring feedback a part of her standard process for essay writing, however the general principles are applicable to any subject and any year level.

This teacher has modified her standard cover sheet for essays. In addition to the description of the task and success criteria, students are asked to identify a specific aspect of their writing they will be focusing on. This can be something the teacher has been covering in class, or it might be something the student has identified based on previous feedback.

Having this focus puts students in their learning zone. They aren't sitting down to simply write an essay, as had so often happened in the past. They are sitting down to write a better essay than before, and they know how they are going to try to make it better.

One student described his focus when writing an essay on Shakespeare's *Romeo and Juliet* like this: 'To use appropriate and varied quotes that support my point. In previous essays I've just tried to include quotes we've used in class, but they didn't always match what I was trying to say.'

Before these students hand in their essay, there is one more step. The cover sheet also provides an opportunity for students to ask the teacher for specific feedback on the element of their writing they'd been focusing on. This helps the teacher give the most valuable feedback to the student.

In this case, the student asked for feedback that was tailored to his goal. He wrote: 'In this essay I've tried to be more careful in choosing quotes that best fit my points. Could you please tell me if I've chosen the best quotes, and if I haven't, how I could choose better ones? In particular in the second paragraph I couldn't decide between using " … some consequence yet honing in the stars" and the one about "fickle fortune". Both seemed to be pretty similar to me, so I couldn't decide.'

Now that the teacher has been primed to give tailored feedback to the student, it makes her work much more focused, she saves time, and the feedback the student receives is much more valuable. Of course, the teacher can give other feedback as well, but tailoring the feedback in this way means it's a perfect fit for the student's learning goals.

Chapter 13
Effort: the currency of growth

We are all capable of growth, but it is not free.

HOW WELL DO YOU SPEND YOUR TIME AND ENERGY?

Challenge is the pathway to growth. A learner's Habits of Mind are the actions which take them down that path. Mistakes and feedback provide a learner with the information they need to keep them heading in the right direction. But, over time, it's a learner's *efforts* that propel them forward to greater and greater growth.

The way we use the word 'effort' in schools is actually pretty vague. Think about the multitude of different ways the word effort is used in your classrooms. The student who's been busy, active and participated in activities all day has put in a lot of effort that day. The student who's worked hard to produce something of quality is praised for their hard work and effort. Another student who has struggled all lesson, but ultimately failed to achieve their goal is also praised, because at least they put in a lot of effort. And the student who is focused, makes mistakes, asks for feedback, corrects their mistakes and ultimately achieves their learning goal is also praised for their effort.

About the only thing these examples have in common is that each student has expended a lot of time and energy. However, how that time and energy have been spent, and what each student has achieved as a result, are all very different.

Like so much of our work with Learnership, we must take a more critical and nuanced approach to understanding effort. This is no different to any other area of expertise. Indeed, the ability to be discerning and deliberate about how you engage in an activity is one of the defining qualities of an expert.

> ❝ ... effort is not the amount of time and energy a learner puts in to a task, it's how well that time and energy are spent.

To say a learner has put in effort is akin to saying the principal dancer in the New York City Ballet moves to the music. Or to describe the work of Leonardo da Vinci merely as paintings. Or to say a master chief cooks a meal. The statements are true, but they are vague and ultimately unhelpful. The descriptions rob the expert of the sophistication and complexity that make them an expert. More importantly, they rob us of the means to understand what they are doing or to learn from their performance.

From the perspective of Learnership, effort is not the amount of time and energy a learner puts in to a task, it's how well that time and energy are spent. More specifically, it's about *how* and *where* that time and energy are spent. Skilful learners understand effort, and they invest it wisely.

THE EFFECTIVE EFFORT MATRIX

Skilful learners understand that effort is the currency of growth. They know that while they are capable of growth, it is not free. It demands an expenditure of *the right type of* effort.

Skilful learners recognise that effort has value. It comes in the form of our time and energy, both of which are renewable, but still limited, resources. We don't get to store them up. Skilful learners recognise their effort can be wasted, spent or invested, depending on what they do and how they do it. They seek to understand and maximise the value of their effort.

The way some learners spend their time and energy is more valuable than others. As an educator you will already have a sense of this. You know when students are wasting their time. There are also moments when you know two students are putting in a 'lot' of effort but getting different results. Both are 'trying hard', but one is growing and the other is not.

The Effective Effort Matrix

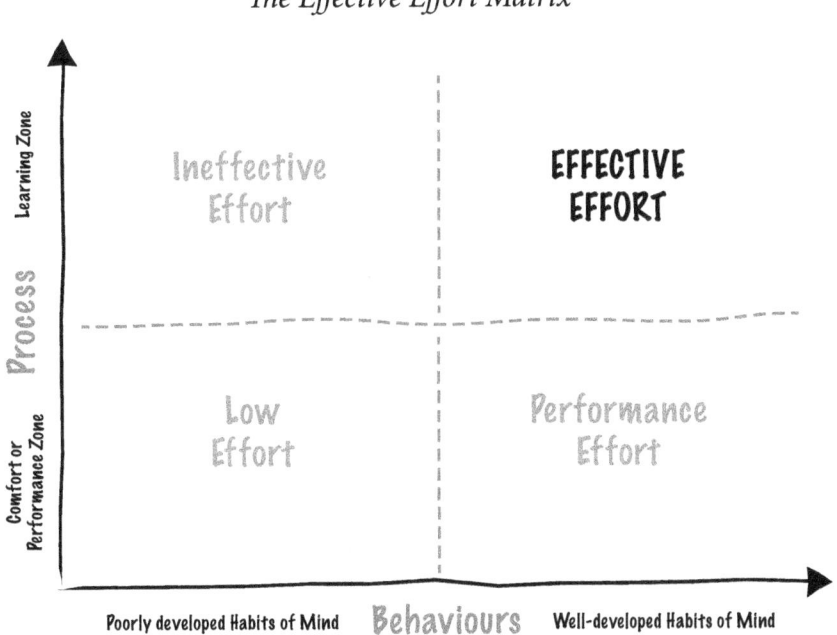

The Effective Effort Matrix illustrates why not all effort is equal. Its two axes help us recognise that it is *where* and *how* our time and energy are being spent that matters. The vertical axis represents *where* the learner is spending their time and energy, either above the bar in their learning zone, or below the bar in their comfort and performance zones.

The horizontal axis represents *how* the time and energy are spent, and asks if the learner is calling on their existing abilities and established Habits of Mind, or if they are going through the process of developing more mature Habits of Mind. The result is these four types of effort:

- low effort – cruising
- performance effort – performing
- ineffective effort – struggling
- effective effort – growing.

Let's consider how each of these types of effort helps us achieve growth, or not.

Low effort – cruising

Low effort is the result of the learner spending time and energy below the bar, in their comfort zone, applying their Habits of Mind to problems well within their current abilities. It's not doing nothing at all. Rather it's when a learner fills their time with things they can do easily, or the easy things they haven't done yet. To an outside observer this looks like the learner is cruising.

Most learners know what this type of effort feels like. It can feel busy, even productive. Tasks are getting ticked off the list. Progress is being made. But the tasks are easy. The value of what's being produced is low. As a leader, when you get stuck in this type of effort you're left with the feeling that your time could be better spent.

That we spend time and energy in low effort isn't itself a bad thing. There are some tasks that just have to get done. That's okay. These can be easy, and simply consume our time with little return beyond the completion of a low-value task. Low effort is an expense we all have to pay at times. The issue for skilful learners is how much time and energy is being spent in low effort, and how they minimise this, because this type of effort doesn't help us achieve growth.

Performance effort – performing

Performance effort occurs in the learner's performance zone, exercising their most well-developed Habits of Mind. It produces their current peak performance. It is the sort of effort required for the learner to do their best – but not any better.

There is a need for performance effort. In schools, teachers often expect students to produce their best in the classroom, demonstrating their current peak standard. Performance effort is where we get the greatest short-term return for our expenditure of time and energy. It is often expected of us in work and other high-stakes situations. It is still an expense, but the task we complete has high value. It doesn't feel like we've wasted our effort, but at the same time it's not an investment either. There's no long-term gain.

As we've already explored, you don't get better by doing your best. When a learner spends too much time engaging in performance effort they allow their best to get in the way of getting better. The issue for the skilful learner is to balance the demands of performance with the need for growth. To balance the expenditure of effort on performance with investment of effort in their growth.

Ineffective effort – struggling

Ineffective effort is a potential drain on resources. It occurs when the learner steps beyond their current best, into their learning zone, but does so ineffectively. They apply old behaviours, their previous best, to new and more challenging problems.

As we've discussed, when it comes to your Habits of Mind, what got you here won't get you there – it is the stretch of the challenge that drives growth. So as they initially step into their learning zone, a learner will find themselves ill equipped for the challenge. They struggle, make mistakes, and achieve little or no progress.

That a learner struggles is a normal part of the learning process. It is part of the investment learners make in an attempt to achieve growth. However, the struggle the learner experiences during ineffective effort can be either productive or unproductive. A wise investment, or a poor one.

Unproductive struggle looks like 'working hard, but going nowhere'. The learner experiences this when they are not able to access, or fail to act on, the information they need to improve. This could be because they are unwilling or unable to act on information available to them in the form of mistakes or feedback. Either way, progress stalls.

This type of unproductive effort is high cost but has little or no return. Time and energy are going up and up, but progress stalls. The wheels are spinning, the engine is revving, smoke is coming off the tyres, but the vehicle is stationary.

Less skilful learners can waste a great deal of effort in unproductive struggle. They keep pouring their time and energy in. Their costs escalate, and they see little return. As we'll see in a moment, this can significantly impact their willingness to invest their effort on future challenges.

Skilful learners are quick to recognise this low return and take steps to gather the information they need to progress. They don't waste unnecessary time in this type of effort, and take measures to change the return they are getting. They shift into productive struggle.

Productive struggle is informative. The learner's mistakes and the feedback they are receiving allows them to make slow, but steady, progress. Each mistake can be followed by a correction that moves them forward, providing a small but important return for every effort.

When a learner is in productive struggle, they focus not just on what they are learning but also on how they are learning. They actively develop their Habits of Mind to build the skills they need to succeed at this new level. This type of effort has the greatest long-term return as the learner is investing not only in what they are producing but also in their own development.

A skilful learner is able to minimise the time and energy spent in ineffective effort by maximising the amount and quality of information they receive, and moving quickly from ineffective effort to effective effort.

Effective effort – growing

Effective effort occurs as the learner develops their Habits of Mind and shifts out of struggle and into growth and achievement. Their time and energy are not simply producing a product, they're doing something much more valuable – they are changing themselves. Their focus on how they are learning allows them to develop and exercise more highly developed Habits of Mind than before.

As the learner develops their Habits of Mind and applies them to this new level, what they used to find hard becomes easy. The way forward becomes increasingly clear. Counterintuitively, this is characterised by time and energy going down, and progress leaping forward. This type of effort has greatest value, as the learner is now operating at a new, higher, level.

> ❝ Skilful learners are keenly aware that effort isn't just 'hard work'. They are focused on the return they are getting on their effort.

At times this type of effective effort can feel like flow. It might feel like the learner has had a breakthrough. They can sense their efforts are paying off. They can do something they weren't previously able to do. The shackles of struggle have fallen off and been replaced by a feeling of progress, even joy.

Skilful learners are keenly aware that effort isn't just 'hard work'. They are focused on the return they are getting on their effort. They manage their time and energy for greatest effect. They realise that some time will be spent in low effort but seek to minimise this. They understand that some time needs to be spent in performance effort and seek to maximise the value they receive from it. They also recognise that learning almost inevitably involves some ineffective effort, but they employ strategies like designing mistakes and tailoring feedback to minimise the cost and maximise the return from this effort.

And the skilful learner will seek to move quickly into effective effort and maximise their investment here.

PRAISING EFFORT EFFECTIVELY

Of course, understanding these four different types of effort also provides teachers with a much more differentiated and targeted way to praise, encourage and teach students how to engage in effective effort.

A group of teachers I was working with recently had fallen into the standard 'great effort', 'good job' and 'you've worked really hard on that' phrases for praising effort. Which is understandable – it's probably what they'd heard growing up too. While their intentions were good, their execution needed work.

To get them refocused, I suggested that instead of 'praising effort' they should praise students for the particular actions which led to growth. I asked them to think specifically of what the student was doing, how they were engaging in learning and what they were doing to achieve growth. To think about how and where the learner's time and energy was being spent, not simply how much time and energy they were spending. Here are some of the alternatives they came up with:

- It was great to see you spend so much time in your learning zone today!
- I really appreciated how, when you made that mistake, you spent your time trying to work out why you got it wrong, rather than giving up or asking for help straight away.
- I noticed that when you had to choose between the easy task and the harder one, you chose the harder one. That's awesome, and the way to grow.
- It's good to see you getting lots of work done, but it looks like those tasks are in your comfort zone. Now what I'd like to see you focus on is something in your learning zone.
- John, how long have you been stuck on that same problem without any progress? It's great you're sticking to it, but when you're stuck at something for a long time, and not seeing progress,

we call that unproductive struggle and it's not a great use of your time. It's a sign you need to get some more information.
- Michelle, over the past few days I've been watching how you've been spending your time. Tell me, how much of that time do you think has been spent doing your best, and how much has been spent trying to get better? Have you been getting better, or just keeping busy?
- Awesome! All that struggle has really paid off. Not only are you doing better, but now that you've developed your Habits of Mind, you're the type of person who can do better! This new standard is just going to get easier and easier for you now.

Notice how a deeper understanding of effort has allowed teachers to be more specific and more helpful in their praise. They've shifted from the amount of time and energy the student expends, to how that time and energy is invested. This is not simply a better way to praise students, it also helps students develop Learnership.

COUNTING THE COST

Recognising and learning to think about effort as the cost of growth is an important step in becoming a skilful learner. However, knowing where and how to get the best return on effort is not the same as knowing how much the cost will be. Will the growth cost a lot, or a little? What does a 'lot of effort' look like? These are questions that skilful learners can answer.

Being able to accurately judge the amount and type of effort required to reach a particular goal is called 'motivation calibration'. It's the ability to know exactly what the cost is going to be. Not in time or energy alone, but in all the elements that go into achieving growth. The need to ask questions and search for answers. The setbacks that will occur. The time that will be lost to ineffective effort, with no progress. All that goes into the messy details of achieving growth and being able to accurately judge the cost of growth.

Some learners are over-calibrated. They incorrectly estimate the cost of growth to be too high. This inflated cost makes the cost/benefit ratio too high. The goal is not worth the cost it would take to achieve it. The value appears low. In this situation, learners tend to put off or avoid challenges.

You have probably experienced moments of being over-calibrated. Have you ever had a goal you thought was going to take lots of effort? You didn't have the resources (time and energy) right now. So you put it aside until you could 'afford the time'. But when you eventually got to the task, it turned out to be much easier than you thought. You might have said something like, 'If I'd known it was going to be that easy, I would have done it ages ago!'

That's what over-calibration feels like. A little bit of over-calibration leads you to put things off unnecessarily. If a learner is very badly over-calibrated, they put things off forever, choosing instead not to waste their effort on something they expect to get no return on. Which would be a wise choice – if true. Unfortunately, it's not that they haven't got enough effort for the task, it's that they don't know how to spend their effort to complete the task.

Spending too much time in ineffective effort is a sure way to become over-calibrated. You begin to expect the cost of growth to be very high.

Under-calibration is the opposite. It is when the learner under-estimates the cost of growth. They think a task is going to be easy, but it's not. In these situations the learner begins but quickly exhausts their budget of effort. This often leads them to quit, with an 'I tried, but I couldn't do it' result. Or to continue with a feeling that they are 'overspending', every extra effort a perceived loss, spent begrudgingly, with all the negative emotions associated with that.

Spending too much time in your comfort zone and performance zone is a sure way to become under-calibrated. In these zones the cost of completion or achievement is relatively low. You come to expect an easy return, but fail to recognise the cost of growth is higher than the cost of completion or achievement.

Research from McKinsey & Company has shown that the ability to accurately calibrate effort – to count the cost – has a significant impact on student performance. As learners come to understand the cost and return profiles of different types of effort, their motivation calibration improves. The ability to distinguish between low effort and performance effort – and the value of returns in each – changes the learner's expectations. The capacity to minimise the expenses lost in the unproductive struggle of ineffective effort and increase returns by knowing how to shift to productive struggle maximises the return on investment in growth.

> ❝ ... the ability to accurately calibrate effort – to count the cost – has a significant impact on student performance.

Understanding effort as the currency of growth is also a significant growth mindset mover. As we discussed in part II, someone with a growth mindset understands it takes a lot of effort to make something look effortless. They recognise the value of effort and the benefits that arise from investing it well.

There's another side of this investment model of effort, and that's the often overlooked cost of inaction. Time and energy are renewable resources. 'I'm going to have more time next week, so why stretch myself this week if I don't have to?' is a question posed by the less skilful learner.

The cost of inaction is the lost opportunity for growth. As we described earlier in our discussion about challenges, the long-term benefit of growth is that it raises the bar, increasing the size of our comfort zone and in effect futureproofing ourselves. Learning communities understand and value this long-term benefit of growth. We are not improving merely to achieve our immediate short-term outcomes, but also to better prepare us for the unknown challenges of the future.

PART IV KEY TAKEAWAYS

- Challenge is the pathway to growth.
- Not all challenges are equal. Understanding challenges requires understanding the zones of learning:
  - The comfort zone: Things you have mastered already, and 'easy things you haven't done yet'.
  - The performance zone: Drawing on the best of your current abilities to produce your current peak performance.
  - The learning zone: The slight stretch beyond your current best. The need to focus on how you are learning, not just what you are learning (AKA the zone of proximal development).
  - The aspirational zone: Beyond your learning zone. Too much of a stretch to be achieved at this time.
- Skilful learners develop a deep understanding and a healthy relationship with challenge. They learn to be comfortably uncomfortable with their learning zone and come to embrace challenges.
- Habits of Mind are the dispositions we develop to succeed at increasingly difficult problems. They are the actions we take as we solve problems.
- Mistakes are about information and action. Not judgement.
- There are six different types of mistakes. Three are useful. Three are not.
- Teachers usually think of feedback as something to be **given**. From the perspective of Learnership we consider feedback from the perspective of how it is **received**.
- Skilful learners maximise the value they get from feedback by tailoring it to their specific needs.
- Effort is the currency of growth.
- Not all effort is equal. It's about how well you invest your time and energy, not how much time and energy you invest.

- The Effective Effort Matrix defines four types of effort:
  - low effort – cruising
  - performance effort – performing
  - ineffective effort – struggling
  - effective effort – growing.
- Skilful learners understand the value of effort and develop very good motivation calibration.

Use the space below to add some of your own part IV key takeaways.

- _____
- _____
- _____
- _____
- _____
- _____
- _____
- _____
- _____
- _____
- _____
- _____
- _____
- _____
- _____

DISCUSSION AND ACTION

- Visit www.jamesanderson.com.au/learnerprofile to learn more about the Habits of Mind Learner Profile tool.
- With your leadership team, discuss the idea of the learning zone.
- Reflect on and discuss the idea of learners (including the adults in your community) who are 'getting busy, not getting better'.
- Consider where there are opportunities for you to design mistakes and tailor feedback for your learners.
- There is often one dimension of Learnership that stands out as needing the most immediate attention. Which might this be for you and your learners?
- Do you think of effort as the amount of time and energy a person spends on a task, or how well that time and energy are spent? To test your default way of thinking, ask yourself this question:

    When a student hands up a piece of work that isn't to the standard expected, which question are you more likely to ask? Are you more likely to ask, 'How much time did you spend on that?' Or are you more likely to ask, 'How did you spend your time on that?' They are two very different questions that represent two very different views of effort.

Use the space below to add some of your own discussion and action items.

- _____
- _____
- _____
- _____
- _____
- _____

WHERE TO FROM HERE?

Now that you have a deeper and clearer understanding of the five elements of Learnership, it's time to look at how a learner's relationship with each of these changes as they develop Learnership. What does the progression from beginner to expert look like? And importantly, why does the world need expert learners?

Part V
The six levels of Learnership

Have you ever seen a Jackie Chan movie? Even in the made-up world of the movies it's not hard to recognise his level of expertise. The flips, the spins, the flying kicks. Even if you're not a fan of martial arts, you can't help but be impressed by his abilities.

You'll be familiar with the white to black belt system many martial arts use to indicate expertise. A white belt represents beginners. You can recognise beginners not only by the colour of their belt, but also by what they do. They have only the most basic skills, but are building a foundation for future growth.

White belts usually don't stay white belts. As a person develops their skills they earn a yellow belt, then an orange belt and green belt. Each belt represents the achievement of a new level of skilfulness. A stop on the path towards expertise. Jackie Chan has been developing his skills for a long time and is a black belt in Hapkido.

Learnership is similar. By observing how a learner is engaging with the five key elements we can describe their current level of expertise with the Learnership Matrix.

Each level illustrates an increasing degree of sophistication and effectiveness in how the learner is engaging in the learning process. It also demonstrates an increasingly mature and effective relationship with each element.

And like the belt system in martial arts, the level represents where the learner is in their journey towards becoming an expert learner. It defines *where they are* and their current level of skilfulness, not *who they are*. With practice, all students can learn to become increasingly skilful learners.

As you explore the levels of Learnership in this part, I invite you to reflect on the learning behaviours you see most often in your learning community, including from your teachers, and yourself.

Chapter 14
The Learnership Matrix

The Learnership Matrix: describing skilful learning.

By now you're probably wanting to know, what are the different levels of Learnership? What does it actually look like to be a skilful learner? I've developed the Learnership Matrix (over the page) to answer these questions.

HOW TO NAVIGATE THE LEARNERSHIP MATRIX

Let's begin by taking a moment to learn how to navigate the Learnership Matrix, and recognise its key elements and some basic characteristics of learners at each level. Once we have our bearings, we'll take a deep dive into each of the six levels in the next few chapters.

Across the top of the matrix are the five elements of Learnership we have just explored. Challenge is listed first, because in many ways it is what drives learning. It provides the stimulus for growth. The other elements relate to how we respond to challenge and achieve growth.

The vertical axis lists the six levels of Learnership. Each level is distinctive and represents an increasingly effective way of engaging in

The Learnership Matrix

	CHALLENGE	HABITS OF MIND	MISTAKES	FEEDBACK	TIME & ENERGY
AGILE LEARNER	EMBRACES	CULTIVATES	DESIGNS	TAILORS	GROWING
INDEPENDENT LEARNER	TARGETS	DEVELOPS	USES	REQUESTS	STRIVING
DIRECTED LEARNER	ATTEMPTS	EXTENDS	CORRECTS	RESPONDS	PRODUCING
PERFORMANCE LEARNER	LIMITS	APPLIES	AVOIDS	SELECTS	PERFORMING
BEGINNING LEARNER	REDUCES	DESCRIBES	RECOGNISES	ACKNOWLEDGES	DOING
NON-LEARNER	AVOIDS	IGNORANT	IGNORES	DISREGARDS	WASTES

© James Anderson | www.jamesanderson.com.au

the learning process, and a maturing relationship with each element of Learnership. Importantly, each level also represents a greater level of agency in the world.

In the middle of the Learnership Matrix is a line that divides the matrix in two. This line loosely represents the performance plateau, or 'the bar' that we discussed in chapter 9. There are three 'above the bar' levels of Learnership, and three 'below the bar' levels of Learnership.

The key difference between above-the-bar learners and below-the-bar learners is their relationship with their learning zone. As we will see, below-the-bar learners don't have a productive relationship with their learning zone. Above-the-bar learners have progressively more mature and productive relationships with their learning zone.

Starting from the bottom of the matrix we see Non-Learners. This is our baseline. At this level of Learnership students essentially aren't engaging in the learning process at all. The way they avoid challenges robs them of the opportunity to grow. Students with this level of Learnership tend to opt out of learning altogether.

At the level of Beginning Learner we see students who run to their comfort zone. They participate in class, but always want the easiest tasks. These students see learning more as a series of activities to be completed rather than a process of growth. They get busy at the expense of getting better.

At the level of Performance Learners we see students who love their performance zone. If you've ever known a student who is more likely to put up their hand with answers (they know) rather than with questions about things they don't know, they are likely to be at this level of Learnership. They love the safety, certainty and the recognition that comes from being in their performance zone. These are the learners who do their best at the expense of not doing better.

Continuing our journey up the matrix and going above the bar for the first time, we find Directed Learners. These learners require a teacher to guide their learning. In many ways this is the level of Learnership our system is designed for. The quality of learning is a direct result of the quality of teaching. At this level of Learnership, learners are responsive, in the sense that they respond to the teacher's instructions. They are learn*ing*, but they are not learn*ers*.

Independent Learners set their own challenges and take charge of the learning process to achieve their goals. These learners are reactive. They react to the challenges they encounter on the way to achieving their goals. They are learners in the sense they are in charge of their learning, independent of a teacher. However, in the absence of their challenges and goals, they stop growing. They are learners, but they are not continuous learners.

> ❝ As we progress up the Learnership Matrix we see steadily improving outcomes. Learners are getting better at getting better. It's not simply the skillset they bring to learning that is improving, it's their relationship with learning that is improving.

Agile Learners are proactive. They are focused on achieving growth, not simply on achieving *goals*. They leverage the challenges that exist in the world around them to achieve continuous growth. This approach proactively prepares them for future challenges. They become futureproofed.

As we progress up the Learnership Matrix we see steadily improving outcomes. Learners are getting better at getting better. It's not simply the skillset they bring to learning that is improving, it's their relationship with learning that is improving. As we'll explore in a moment, with this development comes an increasing degree of agency in the world.

LEVELS, NOT CATEGORIES

It's very natural, and useful, to create an avatar for each level of Learnership. This might be an imaginary student you use to represent each level of Learnership, or it might be a student you know who seems to fit a particular level of Learnership. The avatar serves as a reference point, a cognitive anchor for the ideas associated with each level.

Don't let the avatar you create trick you into categorising students as *being* a type of learner. Our goal is to help students become increasingly skilful learners. Over time, we want to improve how students engage in the learning process, not categorise them.

In part II we saw how it was useful to understand mindset from the perspective of fixed and growth. But to change mindset we had to think of it as a journey along a continuum. The same is true for Learnership. The matrix divides Learnership into six recognisable levels. This helps us understand Learnership. But improving Learnership is a continuous journey.

Students don't jump from one level of Learnership to the next. At any particular time, students will demonstrate behaviours at several levels of Learnership, with varying frequency. As they become more skilful learners, they will engage in the behaviours associated with the next level more and more frequently. As we'll explore in the next part, we measure Learnership in the school by measuring the frequency of behaviours associated with each level.

As you move through this section and become increasingly familiar with the levels of Learnership, you'll find you start thinking about your students differently. You'll walk past classrooms and see students' learning behaviours in a new light. The way teachers talk about students will carry new meaning and new insights. You'll ask questions that hadn't occurred to you before. As you build these new understandings, you'll find it useful to have a copy of the matrix close at hand.

You can download a copy of the matrix to pin on the notice board in your office or keep a copy on your phone or tablet using the QR code. Annotate it with your reflections. Feel free to distribute copies to your leadership team, but I suggest you hold off distributing it to your entire staff until after you've read the rest of the book.

Now that you have a sense of how to navigate the Learnership Matrix, let's take a more in-depth look at each level. As you explore each level, I invite you to reflect on how you, your students and your teachers engage in learning. Annotate the coming pages with your own examples drawn from observations of your own school and classrooms. Make note of how frequently you see behaviours associated with each level of Learnership. Try to identify the level of Learnership that best describes how members of your school community currently engage in the learning process.

Chapter 15
Non-Learners

Opting out of learning.

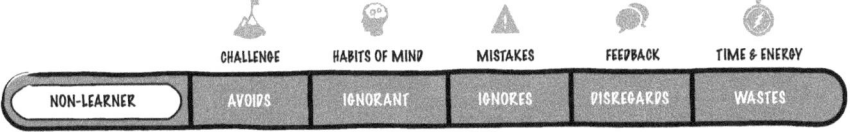

Having been in education for a while, you've probably come across a few students whose default setting is to do as little as possible. They may even refuse to participate in the learning process at all. These are what I describe as 'Non-Learners'.

RECOGNISING THE NON-LEARNER

My description of a Non-Learner is really a baseline for Learnership. It describes what it would be like to not engage in learning at all. I don't believe we have many true Non-Learners in our schools – although we have learners who display some of the behaviours associated with being a Non-Learner some, or even much, of the time. In practice, most students will engage in learning at least to some degree, some of the time – even if it's not in a classroom.

There are a host of reasons why students might not engage in learning that are probably jumping into your mind about now. Lack of sleep. Problems at home. Mental health issues. You're familiar with the list. When students aren't engaging in learning for these types of reasons, it's not really about how they learn. These other factors are stopping them from learning in the same way they might stop even a skilful learner from learning. These types of issues may need to be addressed for individual students before you can start thinking about their Learnership.

Often the root cause behind a student being a Non-Learner is a mindset issue. A Non-Learner might see their abilities as fixed, feel they have reached their limits, and see little or no point in trying. In their eyes it's better to opt out altogether than to try, and fail. These students will say things like, 'I don't want to … ' when they mean, 'If I tried, I'd fail. And I don't want to fail.'

> ❝ Often the root cause behind a student being a Non-Learner is a mindset issue.

Non-Learners avoid challenges. These are the students who would rather do nothing than something. When we offer them options A, B and C, they are likely to ask, 'Do I have to?', and the answer they are looking for is, 'No. You don't have to. You can just sit there and do nothing.'

As we've discussed, challenges are the pathway to growth. It's not that these learners have difficulty achieving challenges – they simply don't enter into anything remotely challenging in the first place. By refusing challenges, these learners are robbing themselves of any opportunity to grow.

Not having had many meaningful experiences of engaging in the learning process, these learners lack an understanding of how learning really works. They have little language for learning and few metacognitive constructs to describe how to engage in the learning process. They are essentially ignorant of their Habits of Mind and how they contribute to their learning and growth. The 'how to' of learning is a bit of a mystery to them.

Because they tend not to engage in the learning process, these learners tend to see no use for the information that would help them grow. Consequently, they ignore any mistakes they might make and disregard feedback.

These learners largely waste their effort. Much of their output is low effort. Time simply passes them by and they are almost entirely unproductive. Any learning that might occur is incidental, almost accidental, a result of casual experience or simply engaging in day-to-day activity. There is no intent or direction to their learning. And the learner remains unchanged.

Students who remain Non-Learners have very limited opportunities as adults. As educational leaders, we have a duty to students and our wider community to ensure no-one leaves our school with this level of Learnership. As we'll see in a moment, these people have very little agency in the world. They are easily derailed by disruption and challenges, they become the victim of their circumstances and often require a great deal of external support.

Take a moment. How often are these types of behaviours occurring in your classrooms?

Chapter 16
Beginning Learners

Taking the easiest option.

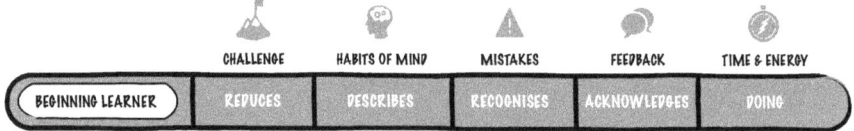

You almost certainly know, or have known, students at this level of Learnership. These are students who always want to be in their comfort zone. They are constantly seeking to reduce the level of challenge, looking for the easiest task, the minimal effort. They search for their path of least resistance through a lesson. They are happy to *participate* in classroom activities but they don't want to be *challenged* by them.

For the Beginning Learner, classrooms are places where they complete activities. They expect to be able to move through tasks and complete them easily. If the activity is easy and they enjoy it, they'll keep doing it. They might even ask to do it again … and again. If not, the quicker and easier it is to get to the end, the better.

RECOGNISING THE BEGINNING LEARNER

The Beginning Learner has lots of strategies to reduce the level of challenge and minimise the effort required. When given problems to solve, they may ask to be given the answer, try to guess the answer, or engage in other distractions to avoid the challenge. Occasionally they'll simply refuse to do a task because it's 'too hard'. In class they may simply stop when they encounter a challenge, or skip over the 'hard parts'. Or they might stretch out their time, wasting it on other things, to avoid getting up to the challenging part of the activity.

These are the students who will hand up a piece of work saying they've finished, but they didn't attempt the parts they found challenging. Finished for them is a point in time, not a standard achieved. They feel 'I didn't know how to do that' is sufficient reason for not doing something. These students spend their energy in the busyness of doing.

At this level of Learnership, teachers find themselves dragging students through the learning process, which leaves them exhausted. Students not only need to be given instructions about what to do, they also need constant monitoring to keep them on task. Teachers sometimes feel they need to trade what the student is meant to be learning for what the student will be prepared to do.

> ❝ At this level of Learnership, teachers find themselves dragging students through the learning process, which leaves them exhausted.

For the Beginning Learner there is very little intentionality in learning. They tend not to effectively plan, monitor or reflect on the learning process. Instead their learning is episodic. One activity after another. They rarely think about how they approach a particular activity, instead working through it moment to moment. As a result, they may fail to see the progression in learning, or connect one lesson to the last.

Beginning Learners can describe how they learn, but only after the fact. They may understand the language of the Habits of Mind but will use it to describe what they did in the last activity, rather than what they need to do in the next.

I recall a student I taught many years ago, Bill. Today I would describe Bill as being at the Beginning Learner level of Learnership. If Bill was asked to go back and make improvements or corrections to a task, he would complain he'd already finished that task. And if the class returned to a topic because I felt they hadn't mastered it the first time, Bill would complain that 'I've already done that!'

Bill would measure his effort by the *amount of time* he spent on a task. Because he avoided struggle, sticking to the easy tasks, all his effort tended to be low effort. He expected to be rewarded for spending more time on a task, regardless of how that time was spent. On the occasions he spent extra time on a task, he would say things like, 'I spent hours doing that assignment – I deserve a better grade!' How the time was spent and what he achieved weren't important considerations for him, only that he had spent the time.

The consequence of being focused on activity and getting easy things done with minimal effort is that the Beginning Learner's effort becomes under-calibrated. They expect all activities to be easy, completed only with the allocation of time. When they are pushed into more challenging tasks, they expend their effort budget well before achieving the results, and then quickly give up.

Unlike Non-Learners who avoid doing anything at all, Beginning Learners like Bill tend to have something to show for their time. It often isn't to the standard required, and the more challenging tasks may be skipped, but something is often 'handed in'. When submitting work, Bill's perpetual question would be, 'Is this good enough *to pass*?' Being at a passing standard meant he could finish. Like all learners at this level, he was more interested in finishing than achieving.

When given classroom tasks, Bill would often ask, 'Why do we have to do this?' Which is a question teachers hear often. His reason for asking was he wanted to do something easier instead.

In terms of our common school measures, Beginning Learners make some progress and cover some breadth in the curriculum. However, as the demands of the curriculum increase, they fall further and further behind over time.

How many of your students sound a bit like Bill? Students that constantly seek their path of least resistance through school?

Chapter 17
Performance Learners

Doing your best, at the expense of not getting better.

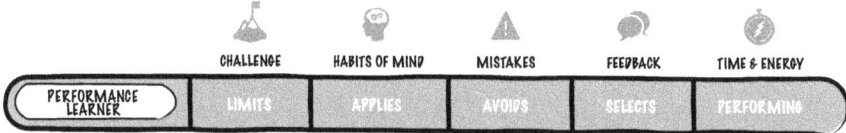

At this level of Learnership, learners are all about their performance zone. These learners love to do their best and show off what they can do well. They love the confidence and certainty that comes with their performance zone. It feels safe. They tend to avoid the uncertainty and discomfort of their learning zone. For these learners, challenge and the idea of doing their best is about refinement, consolidation and performance, not improvement.

Being a Performance Learner does not necessarily mean perfectionism or getting straight A's (although it can). It means they want to limit their challenges to those they know they can complete well and with confidence. Performance Learners love the recognition and satisfaction that comes from doing their best.

RECOGNISING THE PERFORMANCE LEARNER

At this level of Learnership, students will go to significant lengths to target their performance zone. These are the students who carefully select only the problems they know they can do well. In art lessons they might repeatedly produce something similar to their previous work, rather than attempting something new and challenging. In maths, they will attempt all the problems they know they can answer, and leave those they are unsure about unanswered rather than risk getting something wrong. They are slow to seek help, and will switch to a task they know they can do well rather than persist with something they struggle with.

I recall one student I taught who would fill tasks with extraneous detail. They would insert material into assignments that wasn't required to show off what they can do. It didn't matter to them whether what they were doing was part of the assignment or the success criteria. They just wanted another opportunity to demonstrate what they could do, rather than attempt something they weren't confident they could do well.

To teachers, these learners appear motivated. They spend effort on achievement, rather than simply completion as the Beginning Learner would, so their expenditure is higher. They are more focused than Beginning Learners and require less monitoring to keep on task, but still require intervention and support to ensure they are being appropriately challenged.

> 66 To a Performance Learner, 'best' means right or perfect, not better.

The students in your school who are at this level of Learnership often thrive on the rewards of a job well done. In classrooms they want to show the teacher the quality of their work. They are quick to put their hand up with an answer to a question they know, but slow to put their hand up with a question about something they don't know.

They are keen to 'do their best', but relate the idea of doing their best to making their performance more reliable and consistent, rather than making it better than their previous best. To a Performance Learner, 'best' means right or perfect, not better.

Unlike the Beginning Learner who feels that learning finishes when the activity is over, Performance Learners feel like learning finishes when the performance is over. Once the assignment is handed in or the test is finished, learning stops and they move on. Because learning finishes with the performance, they see little need for feedback or reflection.

From a learning perspective, these students are risk averse. They want to remain safe and confident in what they know they can do. Mistakes are avoided, and if they do occur are likely to be ignored, dismissed or disguised. Feedback is similar. These learners select feedback that is affirmational, but will disregard any feedback that might be critical or constructive.

Performance Learners have a reasonably well developed language for learning and can be intentional about their learning. They know what it takes to do their best and can tell you which Habits of Mind will be necessary to repeat a performance or reproduce a previous standard. However, they tend to refer to their Habits of Mind in one dimension. For example, they might say they *are* persistent, or *can* strive for accuracy. They are less likely to discuss their Habits of Mind as something they are working on improving.

Performance Learners live the minimax principal. They want to get the maximum result for the minimum possible effort. When in their performance zone they feel they are getting good value for their effort. Going into their learning zone requires greater effort and comes with less certainty of a positive result. They define achievement by the quality of performance rather than amount of growth achieved.

Performance Learners are generally very poor at understanding the cost of inaction. They constantly spend their effort performing, and value the performance results they achieve. But they frequently fail to appreciate that the time spent in the performance zone is time lost that could have been invested in growth.

How frequently do you see behaviours associated with this level of Learnership in your school? Students who want to do their best, at the expense of not doing better? Take a moment to jot down some examples in the margin.

THE PERFORMANCE LEARNER TRAP

Many adults who were once Directed Learners or even Independent Learners can retreat to the safety and confidence of the Performance Learner. This is particularly true when we find ourselves in performance environments that value and reward performance over growth.

Let me tell you the story of a principal I met a few years back who illustrates the idea of retreating to being a Performance Learner. I'll simply call him Dave.

Dave was a committed educator who'd worked over many years to build his skills as a teacher, leader and principal. He sought challenges, engaged in further education and developed himself as a leader. He wanted to make an impact, to make a difference and confront challenges head on. When he finally got the principalship he wanted, he immediately got to work.

For the first few years, Dave did an outstanding job. He implemented everything he knew and achieved some great results. The school changed for the better. The school community and his regional leaders couldn't have been happier. He started to build a reputation and profile for himself as an outstanding leader.

The job gave Dave a lot of satisfaction. It was rewarding. He could see the results and be proud of what he was achieving. He was a very good principal. Every challenge was an opportunity to prove his abilities.

What Dave didn't recognise was that while he was engaged in the business of improving the school, he'd fallen out of the habit of improving himself. There was more than enough to keep him busy in the job. But the seduction of doing things well was coming at the expense of his own growth. The problems he faced tended to have an immediate answer. He started to manage his time rather than his effort.

As you know, principalship is a dynamic role. The demands change, and personal growth is necessary as you encounter new and more complex challenges. You are, after all, living in the VUCA world we discussed in chapter 1. As time went on, more and more of the role fell outside Dave's abilities. The leader who was excellent in his first few years becomes good in the next few years. Nothing to complain about or affect an established reputation too much – after all, so much had been achieved.

The passing of more time brought more change and more challenges. Dave drew on his significant resources and skills, but increasingly these weren't quite sufficient and his performance started to decline slowly, though the school was still doing well. His response to these challenges and struggles started to be to blame circumstances. Dave's reputation relied more and more on past, rather than current, successes.

By the time he retired, after more than 20 years as principal in the same school, the school community couldn't wait for him to leave. Yes, there were celebrations of a successful career, but the focus was politely on past achievements, the length of service, and more recently, maintaining the school. There was no sense that he'd been driving the school forward. Over a quiet coffee, Dave told me he just didn't know how to deal with some of the complexities of the role these days. He felt powerless in the current climate.

From the perspective of the school board, there was recognition of the challenges ahead and the need to appoint someone who could confront them. They needed someone with the skills required in today's schools. Someone who'd be able to effect change – eerily similar to the description of Dave in the early part of his principalship …

For Dave, the world had changed but he was essentially the same principal he was 20 years before. He'd spent his time in leadership, rather than invested it. He'd fallen into the Performance Learner's habit of demonstrating his abilities rather than developing them. The result: he never made quite the enduring impact he'd wanted to as a leader.

Chapter 18
Learnership and learner agency

You can't 'give' students agency.

Recall our conversation in part I about raising the aspirations and increasing the opportunities for your students. You want students graduating and going out into the world to be powerful, not powerless. They should be masters of their circumstances, not victims. They should act on the world, not have the world act on them. In other words, they should have agency in the world.

The Non-Learners, Beginning Learners and even Performance Learners we've just discussed have significant limitations to their agency. Non, Beginning and Performance Learners are what I describe as 'below-the-bar learners'. Their learning is characterised by staying below the bar, doing the things they know they can achieve easily in their comfort and performance zones.

These learners avoid their learning zone. They draw only on their current abilities, their current level of development of their Habits of Mind, without seeking to increase those abilities. They hope that what got them here will get them there. While these students might be learning and achieving some of our intended outcomes, these tend to be 'easy things they haven't done yet'. Their schooling is characterised by getting busy, not getting better.

HABITUALLY AVOIDING THE LEARNING ZONE

Habitually avoiding the learning zone has two significant impacts on a learner:

- Because challenge is the pathway to growth, without challenge these learners are significantly limiting their opportunities for growth. There's little true improvement.
- Challenge drives the development of a learner's Habits of Mind, so without challenge these students aren't learning to be smarter.

This lack of growth has significant impact on a learner's opportunities in life and their ability to participate meaningfully in a rapidly changing world. It means the challenges that are beyond their reach when they leave school may remain beyond their reach for the rest of their lives. This limits their opportunities, leaving them ill-prepared for the challenges of an unpredictable future. It makes them vulnerable to change, challenge and adversity. In short, it limits their agency in the world.

Recall the learning zone diagram in chapter 9 (shown again opposite), paying close attention to the performance plateau. Everything below the bar a learner already has agency over. They might never have encountered a particular circumstance, but if a below-the-bar challenge arose they would already have the abilities required to succeed at it. But circumstances above the bar are beyond the learner's current abilities, and they have no agency over them. Unless the learner can increase their abilities and raise the bar, the bar will come to represent the limit of their agency in the world.

During times of crisis such as the Covid pandemic, below-the-bar learners are faced with challenges beyond their current abilities – and they duck for cover. They lack the ability to respond effectively, so are forced to wait, and hope, for things to 'get back to normal'. They become a victim of circumstances. A below-the-bar learner's inability to change means they need to either avoid disruptions or be protected from them, which is exactly the type of issue we are trying to address.

The performance plateau

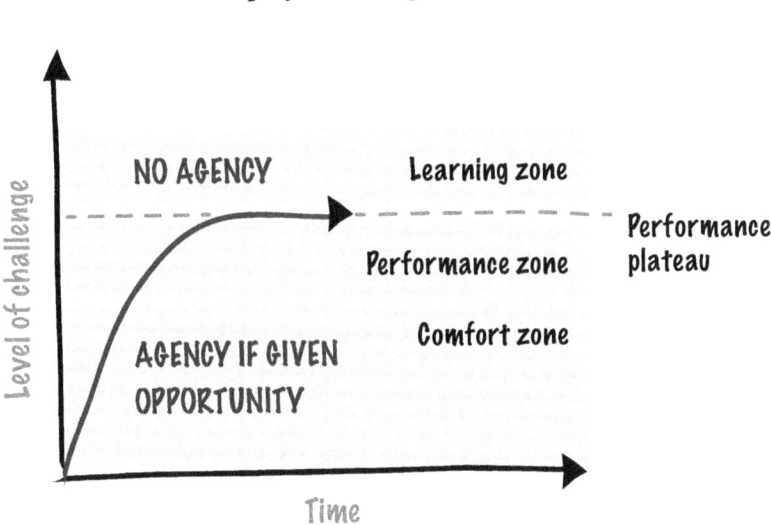

DEVELOPING LEARNER AGENCY

This is where so many schools have gone wrong with their work to improve learner agency. Many schools believe that agency is about having 'voice and choice' in the world – they could give students agency by giving them choices. The problem with this approach, in so many schools, has been they have given students easy choices. Below-the-bar choices.

The 'voice and choice' interpretation of learner agency which is so popular in schools has misinterpreted the concept of agency. It's true that people with agency have a voice in the world, and can make choices and act meaningfully. But simply giving students 'voice and choice' over things they can already do only gives them a *sense of agency*. It does not *develop* agency. The types of choices we give students matters. They must be challenging choices that will raise the bar and ultimately lead to the student's growth.

If your approach to developing agency is to allow students to make choices they already had the ability to make except you previously created an environment that restricted them from making such choices, and if the voice you give them is a voice they already had except you had gagged them, you need to ask, are you giving students the power to act or merely the permission to act?

This is why we can't give students agency simply by changing the environment. We cannot say we are developing agency, and improving a student's life outcomes, if we only change their school environment. True agency is a quality that resides within and is developed by the individual. We can only say we are developing agency when the learner is changing.

> True agency is a quality that resides within and is developed by the individual. We can only say we are developing agency when the learner is changing.

Recall that agency has three interrelated parts: the environment to act, the will to act and the power to act. A growth mindset brings the understanding that it's possible to raise the bar, giving you the will to act. But it's your level of Learnership that impacts how you raise the bar and gives you the power to act. A high level of Learnership makes it possible to succeed at challenges that were previously beyond you.

Being capable of raising the bar has two significant implications for learners. First, it means that in the face of challenge or adversity, students are able to respond effectively and ultimately succeed. Although challenges will come along that are beyond their abilities at the time, they are able to change themselves, develop their Habits of Mind and eventually succeed. They might be the victim of their circumstances in the moment, but their ability to raise the bar means they don't remain a victim.

Second, and perhaps more importantly, raising the bar increases the size of their comfort zone. As they leverage challenges to develop their Habits of Mind there are more 'easy things they haven't done yet' in the world. The number of challenges the world can throw at them that will be outside their abilities decreases. This has the effect of preparing students for the unknown challenges of the future, essentially future-proofing them.

As we move on to explore Directed, Independent and Agile Learners, pay attention to how they raise the bar. Each is capable of raising the bar and developing agency. However, they each go about it in a different way, which significantly impacts their agency in the world which we explore further in chapter 22.

Chapter 19
Directed Learners

Learn*ing*, but not learn*ers*.

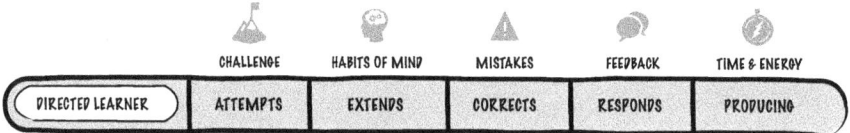

The defining quality of Directed Learners is they are led through the learning process by the teacher. A teacher tells them what to do, and how to do it, at each step of the journey. And the learner does what they are told. They learn and improve, but rely on the teacher to guide the process.

This is the level of Learnership that often comes to mind when we think about schooling. The teacher teaching. The student learning.

TEACHER-MEDIATED LEARNING

The Directed Learner is the perfect fit for an education system that puts teachers at the centre, a system that views teachers as the only variable in the Learning Equation. A system that values quality teaching over quality learning. A system that operates on the principle that learning is the product of teaching.

Directed Learners follow the process of learning laid out by the teacher. They are the consumers of teaching, with learning outcomes being the product of education. They are engaged in the learning process but they are not in charge of the learning process. They are learning, but they are not learners.

When learning is being controlled by teachers, there's a direct correlation between teacher practice and the achievement of learning outcomes. Directed Learners will have the most to gain from 'effective teaching strategies' such as those advocated by Hattie and others. Directed Learners tend to achieve the short-term results valued by our system of education. By following the teacher's instructions and engaging in the learning experiences the teacher creates, students can expect to achieve one year's growth in one year's time.

This type of mediated growth can feel very satisfying for teachers. They can see a direct correlation between their efforts and the results students are achieving.

> ❝ This is the level of Learnership that often comes to mind when we think about schooling. The teacher teaching. The student learning.

RECOGNISING DIRECTED LEARNERS

Think back to the last time you were in a classroom. You'll have no difficulty recognising students at this level of Learnership. These are the students you were trained to teach. In your classroom, the Directed Learners are taking on the challenges you set and asking, 'How do we do this?' When you set appropriately challenging tasks, these students will be in their learning zone. They are putting up their hand asking, 'Can you help me with this please?', or simply, 'I don't get this. What do

I need to do?' They are asking to be guided and instructed. Waiting for the teacher to reduce the effort required and lift the cognitive load for them.

These students will expect the teacher to identify their mistakes, and tell them how to correct them. They'll hand up their work for the teacher to assess, and wait for the teacher to tell them what they need to do differently next time. At this level of Learnership, each step in the learning process requires the teacher's intervention. The reason they take on a challenge is because the teacher told them to. We might go so far as describe them as 'dependent learners'.

In contrast to the three levels of Learnership we've discussed so far, the Directed Learner recognises that learning finishes when growth is achieved, not simply when the activity is finished. Even when learning activities are finished and the tyranny of the curriculum requires the learner to 'move on', these learners will recognise when they 'still don't get that'. The activity might be over, but they know there is more to do before they achieve the learning outcome. For the Directed Learner, learning is measured in growth and achievement, not simply in minutes.

When Directed Learners struggle, they rely on the teacher to guide and support their learning. But as you know all too well, a teacher's time is limited, and they aren't always able to provide timely, targeted, individual support for every student – as much as they might want to.

This means that at this level of Learnership, students can spend a lot of time engaged in unproductive struggle. As a result, these students come to see learning as costly. This leads them to become over-calibrated, overestimating the cost of growth.

This problem is compounded when the teacher intervenes and provides a solution or scaffold that allows the student to experience progress rapidly and with a low effort budget. The student quickly learns there is little return on their effort but a large return on the teacher's effort, so they begin to struggle less, giving up easily and waiting for the teacher to intervene. They may even expect the teacher to do all the heavy lifting of learning for them and simply provide them with the answer.

PRODUCING GOOD RESULTS, BUT …

At this point, Directed Learners have become dependent on the teacher to such a degree that they become almost helpless without constant guidance and intervention. Teachers may describe them as 'passive' learners.

Well-intended teachers, who are often prepared to do more and more of the heavy lifting, can lead Directed Learners through the curriculum and, in some cases, help them achieve outstanding results. We saw an example of this earlier with the year 12 Business Management teacher. We've also heard this with students who claim the only way they'll get better results is if they get a better teacher!

It's entirely possible for Directed Learners to acquire subject area expertise. Directed Learners may go on to higher learning, but will tend to earn their degrees through coursework where their learning can be guided, rather than a thesis where they are expected to be more independent. They may become a career student. In informal contexts and the corporate world they can be recognised as lifelong learners, but it's a lifetime of learning mediated by teachers.

As a school leader, it would be easy to become complacent in a school of Directed Learners. Curriculum goals would be met. Students would achieve expected standards. There would be nothing 'wrong' with the school. As a leader of teachers, you'd be seen to be doing your job, because teachers would be doing a good job and students would get excellent results.

But a community of Directed Learners isn't a learning community, it's a teaching community. It's a community based on the art of teaching, not the art of learning. It's a community where output is measured by the learning outcomes achieved, not the type of learners created.

> ❝ … a community of Directed Learners isn't a learning community, it's a teaching community.

A community of Directed Learners doesn't give learners true agency and doesn't prepare them for a rapidly changing and increasingly complex world. When challenge or adversity come along, Directed Learners need to be told how to deal with it and given support to overcome it. I'm sure you've known Directed Learners who did well in the managed and supportive environment of school but struggled when that support and guidance was removed at university.

As we've discussed, to have true agency in the world and overcome the challenges life throws at you, you need to be able to raise the bar. Directed Learners can raise the bar, and do increase their agency, but *not on their own*. They require the support and direction of teachers to guide them through the learning process, raise the bar and overcome challenge and adversity. In the absence of this support and direction they will remain the victim of their circumstances.

Directed Learners can meet short-term curriculum goals, but we have loftier goals to increase the opportunities, aspirations and agency of all learners. For that we need to create learners who take charge of the learning process and raise the bar independently.

As you reflect on learning in your school, how often do you see the behaviours associated with Directed Learners? How many of your teachers would be satisfied to have Directed Learners in their classroom? How satisfied would you be if students were leaving your school having completed their learn*ing* successfully, but not having become learn*ers*?

Chapter 20
Independent Learners

Taking charge of learning.

	CHALLENGE	HABITS OF MIND	MISTAKES	FEEDBACK	TIME & ENERGY
INDEPENDENT LEARNER	TARGETS	DEVELOPS	USES	REQUESTS	STRIVING

The hallmark of an Independent Learner is they understand how they learn. They don't need to be led through the learning process, they are in charge of it. By this level of Learnership they have become learn*ers*.

Independent Learners have made significant progress along the Mindset Continuum. They have a growth-oriented mindset, and they understand their capacity to grow. They not only want to get better, they are working on the skills required to get better at getting better. They are focused on becoming better learners.

RECOGNISING THE INDEPENDENT LEARNER

An Independent Learner is not simply a student who is able to work unsupervised. Even when students are working on their own for a time, the teacher can still be in charge of the process of learning. For that matter, students might be working on their own but running to their comfort zone and doing only the easy tasks, happy to be left alone and not pushed to do something more difficult.

It's also not true to say that Independent Learners don't need a teacher. They do. The teacher will still provide support, guidance and content knowledge expertise. Independent also does not mean 'learn whatever you want'. The teacher will usually (but not always) decide what is to be learned and provide a learning pathway.

When you see students who are in charge of how they are engaging in the learning process, who are learning and growing effectively without the need for a teacher to guide the process, you are witnessing Independent Learners.

One of the keys to becoming an Independent Learner is to develop an appreciation of the learning zone. Independent Learners understand that challenge is the pathway to growth. They don't expect growth to be easy, but they do expect to achieve it. They are comfortable with the temporary discomfort of struggle knowing this allows them to grow.

> ❝❝ One of the keys to becoming an Independent Learner is to develop an appreciation of the learning zone.

One primary school teacher described working with a group of Independent Learners like this: for a number of weeks the students had been consolidating their reading skills – working largely in their performance zone. They had become confident at their current reading level and had been experiencing a lot of immediate success. Several of the students were able to recognise their mastery and approached the teacher to say they were ready to move on. So the teacher chose a reading task for the students that was just beyond their current abilities.

When the students didn't experience the immediate success they'd become familiar with, instead of quitting or immediately asking for help, they doubled down to direct their own learning and work it out. Mistakes were made, then analysed. They consulted resources and applied the strategies they'd previously been taught. This resulted in some progress, but there were still parts of the exercise they didn't understand.

It was at this point – when progress had slowed – they recognised they were in ineffective effort. They were struggling, without progress. So they sought the teacher's help. Instead of asking for the answer or asking what they needed to do, they requested guidance on their approach so they could work it out for themselves. They asked if they were on the right track or going about it the right way. Eventually they narrowed down exactly what they didn't know, and recognised they needed some information they didn't have. It was then that the teacher sat down with them to show them some new strategies and give them some information they needed.

In this way, teaching independent learners can feel quite rewarding for teachers. They are seeing students set out on their own and taking charge of learning. Instead of dragging students through the learning process, they are given some of their energy back.

FROM TEACHING TO COACHING

Notice how an Independent Learner still needs a teacher, but the role of the teacher has expanded slightly. Some might describe this as the shift from 'sage on the stage to guide on the side'. I call it the shift from teaching to coaching. Students still require input, but it's on their terms. The teacher is no longer the sole driver of the learning process; they are there to facilitate, to provide subject area expertise and to identify where learners need additional support and guidance. In a coaching role, the teacher becomes far more focused on the *how* of learning, rather than simply on the *what* of learning. They are focused on the learning strategies that are a central theme of this book.

It's also worth noting that our system has often advocated for moving from 'sage on the stage to guide on the side', setting rich, open-ended, problem-based learning tasks. But teachers often find students struggle with these. That's because these pedagogies require students to have the skills of Independent Learners. Many students don't, and schools have lacked a systematic understanding of how to develop these skills.*

Teachers who aren't used to Independent Learners can feel lost when such students show up in their classroom. For the first time the teacher isn't solely in charge of the learning process. Rather than guiding learning, they are along for the ride. Many who were trained in the teacher-centred culture lack the skills – or the understanding of the learning process – to deal with Independent Learners. They don't know what to do when the student takes charge of learning.

I was like that. In my middle school classroom I had a number of students who I'd describe today as being at the Independent Learner level of Learnership. These were students who would (mostly) take on challenges willingly, and even seek them out. They would work through problems on their own. They required very little intervention from me. And they tended to achieve the short-term learning outcomes demanded by the curriculum.

It pains me to say this, but in retrospect, I failed these students. I tended to leave them to their own devices and let them get on with their work. Instead of supporting them in further developing as learners, I redirected my limited resources to the students at the Beginning, Performance and Directed Learner levels of Learnership in my classroom. Armed with the understanding of Learnership I have today, I wouldn't make that mistake again. I'd be able to help them continue their journey and become even more skilful learners.

Independent Learners focus not only on *what* they are learning but also on *how* they are learning. They are very conscious of their Habits of Mind. They recognise that what got them to their previous standard will not necessarily be enough to get them to the next standard. So they are quick to understand when their Habits of Mind are not well enough developed to achieve their goals, and set out to develop their Habits of Mind as required.

Notice also that being an Independent Learner does not necessarily mean the learner has highly developed Habits of Mind or sophisticated

---

* We discuss more about how raising the level of Learnership in schools allows teachers to engage in more effective, more rewarding pedagogies in part VII.

learning skills. It simply means the learner no longer relies on the teacher to extend their Habits of Mind. Instead they are actively developing them to meet their needs. The learner is in charge of their growth.

Independent Learners understand that effort is the currency of growth, and are prepared to invest that effort in striving towards their goals. They become increasingly aware of the return on their effort so they become discerning about how they spend it. When these students ask, 'Why do we have to do this?', they aren't asking for something easier, they are asking if it's important enough to invest their valuable effort into.

This understanding also means they are better at appreciating the effort that goes into other people's backstories. Consequently they are far more likely to celebrate and find inspiration in the success of others, rather than feeling threatened by it.

Take another moment to reflect on the students you've known who demonstrate the skills of the Independent Learner. How often do you see this level of Learnership in your school? What type of results are these learners achieving, both in terms of our short-term learning outcomes, and our longer term educational goals? How might your learning community change if you had more students at this level of Learnership?

INDEPENDENT LEARNERS DO NOT 'TEACH THEMSELVES'

Becoming an Independent Learner doesn't mean learning how to 'teach yourself'. By now it should be clear that while there are some commonalities, the skills of teaching and the skills of learning are not one and the same. They complement each other.

For example, when teaching someone, the teacher is generally expected to have a sound understanding of the subject matter being taught. In fact, there was a time when the only criteria for being a teacher was to be a subject expert. When teaching something they are familiar with, the teacher is not struggling in the learning zone. More likely the material being taught is in the teacher's comfort or performance zone.

This is not true for a learner who is venturing into the unknown. They are in their learning zone where there is uncertainty and discomfort. They are focusing not just on what they are learning, but how they are learning. They are looking for the information that may be apparent to a teacher but is not immediately apparent to them. In this sense, it's impossible to 'be your own teacher'.

If being an Independent Learner was simply a matter of learning to be your own teacher, every teacher would be a skilful Independent Learner. And every Independent Learner would be a skilful teacher. Further, the method of teaching someone to become an Independent Learner would be as straightforward as teachers explaining their teaching strategies to students so they can use them on themselves. Which is clearly not the case.

This raises another sticky problem for developing a learning community, which may have already occurred to you. If teachers are going to develop Learnership and an important aspect of teaching something is that you have subject area expertise, teachers will need to become better learners! As one principal put it, 'When it comes to teaching Learnership, the "I do, we do, you do" model for learning is limited by the "I do" part!' We'll explore this important issue later.

INCREASING AGENCY

An important characteristic of Independent Learners is they are the first level of learners capable of raising the bar *on their own*. Directed Learners can raise the bar and succeed at true challenges with the guidance of the teacher. An Independent Learner can take charge of their own learning, giving them the power to grow independently.

Independent Learners are adaptable. They set goals, and when circumstances change, or the environment demands it, they can change their goals. You'll have recognised Independent Learners during the Covid pandemic; rather than asking for help and guidance, they were the learners who were able to 'pivot' to a new goal when circumstances demanded.

This ability to guide their own learning and respond to emerging challenges gives Independent Learners more agency in the world. Being in charge of the learning process, they can change themselves. They are powerful, not powerless, in the face of adversity.

BECOMING WHO YOU WANT TO BE

I'm sure you know a lot of Independent Learners. These are the people who are setting goals and striving towards them. Often they appear driven. You might even recognise many of these qualities in yourself, or your peers. At some point in their career they decided they wanted to be a principal, and then set out on the path towards achieving that goal. Independent Learners tend to get good at something. They specialise.

We see Independent Learners in all walks of life. Business. Sciences. The arts. They are self-directed and self-managing. And in some ways, they are selfish. I mean that not in a derogatory way, but rather to point out that the Independent Learner's goals are their own. They choose them for their own reasons. Einstein was an Independent Learner. No-one told him to delve into how the universe behaves at the speed of light, and there was no pressing need to do so. He just did it because he chose to.

Many athletes and artists are similar. They push themselves towards their next goal, and their next, each time driven by the target they place in front of themselves. Many people achieve a lot this way.

With time, the right type of effort and a little luck, Independent Learners become the person they *want* to be. Why luck? Because things don't always turn out the way you plan. To be able to set your goals and not have things beyond your control get in the way requires a bit of luck. Perhaps there was a time when you could be confident that the world wasn't going to happen to you, that you wouldn't need to adjust. But that's not today.

If the world was evolving slowly, Independent Learners could pivot, adjust their goals and evolve with it. But that's not the world we live in either, and not the world we are preparing students for. The world is changing rapidly, and is more challenging. The chances that circumstances will stay aligned to a student's goals are small.

As we move on to consider the Agile Learner, I want to leave you pondering this question: what if, as an Independent Learner, the person you *want* to be in the world isn't the person you *need* to be in the world?

Chapter 21
Agile Learners

Masters of learning and growth.

AGILE LEARNER	EMBRACES	CULTIVATES	DESIGNS	TAILORS	GROWING
	CHALLENGE	HABITS OF MIND	MISTAKES	FEEDBACK	TIME & ENERGY

This is what you've been waiting for. It's time to answer the question, what do the most skilful learners do? And why, when we can achieve so many of our short-term educational outcomes with Directed or Independent Learners, should we be seeking to create Agile Learners?

MASTERS OF GROWTH AND LEARNING

Agile Learners are masters of growth and learning. They are the learners who have refined the process of achieving growth from an act to an art. Their learning is characterised by its proactive nature, its intentionality and its effectiveness in preparing them for an unknown and challenging future. They gain more out of every learning situation than any other learner.

Agile Learners are keenly aware of the increasingly complex and rapidly changing nature of the world, and they proactively seek to prepare themselves for it. They do this by taking on the challenges the world presents them with today, and leveraging those challenges to help them raise the bar and grow. In doing so, they are increasing the size of their comfort zone, filling the world with 'easy things they haven't done yet', preparing them for the world of tomorrow.

Agile Learners recognise that the value in tackling challenges stretches well beyond the immediate solution; the real value in challenge lies in its ability to drive growth. They understand that every time they go into their learning zone they give themselves the opportunity for personal growth. So they *embrace* challenges, in the spirit of JFK when he said, 'We do these things not because they are easy, but *because they are hard*'. This differs greatly from what an Independent Learner does.

It is the motivation of the Agile Learner that really sets them apart. At this level of Learnership, students have a highly growth-oriented mindset. They understand themselves as learners. They have deep awareness of their capacity to create their own abilities, and a deep appreciation that their greatest resource is their ability not simply to change themselves, but to change how they change themselves. To get better at getting better. So they are motivated by the achievement of personal growth, not simply the attainment of goals.

RECOGNISING THE AGILE LEARNER

Agile Learners take on challenges because they want the growth only a challenge will bring. Their time and energy is invested in themselves. The return on their investment is measured in their personal growth. They take on challenges because they *want the challenge* – it's their pathway to growth. They recognise that the solution to the problem might be of immediate value, but the personal growth that results from taking on a challenge has enduring value. In many ways the solution itself is of secondary importance.

Not that Agile Learners take on challenges without purpose. They also have goals, and encounter adversity that must be overcome.

The challenges they take on must be worthwhile. But Agile Learners see purpose and value in any challenge that helps them grow, not just the ones that help them reach an immediate goal. So when there is opportunity to take on a challenge they embrace it.

If you've ever met an Agile Learner, they were probably very good at something. Like anyone else, they have their interests and their goals, and they've pursued those. But they are also pretty good at a lot of things. They are aware the future is unpredictable, so they leverage the challenges of the present to prepare for the future. As a result, they tend to have a breadth of experience and range of abilities that leaves them highly versatile. They have more skills, and can more easily 'turn their hand' to a new challenge than most people.

> Agile Learners recognise that the solution to the problem might be of immediate value, but the personal growth that results from taking on a challenge has enduring value.

For the Agile Learner, challenges are a bit like deciding to take the stairs instead of the lift. The time will come and go whichever choice is made, so the question becomes how will you use that time? Standing in the lift or walking up the stairs? There is an opportunity to grow. Will you embrace it, or will you let it pass by? Why accept little or no return on that time, when you can gain so much from it?

Agile Learners understand their Habits of Mind are their greatest asset, so place particularly high value on developing them. They recognise the intimate relationship between challenges and the development of their Habits of Mind. So when there's a range of challenging opportunities in front of them, they'll tend to choose the ones that develop their weaknesses, rather than the ones that lean on their strengths. In this way, they are continually cultivating their habits.

This represents a significant change from other learners. Below-the-bar learners simply use the Habits of Mind they have. Directed and Independent Learners develop their Habits of Mind to succeed at their immediate challenges. But Agile Learners use today's challenges to develop their Habits of Mind in preparation for future challenges.

Agile Learners place high value on their time and energy, and seek the greatest possible value from these limited resources. They want them invested for maximum growth. They are very quick to recognise ineffective effort and to seek out support and information that will help them move into effective effort and growth.

Agile Learners recognise that information drives growth and helps move them into effective effort, so they are proactive in gathering information. They become experts at designing mistakes and tailoring feedback, effectively targeting and gathering the information they need.

BECOMING WHO YOU NEED TO BE

As we've discussed, below-the-bar learners lack agency. Their tendency to focus their efforts in their comfort and performance zones mean that challenges beyond their current abilities remain beyond their current abilities. They lack the capacity to grow.

Above-the-bar learners are capable of growth. They develop their Habits of Mind, raise the bar and make things that were once impossible, possible. This results in them having greater agency in the world. When they encounter challenges and adversity, they are able to take charge of their circumstances. They have the power to act.

Agile Learners have a unique and powerful advantage that gives them the greatest agency in the world: they know they can't predict the future. They can't know specifically what challenges will come their way. But they do know the future will be challenging. So rather than reactively responding to challenges as they arise, they are proactive about preparing themselves for a challenging future. By proactively embracing challenges, cultivating their Habits of Mind, developing a well-rounded profile and investing their time and energy in growth, they are constantly raising the bar. This increases the size of their comfort zone. This has a twofold effect:

- It makes many of the challenges the future may present 'easy things they haven't done yet'.
- It keeps them getting better at getting better.

Unlike Directed and Independent Learners who must respond to adversity as it arises, Agile Learners are futureproofing themselves. Of course, some challenges will still arise that are beyond their current abilities, but many challenges will occur that they'll find themselves well prepared for because of the way they have embraced challenges and cultivated their Habits of Mind. They'll find they are equipped and powerful in the face of change. They are more likely to be the master of their circumstances, not the victim.

During Covid, the Agile Learner had one of two responses. They either recognised the pandemic as a 'once in a lifetime learning opportunity' and embraced the unique challenges it offered as a means to further their growth. Or, they were grateful that over the preceding years they'd sought opportunities and developed abilities that would now serve them to confront the pandemic more successfully.

This proactive approach of embracing challenges as opportunities to grow, and preparing for the unknown challenges of the future, is uniquely powerful. It means Agile Learners are the only truly lifelong learners. It results in the Agile Learner going beyond resilience. The Agile Learner becomes antifragile, a concept we'll explore in the next chapter.

Agile Learners can become the heroes of their own story. Rather than becoming the person they necessarily want to be, they become the person they need to be in the world.

As you consider the level of Learnership in your school, how frequently do you see the behaviours associated with Agile Learners? Learners who are embracing challenges, who cultivate their Habits of Mind as their greatest asset? Learners who are proactively designing mistakes and tailoring feedback? Learners who are investing their effort in growth? If students are leaving your school, and are not on the path to becoming Agile Learners, can we really say we are preparing them to thrive in a rapidly changing and increasingly challenging world?

Chapter 22
Why the world needs Agile Learners

Futureproofing yourself against an unknowable future.

The pace of change has continued to increase, and there's no sign of it slowing down. The details vary depending on who you listen to, but the trends are clear. It is no longer an expectation that people will merely change jobs or even roles several times in their lives. Today's learners will change *careers* several times. By some estimates, students in your school today will have up to seven different careers! Many will be working with technologies, solving problems and employed in industries that are just now in their infancy, or don't even exist yet. The rise of the 'gig economy' means even the concept of having a 'job' is dramatically changing.

In a world where change is the only constant and uncertainty the only certainty, we need a different type of learner. Students with Learnership at the level of Directed or Independent Learners won't be enough. They won't be able to keep up with the rate and nature of this change. If the duty of the education system as a whole is to prepare our youth for the future, we have to create Agile Learners.

To be clear, I'm not making a case that developing Learnership and creating Agile Learners would be a *nice thing for schools to do*. Some sort of value add, or a goal for our top schools or a select group of our students. I'm making the case that developing Agile Learners needs to be a goal we achieve for *all* our students in *all* our schools.

> ❝ ... developing Agile Learners needs to be a goal we achieve for *all* our students in *all* our schools.

GOING BEYOND RESILIENCE

As you read the descriptions of the different levels of Learnership in the previous chapters, I'm sure you recognised many of the students in your school. At least some of your students, possibly many, have low levels of Learnership. They are Beginning, Performance and Directed Learners. These are the students you worry about. These are the students who are going into the world with low aspirations and limited opportunities. These are the students who lack agency in their lives.

We are already seeing the negative impact of relatively low levels of Learnership in our students. Those with low levels of Learnership don't cope well with change and challenge. Particularly in a post-Covid world, we find them struggling. The fact that many of our students are not coping is reflected in what has become a global focus on resilience.

It seems every school I visit is talking about resilience. Many schools have included building resilience as part of their strategic plan. Some have even made it part of their motto. At every conference I've gone to in the last five years, someone is talking about resilience.

And it's not just schools – businesses are talking about resilience as employees with low levels of Learnership struggle with challenge and uncertainty. You live and work in this environment too. As a leader of teachers, Learnership is as relevant to you and your team as it is for your students (something we'll explore further in part VII).

The problem with this focus on resilience is that, for the most part, it's a reactive approach. The world has already happened to the student, and we talk about the need to 'bounce back'. Or we talk about the need for 'protective strategies'. The model is that the big bad world is going to come along and our students need to protect themselves from it, and bounce back when that doesn't work.

But what if challenge and uncertainty weren't things to be feared? What if they were to be embraced? What if instead of having to protect your students from disruptions and help them bounce back from setbacks, you could use those disruptions to help them grow? What if instead of worrying about your students being fragile, they were antifragile?

Becoming antifragile: benefitting from disruption

In his 2012 book *Antifragile: Things that gain from disorder*, Nassim Nicholas Taleb describes the concept of being antifragile. It's a massively important concept that most people don't have an intuitive understanding of.

When you think of something that's fragile, what comes to mind? Perhaps something like glass, or a delicate china cup – something easily broken. Things that are fragile need to be protected from disruption.

Some of our students are like that – fragile. Students at the Non-Learner and Beginning Learner levels of Learnership don't cope well with disruption. Their limited capacity to change themselves means they are sensitive to problems. When the world happens to them, they don't know how to cope. So they need us to protect them. This is one of the reasons we hear so much about schools needing to provide a safe and supportive environment.

This inability to cope with disruption is also why, when Covid (or any other significant challenge) came along, below-the-bar learners ducked for cover. They didn't have the skills to cope with this new world, and they couldn't easily change themselves into someone who could. Their only strategy was to wait and hope for things to get back to normal.

What about when you think about the opposite of fragile? What idea does that bring to mind? For most people the ideas that come to mind for the opposite of fragile are strong, robust or even resilient – things that don't break easily.

But Taleb would say you've missed the point. The opposite of fragile is not something that doesn't break. Taleb points out that things that are fragile break easily when disturbed, whereas something that is strong or robust withstands a lot of disturbance before it eventually breaks.

Things that are resilient bend and bounce back after disruption. The word resilient is derived from the Latin verb *resilire*, meaning 'to leap back'. Students at the Directed level of Learnership are resilient. We can show them how to prepare and protect themselves, and to bounce back after disruption. Independent Learners are robust and adaptable. They can withstand change by adapting to the disruption.

Adaptability has its limits though. Too much change, or when change happens too rapidly, and even an adaptable system will break.

Being antifragile is different. Taleb describes systems that are antifragile as systems that *benefit from disruption*. These are systems that don't just survive when disrupted, they thrive.

> ❝ Taleb describes systems that are antifragile as systems that *benefit from disruption*. These are systems that don't just survive when disrupted, they thrive.

Taleb points to many real-world examples that are antifragile. Think of a small hedge plant. Plant it in the ground and leave it to grow and it becomes a sticky hollow tree. But come along each season and disturb it a little by trimming the tips, and it responds to the disturbance by sending forth new branches. It grows lush and strong because of the disturbance. This is what it means to be antifragile. Minor disturbances make you stronger.

Evolution is antifragile. It is driven by the disruptions that provide selection pressures. Our immune system is antifragile. By exposing ourselves to minor pathogens as a child, we build immunity as an adult.

This is why we should let children play in the dirt every now and then and not keep them in a sanitised world.

Once you know what you're looking for, you'll see antifragile systems everywhere.

Antifragile systems benefit from disruption. They need it. More than that, they thrive on it. But the disruptions have to be the right size, enough to stimulate growth. If you prune your hedge by cutting it off at ground level, it's not going to survive. But if you don't prune it at all, there's very limited growth.

This is why our learning zone is so important. It provides the right amount of challenge to stimulate growth. Schools that have taken the idea of providing a safe and supportive environment to the point of protecting their students from challenge and struggle are doing them a disservice. They are keeping their students in their comfort and performance zones. We need to make our school environments safe and supportive while still being challenging.

AGILE LEARNERS ARE ANTIFRAGILE

By deeply understanding the learning process, Agile Learners become skilful learners who embrace challenges, leveraging them for the opportunity they provide to help them grow. Each time they leverage a challenge, any challenge, to help them grow, they raise the bar. Raising the bar fills their world with 'easy things they haven't done yet'. They go beyond learning how to survive in a rapidly changing and increasingly complex world, and can't help but thrive in it.

Taleb points out that we can't predict the future. Not because it is difficult to do, but because the nature of change is such that it is impossible to do. We are going to face what he calls 'black swan events'. These are highly improbable but highly impactful events we can't predict. But we can prepare for them.

In a rapidly changing and increasingly complex world, the only way to prepare for future challenges is to leverage the challenges and adversity in front of you to grow today. That's what Agile Learners do, and that's how they go beyond resilience and become antifragile.

The learners we seek to create are Agile Learners. They have the greatest agency in the world. These learners don't need to be resilient, because they are antifragile. They don't need to be protected from adversity, because they know how to take on challenges. Agile Learners understand they are capable of growth (a growth mindset) and they understand how to go about achieving that growth. They face a rapidly changing and increasingly complex world as an opportunity to grow, with both the will to act and power to act. They move through life the master of their circumstances, confident in their ability to overcome adversity, achieve any goals they choose and make a difference to the world around them.

> 66 In a rapidly changing and increasingly complex world, the only way to prepare for future challenges is to leverage the challenges and adversity in front of you to grow today. That's what Agile Learners do, and that's how they go beyond resilience and become antifragile.

PART V KEY TAKEAWAYS

- The Learnership Matrix describes increasing levels of skilfulness on the journey from Non-Learner to Agile Learner.
- Non-Learners don't participate in the learning process. They opt out, choosing to do nothing rather than something.
- Beginning Learners see learning as an activity that fills time and finishes when the activity finishes. They look for the easiest, least demanding options.
- Performance Learners do their best, but at the expense of not pushing themselves to do better. They are masters of the minimax principle: maximum (current) performance for the least effort.
- Below-the-bar learners (Non, Beginning, Performance) have little agency in the world. They become victims of their circumstances, and powerless in the face of challenge and adversity.
- Directed Learners improve, but their learning is entirely controlled by the teacher. They are learn**ing**, but are not learn**ers**.
- Independent Learners take charge of the learning process. They are goal setters. In the absence of goals, their learning stops.
- Agile Learners are the only truly lifelong learners. They embrace challenges, in the spirit of JFK's 'we do these things not because they are easy, but because they are hard'. They recognise the long-term benefit of growth is it prepares them for an unknowable future.
- Above-the-bar learners are capable of growth, so can increase their agency in the world.
- In a VUCA world, where change is the only constant and uncertainty the only certainty, we need to develop – and become – Agile Learners. These learners' habits of embracing challenge and cultivating their Habits of Mind mean they are constantly raising the bar, which has the effect of making them antifragile, and essentially futureproofing them.

Use the space below to add some of your own part V key takeaways.

- _____
- _____
- _____
- _____
- _____
- _____
- _____
- _____
- _____
- _____
- _____
- _____
- _____
- _____
- _____
- _____
- _____
- _____
- _____
- _____

DISCUSSION AND ACTION

- With your leadership team, reflect on the level of Learnership you tend to notice from:
    - students
    - teachers
    - yourselves.
- What might be some of the barriers to achieving greater levels of Learnership in your school? How might these be addressed?

Use the space below to add some of your own discussion and action items.

- _____
- _____
- _____
- _____
- _____
- _____
- _____
- _____
- _____
- _____
- _____
- _____
- _____
- _____
- _____

WHERE TO FROM HERE?

Now that you have an understanding of what skilful learning looks like, it's time to ask two important questions. Firstly, what level of Learnership have your learners achieved? Secondly, what are the forces, or culture, driving the development of these types of learners in your school?

In the next part we delve into the concept of culture, and I invite you to use a powerful tool to measure the level of Learnership and your school culture as it relates to learning.

Part VI
Creating a culture for Learnership

You've heard of a culture referred to as 'the way things are done around here'. It's the norms of a community that create a default way of behaving and working. This reflects what we believe and creates what we see, hear and experience in our community. But culture is shaped just as much by what's not there as by what's there.

In this section I encourage you to think of your school culture not just as what you see, hear and experience, but also what's missing. For example, in the teaching culture so prevalent in our current educational climate we see quality teaching and achievement of (short-term) learning outcomes – both of which are desirable. But while this teaching culture is doing a great job of producing learn*ing*, it isn't doing a great job of creating learn*ers*.

It's not always easy to measure culture, so in this part I offer you a practical and easy-to-use tool for identifying your school culture as it relates to learning. I give you powerful insights for understanding the forces driving your current culture, helping you to see what's there as well as what's not.

Let's begin by addressing some of the cultural challenges principals face and recognising how, by developing a culture of learning and growth, you can establish ways of working that make it easier to reach your long-term goals. With the right culture – focused on growth and Learnership – it would be difficult *not to* reach your long-term goals!

Chapter 23
Assessing your learning culture

This is the way learning gets done around here.

When I arrive at a school, I always invest some time identifying its culture towards learning.

I walk around the school and ask myself, what am I experiencing? What are the most common behaviours I'm observing? How do students, teachers and leaders experience the school? I look at what's hanging on classroom walls. I listen to teachers' conversations in the staffrooms. I pay close attention to the language used. I watch the students in the classrooms. Most importantly, I ask myself, what are the underlying beliefs and assumption about learning that are driving what I'm experiencing?

I do all of that before I look at the website, read the school's prospectus or review the three-year improvement plan. Culture is what you actually experience. And that's not always the same as what you'd like to have people experience, or necessarily what you say it is.

In the context of our focus on Learnership, we are interested in a school's culture as it relates to learners and the process of learning, what I refer to as its 'learning culture'. Culture in its broadest sense encompasses more than this, but in this book I focus on a school's learning culture as this drives how students engage in the process of learning.

Put simply, a school's culture is 'the way things get done around here'. Culture is driven by a set of often unspoken rules and assumptions about learning. Like a learner's mindset drives their individual behaviours, a school's culture drives the community's collective behaviours. The result is the emergence of a particular level of Learnership. Get the learning culture right and not only will you create Agile Learners, it becomes hard not to!

> Put simply, a school's culture is 'the way things get done around here'.

So as I walk around a school I'm trying to discern, what are those unspoken rules? What's driving the way students (and others) engage in the process of learning? What's driving the learning culture? And I'd like to encourage you to do the same.

One thing I've learnt is that paying attention only to what you experience can give an incomplete and sometimes misleading picture of culture. We need to look closer. It's at least as useful (and possibly more so) to think about a school culture by looking for what you *don't* experience, and to ask 'what's missing here?'

For example, a primary school I once worked with appeared to have a beautiful culture. Walking around the school I could see from the student work adorning the walls that the community took great pride in the students' work. Learning intentions were displayed clearly in the classroom. In the staff meetings teachers were talking about pedagogy. There was a data wall showing student standards. Informal conversations in the staffroom centred on student welfare, resilience and wellbeing. The anecdotes teachers shared with me were about creating a safe and caring environment for the students, a protected place. Moreover, students were smiling. The school just 'felt' safe and caring.

On first inspection, this school's culture might seem satisfactory, even desirable. There was nothing overtly 'wrong' with what was there. Nothing we might want to subtract from the culture. Certainly the school leadership and the wider community were happy.

But the longer I spent with the school, the more I got a sense of, 'Yeah … but …'. I started to experience a nagging sense that while what I could see was good, and there wasn't anything jumping out at me that was bad, there was something … missing. Something wasn't quite right. That's when I knew it was time to look for what was not there.

In this school the focus on caring for students' wellbeing was being carried to the point of protecting them from the struggle of learning. Teachers' beliefs that students needed to be protected from discomfort meant that learning activities became activities designed for students to complete and experience (easy) success and enjoyment. The data wall was being used to identify what students could do, rather than where they needed to go. The work displayed so prominently on the walls was largely about presentation and demonstration, not growth and improvement.

What was absent from this culture was a focus on growth. While there was lots of activity, there was little learning. And where there was learning, it was nearly always teacher directed. There was little focus on students becoming learners.

LEARNING CULTURES

Each level of Learnership emerges easily and naturally from a school's underlying learning culture. Each action relates to and supports the next. There is a consistency and coherency that gives any culture its strength, and helps it endure – for better or worse.

In the example above the dominant underlying beliefs driving the culture were about the need to 'protect' students and 'keep them safe'. Students who were thriving should be enjoying school. From this set of beliefs, all the actions – developing curriculum based on engagement and enjoyment, focusing on what students could do (easily), rather than where they needed to go, over scaffolding and doing all the heavy lifting of learning – make sense. Each action is aligned with the others and the underlying beliefs driving them.

Once all those practices are in place and the culture is established, any new practice will be shaped by the existing rules and beliefs – that's what culture is. Everything aligns naturally and easily with the existing culture.

With practice you'll become adept at identifying the drivers of a school's learning culture. As we explore the six cultures associated with each level of Learnership, look for the internal consistency within each – how each element weaves together to almost naturally produce the level of Learnership. These are:

- Culture of avoidance – Non-Learners
- Culture of activity – Beginning Learners
- Culture of performance – Performance Learners
- Culture of teaching – Directed Learners
- Culture of learning – Independent Learners
- Culture of growth – Agile Learners.

Although I describe six distinct cultures, in practice most schools are best described as a mix of two (or sometimes three) of the cultures. As a leader, you're not trying to identify 'your level' but the extent to which each level applies to you. Once we've done that, we will discuss what needs to be done to create a culture of growth.

> ❞ ... creating a culture of learning and growth will bring out the best in your existing culture, and makes the development of Agile Learners easier to do than to not do.

You may already be developing a sense of your school's learning culture. As you read part V you probably recognised the level(s) of Learnership most common in your school. At the end of this chapter I invite you to assess your school's learning culture using the Learnership

Diagnostic. This tool will show you the frequency of behaviours associated with each level of Learnership, measuring the learning behaviours present in your school, identifying your dominant learning culture, and produce a graph similar to the ones below.

But for now, follow along as we look at each of the six cultures, examining the underlying beliefs that drive them and how these create the conditions for different levels of Learnership to emerge. Each culture has valuable characteristics. However, we also consider how Learnership can be improved by developing a culture increasingly focused on learning and growth.

In the rest of this section, we look at how creating a culture of learning and growth will bring out the best in your existing culture, and makes the development of Agile Learners easier to do than to not do.

NON-LEARNERS: CULTURE OF AVOIDANCE

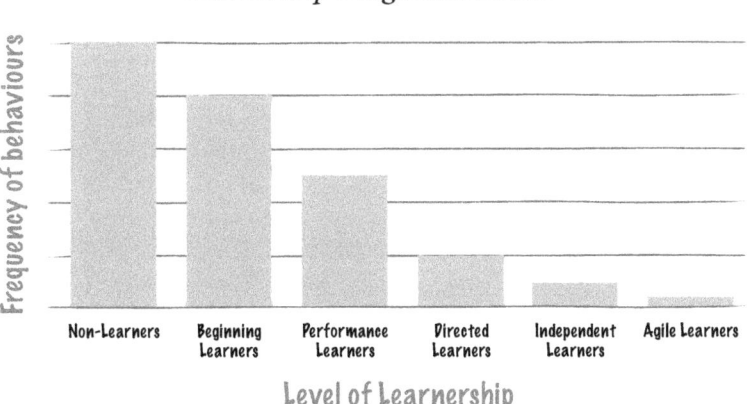

Learnership Diagnostic results

In schools where the most common behaviours are associated with Non-Learners, we find a culture of avoidance. The way things are done is to avoid learning. Within this culture, learners are not participating in learning as much as possible, choosing instead to seek or create distractions or simply not attend lessons.

A culture of avoidance is often symptomatic of students being towards the fixed end of the Mindset Continuum. These students don't understand their capacity to change. They see school as one long test to discover their abilities. And in their eyes, it's a test they have been failing.

Walking through the school observing classrooms, you see many students off task or engaging in avoidance activities – creating distractions, or quietly doing nothing. Teachers must constantly check students are doing what they have been asked to do and keep them on task.

Students can be heard to ask, 'Why do we have to do this?', hoping for a way to escape the task. They'll tell teachers they don't care about the topic, or school, so why should they have to do it?

These behaviours can often give rise to classroom discipline issues, so displays of classroom behaviour expectations and rules are prominent. Some teachers can become despondent and may adopt an attitude of, *if they don't care, why should I?* Other teachers exhaust themselves trying to drag and cajole students through the learning process. For school leaders, staff wellbeing becomes a significant issue.

> 66 The way things are done is to avoid learning.

Unsurprisingly, the learning outcomes for many of these students are well below expected standards. They fall further and further behind benchmarks as time goes on. Having fallen behind, students who attempt to re-engage at the expected standards frequently struggle and fail. This repeated experience of failure is a powerful fixed mindset mover, which results in students being pushed more and more towards the fixed end of the Mindset Continuum, compounding their disengagement from learning and reinforcing the culture of avoidance.

Leaders in schools with this culture are often faced with issues of student attendance and truancy. Just getting students to school and in class regularly is a challenge. Significant resources are often required to cater for students who, at best, are reluctant to engage in learning, and at worst, are actively avoiding it.

The high frequency of well-below-standard performance from students leads to significant numbers of learning interventions. Many students are placed on modified learning programs, all of which consume teachers' time and resources, preventing them from focusing on other more growth-related activities.

Students who are not taking part effectively in the learning process negatively impact the overall performance of the school. The school performs poorly on standardised tests and other measures, which can lead to reviews of school performance. As we saw in chapter 2, this can lead to scrutiny of teacher standards and blaming of teachers for students' poor performance.

Outcomes and challenges for students who emerge from this culture

As students reach leaving age, the question of pathways into the workforce becomes a significant issue. The number of students leaving school early is high. There is very little emphasis on pathways to further or higher education in the school, as these students are unlikely to see these as options for them. The school becomes unconcerned with pass rates and more concerned with retention rates.

Students who have experienced little success in school have very low aspirations, and they don't expect things to change. School leaders lament the low expectations and limited choices these students see for their future.

Clearly, a culture of avoidance is not conducive to learning. Like the Non-Learner represents a baseline for learning, the culture of avoidance represents a baseline for a learning culture – essentially a culture where little learning happens. Fortunately, even schools with a significant proportion of behaviours associated with Non-Learners will also have elements of a culture of activity as well.

BEGINNING LEARNERS: CULTURE OF ACTIVITY

Learnership Diagnostic results

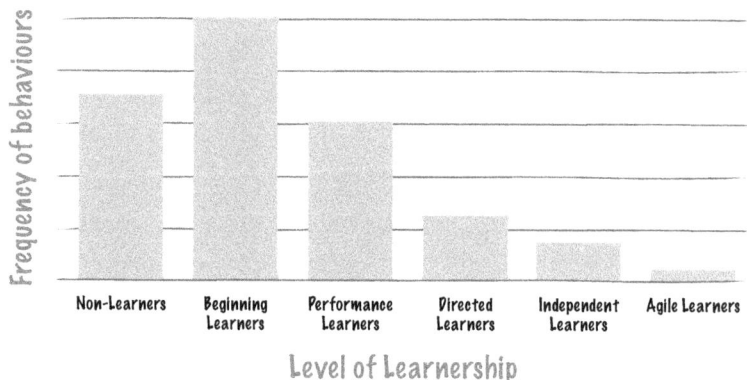

In schools where we find the behaviours commonly associated with Beginning Learners, we find a culture of activity. While Beginning Learners are active, they avoid struggle, so this activity is often at the expense of challenge. The way things are done around here is to keep students busy.

> ❝ The way things are done around here is to keep students busy.

Walking around a school with an activity culture, it feels like a busy place. Things are happening. Classrooms are active. Students are engaged.

The conversations you hear in the staffroom at the beginning of the day are about what students will *do* in class that day. You hear a description of the activities they'll be completing. The part of the activities being emphasised is that they are fun and engaging for students.

Walking into a team or faculty meeting, you notice that curriculum planning is very focused on student engagement. The priority is keeping students on task. Teachers are constantly seeking more effective ways to keep students interested and taking part in learning. When you ask a teacher why they are doing a particular activity, their first answer is likely to be because the students really enjoy it.

I worked in a school with an activity culture in my first few years of teaching and quickly fell into line with this thinking. Like many teachers, my first step in planning a unit of work was to look for the activities I thought students would enjoy. Curriculum planning was about what students would do (and be willing to do) in class. I'd plan these activities, and only then identify the learning outcomes they would achieve. As a faculty, we created activity banks we could draw on year after year of the most successful activities. The entire process was driven by making classrooms fun and engaging.

At the end of the school day, the most common questions you hear from parents are:

- 'What did you do at school today?'
- 'Did you have *fun* at school today?'
- 'What do you *enjoy* about school?'

Questions about what students are working on, learning, struggling with or the goals they are setting will be far less common.

Students can still be heard to ask, 'Why do we have to do this?', but their reason for asking is they are finding the task challenging and would prefer to do something less challenging. They are happy to do something, just not something hard.

Reading student reports can feel like reading a list of the activities students completed, annotated with comments about how students engaged in them or how much they enjoyed them.

In this culture, rewards are given on completion, participation, reaching the end of a task or milestones that involve the passing of time or completing a volume of activities. Assessment is often based on the learning being satisfactory or not satisfactory, rather than the achievement of increasing standards.

Walking into the classroom at the start of the term, you will notice the walls are covered with information about the topic being taught. At the end of the term, you will notice the walls are covered with multiple samples of student work, illustrating that all the students have finished the task. Teacher mark books are filled with records to show what tasks have been completed. For learners there is a sense that school is a series of activities, and learning finishes when the activity finishes.

Good, but could be better if ...

Of course we want students to be engaged in their learning. We expect learning to involve students in activities they find engaging and that connect to their interests. These are positive elements in this culture. However, we will want to realign them towards growth.

The reason for the activity must not be activity itself. Active and engaged in the absence of a focus on growth is simply busy, and keeps students in their comfort zones. The activities teachers design must be geared towards achieving growth, not merely participation and completion.

When students stay in their comfort zones, they measure success by completion. They come to expect achievement to be easy, a tick-the-box exercise. They are robbed of challenge, and understanding that struggle drives growth. Struggle becomes undervalued, even undesirable. 'Hard' is seen to be something that takes a long time, rather than something that stretches them. As a result, these students' efforts become under-calibrated.

Outcomes and challenges for students who emerge from this culture

In a culture of activity, through sheer participation and the fact that the curriculum often demands only breadth and not always growth in learning, students see some progress against short-term outcomes, but it is less than expected. Students slowly and steadily fall further and further behind expected standards of achievement.

By the middle and senior years of schooling, most students' abilities have plateaued and they experience little, if any, growth. These students increasingly encounter challenges beyond their current abilities. However, their lack of experience in their learning zone has resulted in them having a poor understanding of how to develop their Habits of Mind and an undervaluing of effort. This leaves them ill-prepared to succeed at these challenges.

As students approach school-leaving age, discussions in the school focus on retention. To improve their opportunities in life, leaders make efforts to keep students in schools for as long as possible. Secondary schools often offer alternative pathways into employment. Not because these pathways aren't valuable but because these students' inability to engage successfully in the learning process means they have limited choices, and these are the only pathways open to them.

Because these students have failed to achieve significant growth and have not significantly developed the skills of Learnership, as adults they require protected or controlled environments that keep challenges within their abilities. This often restricts their opportunities for work to relatively menial, low-level, task-centred, supervised jobs.

> ❝❝ Because these students have failed to achieve significant growth and have not significantly developed the skills of Learnership, as adults they require protected or controlled environments that keep challenges within their abilities.

Adults who remain Beginning Learners become fragile and so are highly sensitive to changes in their environment. As challenge or adversity come along, they are likely to find themselves out of their depth. They often cannot overcome even relatively minor disruptions on their own and need significant levels of outside support. They easily become the victim of their circumstances, powerless to effect change. As a society, we are left to support and protect these individuals.

PERFORMANCE LEARNERS: CULTURE OF PERFORMANCE

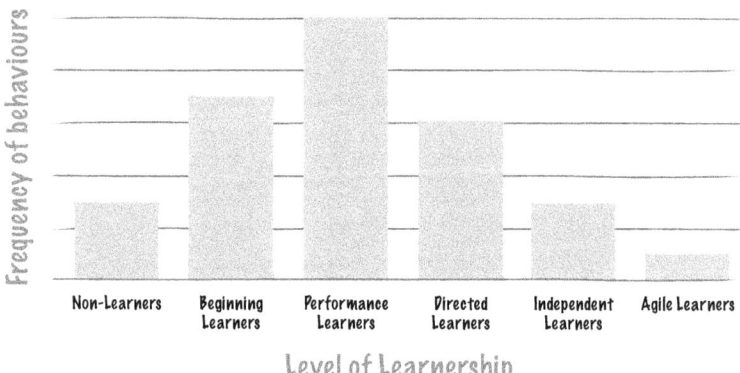

In schools where we commonly see the behaviours associated with Performance Learners we find a performance culture. The way things are done around here is to demonstrate what you can do well, and to be known for what you can do. The spotlight is on student performance.

> ❝❝ The spotlight is on student performance.

The belief guiding a performance culture is that performance is the pinnacle of achievement. The result is students feel it's better to show what you can do rather than struggle to achieve something you can't currently do.

A school I worked with was deeply entrenched in a performance culture. Walking through this school you could feel there was a strong sense of celebration and achievement. There was a belief and an energy around performance, and students demonstrating abilities, that was almost contagious. The halls were covered with badges, stars, plaques and winners. They covered classroom walls with only the best student work.

It felt like the most important reason for doing something was so you could show off what you can do. Students were constantly expected to be in their performance zone. Demonstrating achievement breeds a sense of pride that was palpable in the school.

Listening carefully, I noticed the odd way the term 'high standard' was used. The idea of students achieving a 'high standard' was about perfection and reliability, rather than increasing difficulty and complexity. The school rewarded students more for being perfect at a slightly lower standard than slightly imperfect at what might reasonably be referred to as a higher standard. This practice tends to keep students in their performance zone.

A performance culture can also breed a sense of perfectionism among some students. The focus and rewards for performance mean students come to feel it's more important to demonstrate perfection at the current level rather than moving on, growing, and doing well at the next.

In an environment that's all about performance, effort and struggle are not highly valued. This can lead students to habitually seek their performance zone. They set easy goals and avoid mistakes. Where effort is required, we see students hide their effort or downplay how hard they had to work. Rather than embracing challenges in their learning zone as the pathway to growth, students nibble away at the edge of their learning zone, where risks are low.

In the car park, parents discuss what their child is good at, what performances they are working on, and what achievements and awards their children have received.

It's common that a performance culture breeds a strong focus on assessment. Teachers focus on the standards that need to be demonstrated and on how students will do this. The question of 'what's going to be on the test?' is often heard, coming from both teachers and students.

The verb often heard in classrooms is to 'show' or 'demonstrate'. Teachers want students to 'show me you can … '. Sometimes, this can lead to a unit of work being one long demonstration and assessment piece.

Good, but could be better if ...

Here again we can recognise much in a culture of performance that is valuable. We want student achievement to be celebrated. However, we need to ask *what* is being celebrated, and look to realign our celebrations to growth.

In a performance culture, it's the standard of the performance that sets the criteria for success. The focus is on what students can do, and do well. Faultless performance is valued. If we instead shift the focus to growth, you shift the criteria for success and celebration to be about the amount of improvement the performance represents. You value the backstory of the achievement, not just the achievement.

We can describe the shift from performance to growth as a shift from perfection-ism to improvement-ism. Instead of creating an environment where students are expected to be *perfect*, the culture creates and values a desire to be *better*.

When performance is a goal unto itself, the rewards go to the best performance. But in a culture of growth, we remember that your best is only your best when you measure by yesterday's standards. By tomorrow's standards it's going to be your second best. Your standard is temporary. When we focus on growth, change becomes more important than standards.

> ❝ ... describe the shift from performance to growth as a shift from perfection-ism to improvement-ism.

One thing we see a lot of in a performance culture is energy. What we might miss is that this effort is often performance effort, not growth effort. Valuing performance so highly, students are more inclined to spend their effort in performance rather than invest it in growth. When we hear students asking, 'Why are we doing this?', it's because they are being pushed into their learning zone where they feel uncomfortable.

They are asking if they can lower the bar and perform to a standard they can do well. This hinders their long-term growth. In the absence of a strong growth focus, there is lots of dazzle and often not much depth.

Outcomes and challenges for students who emerge from this culture

Performance Learners are more active and engaged in classrooms than Beginning Learners, but they limit their growth by preferring to spend most of their effort in their performance zone.

Performance Learners give teachers a sense they have the resources to do better, but are not applying themselves in quite the right way. Teachers often identify them as 'underperforming' or use fixed mindset terms like 'not working to their potential'. They are 'good kids' who *could do better*.

Teachers feel like the students need to be pushed a little harder. Unfortunately, teachers are as influenced by the performance culture as students are. It's countercultural to push students into their learning zone where they will struggle, when they could be performing. So students are instead pushed to consolidate standards and increase reliability, rather than raise the bar to new levels.

As a leader in a culture of performance there is much to celebrate. However, results tend to slowly fall behind expectations, and you may find yourself increasingly concerned about achieving 'one year's growth in one year's time'.

When students leave school with the skills of a Performance Learner, they become performance centred. They are sensitive to change. They like to find something they are good at and stick to it, repeating that performance over and over again. The problem, of course, is that to do this, they need a very structured environment that demands the same outcomes all the time. Which in today's world is becoming rarer and rarer. Gone are the days when you could leave school with a set of skills and continue to apply those same skills over and over for the rest of your life.

DIRECTED LEARNERS: CULTURE OF TEACHING

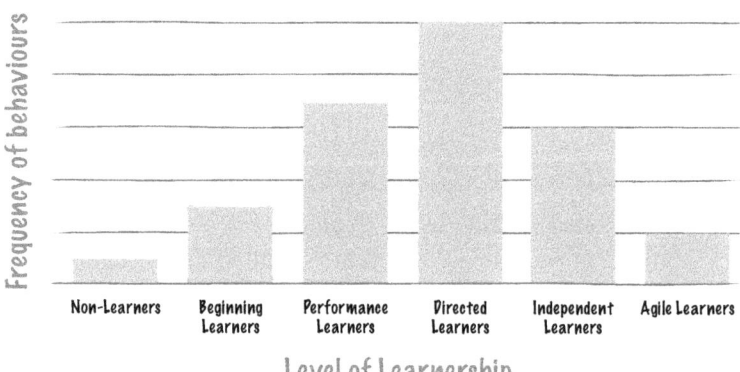

Learnership Diagnostic results

Where we find the dominant behaviours of students associated with Directed Learners we find a culture of teaching. In this environment, the underlying belief is that educational outcomes are largely the result of what teachers do in the classroom. So the way we do things around here is through teaching!

The story I shared in chapter 7 of the teacher achieving great short-term results was an example of a teaching culture. That teacher was doing all the heavy lifting for the students. The students were learning, but they weren't learners.

The teaching culture is perhaps the dominant culture in our system of education today, and has grown out of the intense focus on quality teaching practice over the past 15 years. Even if your school culture does not resonate with the description below, you'll recognise it in the culture of our education system as a whole.

As you walk through a school with a teaching culture, you notice it's the teachers who take centre stage. They are the lead actors, responsible for making sure learning outcomes are met. It might take a little while to tune into it, but you soon notice nearly every problem is a teaching problem. Every solution comes down to what teachers are going to do.

You notice that classroom walls are full of scaffolds and strategies to help students achieve learning outcomes, or other 'how to' displays. These are often subject or topic specific, such as steps for writing an argumentative essay. The posters remind students of what the teacher has told them to do. Exemplars that illustrate standards are also common. Where student work is displayed, it's often used to illustrate how a strategy was applied, with the process and standards highlighted.

In this environment, students step out of the performance spotlight and become consumers of education. Their outcomes are the result of what teachers do. The pervasive influence of learning being the teacher's responsibility leads to the creation of passive learners. So the longer you are in this culture, the more you hear teachers talking about wanting students to take initiative, and how so many students these days are passive learners.

Staffroom conversation and teacher professional learning are dominated by conversations about which teaching strategies are the most effective. To identify these practices, peer coaching and teacher observations are common. Leaders talk about sharing best practice. The driving belief behind these practices is teachers make *the* difference, and improving teacher quality is the way to improve learning outcomes.

In a teaching culture, the word 'learning' is almost always used as an adjective. As in, 'this is what we will be learning'. Explicit learning intentions (which the teacher decides on) are displayed in the classroom. The goal is that these be achieved.

When teachers and leadership teams talk about making learning visible, they are talking about making what students have learned visible. Teachers measure student progress towards the desired outcomes. This information is used to measure teacher effectiveness and assess student outcomes. Teachers reflect on this progress by asking what else they need to do to ensure students achieve the learning goals.

In this environment, the natural focus is on value adding. The primary question is what can we (the teachers and school leadership) do that's going to enhance student learning outcomes? Some of the focus will be on providing resources and on making it easier for teachers to do their job. Much of it will be on improving the quality of teaching, professional learning and sharing 'best practice'. The belief is we can solve all learning problems with better teaching.

In a teaching culture, meeting standards is at the front of teachers' minds. You are likely to hear conversations about the number of students below, at or above standards, and if that meets expectations. Rather than how far students have moved.

As you spend more time in a teaching culture, you notice how often students are spoken about as a collective. We measure teacher success based on the number of students at, below or above standards. The school is data rich, and analysing data is a priority. But individuals are often missing from the analysis.

The teaching and learning role (aka curriculum and assessment leader) is focused on ensuring quality teaching and measuring that quality based on the achievement of student learning outcomes across cohorts. They give scant attention to how students engage in the process of learning, beyond ensuring teachers are providing an engaging curriculum. There is little, if any, focus on how students can become better learners.

In terms of the Learning Equation, most of the focus in this environment is on what the teacher does. There is often a pervasive, if unspoken, fixed mindset belief that the student input into the Learning Equation is limited. The teacher's job is to 'get the most' out of students.

In terms of how students engage in the learning process, the focus is on the quantity, rather than the quality, of their engagement. Conversations will focus on students 'working harder' and putting in 'more effort'. Teachers encourage students to work hard and participate in the lessons they are giving so students can achieve the desired outcomes. Once students are working hard, it's up to the teacher.

As we saw in the previous chapter, this belief that teachers are in command of the learning that occurs leads to teachers getting the credit (and responsibility) for improving student performance. We celebrate teachers when students do well. Of course, they also get the blame when students don't perform to standard.

Good, but could be better if ...

Here again, we can see much we value. Quality teaching is important and will form a large part of the growth culture we are seeking to build – but it's not *everything*. What we don't see in a teaching culture is the learner. We have pushed them to the background, a passive statistic behind the important role of the teacher and the learning outcomes we are trying to achieve.

While a teaching culture uses the term 'teacher impact', a growth culture might use the more subtle, more gentle term of 'teacher effect' when referring to the contribution teachers have on student learning. To affect a student is to make a difference or produce a change. It's not about force, it's about influence. Importantly, this does not minimise the role of the student in their own learning. There can be many influences on student learning outcomes. The teacher is one. The student is another. Ultimately, we want the student to be the major agent in their own learning.

In a teaching culture, we have learn*ing*, but not learn*ers*. This intense focus on teacher practice, and how teacher practice influences learning, is at the expense of the learner learning how to learn for themselves. Teachers teach. Learners *consume*. Learning outcomes are being achieved but learners aren't being created.

In a growth culture, the word 'learning' is nearly always used as a verb. It describes what learners do, the actions they are taking to gain new knowledge, understanding and abilities, and achieve growth.

With a focus on growth, the teaching and learning role in the school expands to include the role of the learners in the learning process. Teachers are responsible not just for quality teaching but also for quality learning.

In the absence of a focus on the growth of the learner, we might achieve short-term learning outcomes, which might be enough to tick the boxes of a system focused on short-term educational results. But students are not learning to take charge of the learning process. They become dependent on teachers. And we fail to meet our long-range educational goals.

Outcomes and challenges for students who emerge from this culture

This environment can feel satisfying for teachers and leaders alike. Teachers' hard work is recognised, and they can see the results they are achieving. Students are typically achieving one year's growth in one year's time, so teachers are deemed to be 'doing their job'. There is a certain satisfaction that comes with knowing your actions are having an impact. Being perceived as the major controllable variable in the Learning Equation elevates their perceived importance.

Schools with this type of culture tend to meet expectations, or at the very least feel they are in control of expectations being met. Some students are doing well. A few need support. Most are progressing as expected.

As adults, Directed Learners can be resilient. We can show these learners how to deal with adversity. The world will still present difficulty and challenge, but with support, the Directed Learner can 'bounce back' and recover from adversity.

For example, in a changing world some industries (such as manufacturing) have faced massive changes. Entire workforces have been displaced as technologies change. Of course this has happened before, but it's happening more rapidly now. Directed Learners in these industries need to be offered new opportunities, to be reskilled, retrained or to have governments create other opportunities where their existing skillsets can be used.

While the Directed Learner can change, their environment needs to be managed for them. Their learning almost always takes place *after* the adversity, in response to challenges that have arisen. The world happens to them, but as long as the structures are there to support them, they can respond, and while they might not be the masters of their circumstances, they eventually, with support, overcome their difficulties.

INDEPENDENT LEARNERS: CULTURE OF LEARNING

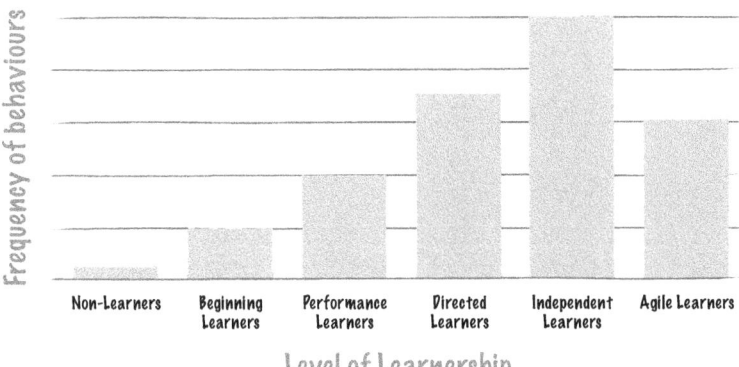

Learnership Diagnostic results

When the behaviours associated with the Independent Learner dominate a school, we find a culture of learning. The focus has shifted from the teaching process to the learning process.

'The way things are done around here' focuses on the process of learning and helping students – and the wider school community, including teachers – become better learners.

As you walk around a school that has a culture of learning, you notice it feels altruistic. The community has its sights set on the long-term benefit of each individual student. Teachers know there are 'shortcuts' to achieving learning outcomes, but they recognise those don't serve the students in the long run.

Talking to teachers in a culture of learning, you recognise they rise above the noise of the short-term mandated outcomes. They understand quality teaching practice is important, and that part of being a quality teacher is ensuring students are becoming quality learners. All teachers become teachers of learning, not just of content. There is an understanding and intentionality around developing Learnership.

Teachers no longer see the curriculum as merely a set of outcomes to be achieved. While achieving outcomes is important, the curriculum is now leveraged as a vehicle to help students develop as learners.

Planning explicitly has the *dual focus* of achieving learning outcomes and helping students become better learners.

> ❝ The focus has shifted from the teaching process to the learning process.

Something that stands out in a culture of learning is that teachers are … different. They have more energy. They are less stressed. As students more clearly recognise their role in the learning process, they are not sitting back passively waiting for learning to 'happen' to them. Students are lifting more of the cognitive load in the classroom.

As students take charge of the learning process, the curriculum can become richer. The possibility of negotiating outcomes with classes and individuals increases. Increasingly, teachers can think of their role as coaching individuals, rather than teaching a class. Walking through a school rich in a learning culture, you notice it is typically much less focused on cohorts and much more focused on the individual.

In a culture of learning, students are goal setters. They are in charge. They understand themselves as learners and take charge of where they want their learning to take them. Teachers will still hear students ask, 'Why do we have to do this?', but the reason they are asking is they want to be assured the learning applies to their goals.

Observing lessons, you notice there is a rich language of learning. As learners explore different topics and subjects, you hear discussions about the Habits of Mind, terms like 'learning zones' and 'effective effort' are used often. Students are focused on how they are engaging in the learning process, not simply on what they are learning. The walls of the classroom include messages about the value of effort, the importance of challenge, what it feels like to be in your learning zone, and more.

As well as the word 'learning', a verb frequently used by teachers is 'reach'. Teachers are helping students reach their goal. Learning finishes only when the goal has been reached. Until then, learners continue to strive.

Good, but could be better if ...

There is much to value and amplify in a culture of learning. Students are taking charge of their learning. Short-term educational outcomes and many long-term educational goals are being met, and exceeded. In this learning culture, there are learners, but there is no continuous growth. For Independent Learners, learning is about setting and reaching goals. So, in the absence of goals, learning can stop.

Independent Learners will often achieve well when compared to the fixed standards we provide in school. They'll get good grades. However, in the long run, this can hinder their growth as learners. When their goals are provided by the school, and the goals are being achieved, there is nothing to continue to push them forward. Students will stop learning when they achieve the desired grade.

Outcomes and challenges for students who emerge from this culture

With a focus on both elements of the Learning Equation (teacher action *and* student action), short-term educational outcomes begin to be exceeded. The school may become a 'school of choice', recognised for its achievements. More satisfying is the way the school community recognises that teachers are developing the whole child, not simply achieving educational benchmarks.

Ironically, as the culture steps beyond the prevailing teaching and performance cultures that dominate our system of education, teachers in the senior years can feel a tension between lifting the cognitive load for students (the quick and easy route to outcomes) and teaching students to do it themselves. Our system still rewards the short-term results, not the long-term goals. So a challenge facing leaders is to continually support teachers to recognise they can achieve the system's short-term goals *better* by focusing on the learner.

Independent Learners are taking charge of the learning process themselves, so they don't need teachers in the traditional sense. They need the teacher to act more like a coach. The difference is a teacher's primary concern is *what* you are learning. A coach is less concerned with what you are learning and more concerned with *how* you learn. This poses a challenge for many of our teachers who have been trained as teachers. They may be expert teachers. But they may not be very skilful learners, and will need to be supported in developing a deep understanding of how to build Learnership.

AGILE LEARNERS: CULTURE OF GROWTH

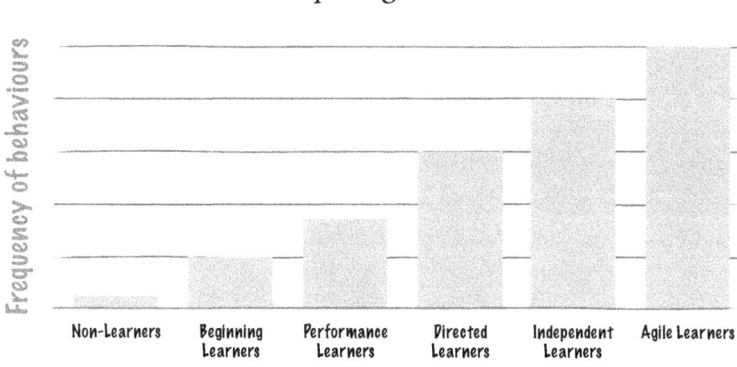

The behaviours associated with the Agile Learner thrive where there is a culture of growth. There is still the need to meet learning outcomes and to engage skilfully in the learning process, but the reason for doing this is to achieve growth. 'The way we do things around here' is to foster continuous growth and improvement.

> 66 'The way we do things around here' is to foster continuous growth and improvement.

When you experience a culture of growth, you recognise it is founded on a growth mindset. The community recognises learning is about creating learners' abilities. Students, teachers and the wider community understand and value each student's capacity to change their most basic characteristics. That who they are and what they can do today is a shadow of who they'll be and what they'll be able to achieve in the future. They are interested in developing those abilities most effectively and developing Learnership.

The school community has a deep appreciation that schooling is about far more than achieving outcomes. It's about raising the aspirations and capacities of learners to lead rich and fulfilling lives. School is about developing agency in the world. To achieve this, learners must have the capacity to become whomever they want or need to be. This requires growth, both in the domains they are pursuing and as a learner.

Not that a culture of growth does away with the curriculum and allows students to pursue their own goals. Students will still need to develop understandings in key learning areas. They'll still need to develop foundation skills. Teachers will still shape a curriculum to achieve this. Particularly in the early years, while students are developing their skills as learners, many lessons will look the same. But the reason for doing them isn't simply the outcome being achieved. Nor are teachers only leveraging the curriculum to help students become better learners. The underlying reason that drives decisions is to achieve growth.

There is a deep appreciation that challenge is the only pathway to growth. So the focus for curriculum design becomes about setting challenges and leveraging them to achieve growth. This means teachers teach to students' learning needs, rather than making them learn to their teaching needs. They set challenges that match students' learning zone, which might be substantially above or below where the curriculum says the learners should be.

In a growth culture, goals are recognised and celebrated in light of the backstory that allowed them to be achieved. The achievement marks a point in time in a longer journey.

Conversations focus on change and improvement. Whether a student is at, above or below an arbitrary standard is almost irrelevant. What's important is how much the student has improved, how much growth has been achieved, and how attaining that growth has helped them improve as a learner.

There is a rich dialogue about the learning process and the development of Learnership. The development of Learnership is explicit and valued. Students' progress towards becoming better learners will be structured, intentional, monitored and reported on like any other valued outcome of the school.

At appropriate times, they will give students the option to pursue challenging goals of their choice. The school recognises these as an opportunity to develop agency. They aren't pointlessly mimicking agency by giving students 'voice and choice'. They are deliberately allowing students to select challenges that will facilitate their growth. In this way, teachers act as mentors, creating the environments in which we present students with the challenges that will help them grow.

What you don't see

What you don't see in a culture that values growth is overt competition. Like the Federer example we used in chapter 4, competition is used to improve, not prove, yourself. It's a means of creating challenge.

Students have emerged from being a statistic, part of a cohort, and are truly individuals in the system. The measurements and comparisons students use are predominately focused on being better than themselves. There is much less ranking and comparisons between students.

In a growth culture not all learners will be Agile Learners, but all learners are becoming better learners. Some will still be at the Directed and Independent level of Learnership. A culture of growth is one that encourages and allows the behaviours associated with the Agile Learner to develop. In a culture of growth, when a student asks, 'Why are we doing this?', the teacher can confidently answer that it's to help them grow.

Outcomes and challenges

A culture of growth produces students who are antifragile and have greater agency in the world. Because they are driven by growth instead of standards or goals, they leverage every learning opportunity to grow. The end result is they futureproof themselves.

This environment is energising for teachers, students and the broader community. Skilful teaching meets skilful learning to produce the kind of buzz that led many teachers to education. With students taking charge and skilfully engaging in learning, opportunities for developing rich, challenging and rewarding curriculums blossom.

With an environment steeped in growth mindset movers, students develop a deep understanding of their capacity to change and grow. This 'un-limits' them and gives them the will to act – they recognise they have free will, and the capacity to freely choose their path in life. They can lead an aspirational life, instead of a limited one that lacks ambition.

Combining their will to act with their development as skilful learners, they also have the power to act. Heading out into a world rich in challenges, they now have agency. They are ready to go into the world the masters of their circumstances, not victims. To be powerful in the face of challenge and adversity, not powerless. To not merely survive, but thrive.

THE LEARNERSHIP DIAGNOSTIC

By now you're probably starting to develop a sense of the learning culture of your school. From part V you've gained a sense of the most common level of Learnership in your school. In this chapter you've recognised many of the wider cultural elements present in your school and perhaps identified some of the underlying beliefs driving these. You've got a sense of 'how things are done around here' in relation to learning and your learning culture.

> 66 The Learnership Diagnostic allows you to measure the learning culture of your school.

But hunches and feelings aren't as powerful as hard data. The Learnership Diagnostic allows you to measure the learning culture of your school. It asks teachers (or students) to record their observations of the frequency of behaviours associated with each type of learner. It then generates a graph similar to the ones above that, at a glance, easily shows you the level of Learnership commonly observed in your school.

Unlike the idealised graphs above, the graph generated from observations of your students is richer in several ways. Schools that have completed the diagnostic with their full staff have found it enormously insightful. Your Learnership Diagnostic results highlight the dominant two or more learning cultures in your school. Other features of the diagnostic help you identify issues specific to your school. I've included several sample diagnostics to illustrate this point. The report you receive after completing the diagnostic includes case studies of schools with similar profiles.

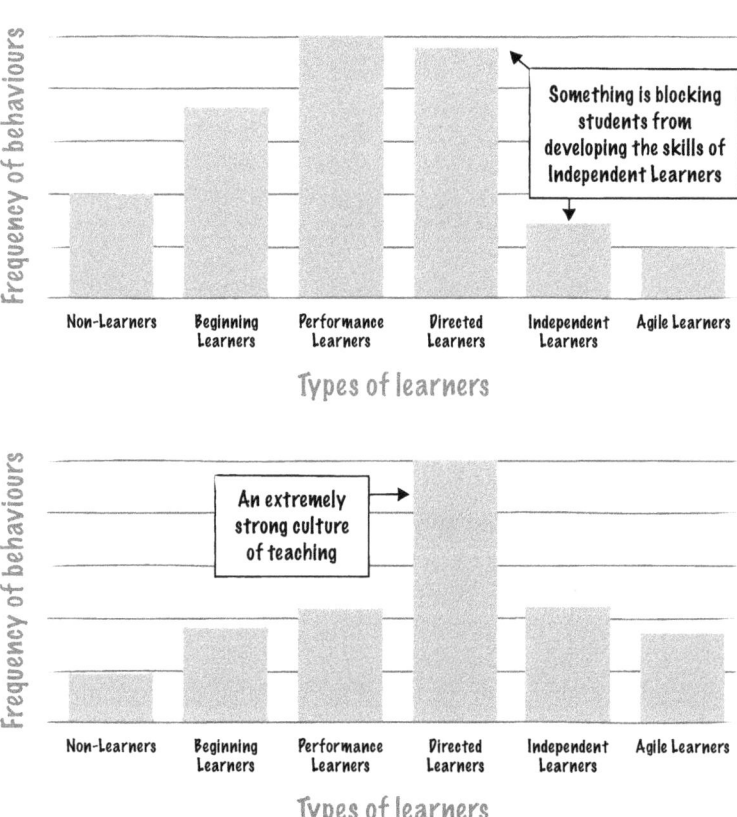

Learnership Diagnostic results

Completing the diagnostic with your leadership team or entire staff is incredibly powerful. It provides teachers with an incredible level of ownership of the data. It also works to validate teachers' observations so they feel heard. As we will see in chapter 26, we can use the diagnostic to paint a picture of what the future can look like, which is incredibly motivating.

Importantly, the Learnership Diagnostic allows you to answer four important questions:

- **What is the degree of Learnership at your school?** The Learnership Diagnostic gives a snapshot of the current degree of Learnership in a school. It uses teachers' observations, not guesswork, to tell you how well students are engaging in the learning process.
- **What is the prevailing learning culture at your school?** As we've discussed, the behaviours we observe reflect the underlying beliefs of the school community. They reflect attitudes towards teaching and learning. This helps to reveal the often unspoken rules driving your learning culture.
- **How do I develop a more growth-oriented culture?** Identifying your prevailing learning culture helps you target interventions to develop a more growth-oriented culture. We discuss this further in chapter 26.
- **Am I changing the learning culture in my school?** Finally, deployed regularly over time, the Learnership Diagnostic allows you to map and track changes in the degree of Learnership in your school – as Hattie would put it, to 'know thy impact' of your interventions.

The Learnership Diagnostic is a free tool. It can be accessed from www.learnership.app. Simply enter the code 'from an act to an art' and check your email for further instructions on how to use the tool.

The diagnostic value is greatly increased by aggregating observations from multiple sources. Although you could complete the diagnostic based on your own observations, consider including your leadership team or your entire staff in creating your school profile. Further details on how to use it with staff are provided in chapter 27.

Chapter 24
Creating a culture of learning and growth

Focus on learning and growth. Achievement and success will look after themselves.

GREAT CULTURES DON'T HAPPEN BY ACCIDENT

As a school leader, arguably your most important role is to lead the culture of your school. A great culture won't happen by accident. You must create it. You must establish the vision for your school and create the conditions that not only generate a culture of learning and growth but also sustain it.

Every school has a culture. Sometimes it comes about by design, other times by accident. Whatever the case for your school, your culture is the sum of what people see, hear, experience and believe. It exists.

The previous two chapters and the Learnership Diagnostic have helped you identify your current school culture as it relates to learning. Chances are you've identified positive aspects – things you'll want to capitalise on and amplify. And you've probably recognised there is some work to be done to create a culture of learning and growth. The type of culture that creates Agile Learners.

Creating and leading a culture is something that entire books are written about. One of the best going around is *Culture Rules* by Mark Miller. In this chapter I elaborate on his excellent work and give you some key steps to applying it to your school to create a culture of learning and growth. The four key areas to focus on are:

- **Aspire:** Define learning and growth as the culture you want to establish.
- **Amplify:** Make the message clear.
- **Adapt:** Take the best of what you have already.
- **Realign:** Nudge the parts of your existing culture that need to be brought into alignment.

Aspire

Your first step in creating a new learning culture is to clearly define the aspiration you are trying to achieve.

You are seeking to create:

A learning community that increases the aspirations and opportunities for students so they can thrive and have agency in a rapidly changing and increasingly complex world. This learning community is founded on the understanding of every individual's capacity to grow (having a growth mindset), and fuelled by their development of Learnership. It raises the status of learning from an act to an art.

Define your vision in ways your community will understand. Keep it simple and straightforward. Exactly how you phrase it, the imagery and language you use are likely to be shaped by the community you serve. The important aspect is your vision has to be clearly captured and communicated – you can't lead something you can't articulate.

If it's part of your leadership style to create and shape the statement collaboratively, do that. We'll discuss how you get buy in for your vision in the coming chapters, but be clear that you are leading this. The vision is not up for negotiation. You're not deciding on the type of culture you want to create, only how you express that vision and go about implementing it.

Capture your vision clearly, and refer to it often. It's not a document that is created and filed away, like so many mission statements. It's the guiding document for your school. Use it. It will help to shape the day-to-day and long-range decisions of your school community.

Amplify

Once you have your vision locked in, amplify it!

This doesn't mean shouting it from the rooftops or spending money on glossy posters. Amplifying your message is about getting it above the constant background noise of our education system. Create a message which transcends the fads, so that your culture of learning and growth becomes a constant for your community in a sea of change.

Throughout this book I've been advocating that nurturing a growth mindset and developing Learnership helps us hit our short-term outcomes on the way to achieving our long-term educational goals. Amplifying your growth culture is about showing your community how maintaining a focus on learning and growth helps you excel at meeting your short-term outcomes and achieve your long-term goals.

Teachers are weary of constant change. New curriculum initiatives. This year's focus on literacy. Next year's focus on numeracy. The need to build resiliency. My School. Naplan. National Curriculum x+1. Show your community how your culture helps you rise above these changes. Each time a new initiative comes along, show how, through your focus on learning and growth, you're already addressing it.

Think of your school. How many of the last few initiatives or national priorities that have come down the pipeline would have been successfully addressed through a focus on nurturing a growth mindset and developing your students as better learners? There may have been some finetuning to be done, a change of emphasis here, a slight realignment there. But what valid educational goal would *not* be addressed by ensuring students have a deep understanding of themselves as learners and are developing the abilities of skilful learners and building agency in the world?

Amplification also happens when you find opportunities to repeat the key messages of your culture. These might be in public spaces such as staff meetings, assemblies or newsletters. They might be in more strategic places, such as policy documents that lock in key elements of the culture. Or they might occur spontaneously during interactions with your community. Each time you do that, you're again showing how the culture you're leading helps your learning community meet their goals. Strategic repetition is your friend.

> ❝ You can't force a culture. You need to get people committed to it.

While you may establish and lead the culture, ultimately it belongs to the community. You want the environment you establish to outlast your tenure as principal. One way to achieve this is to ensure the essence of the culture is woven into those parts of the school that are regularly revisited, renewed and recommitted to. Weave the key elements into existing and new policies, practices and traditions of your school community.

You can't force a culture. You need to get people committed to it. In particular, you need to have teacher buy in. We discuss this important step in part VII.

Adapt

Amplifying the message, getting people on board and spreading the word are important, but are only part of the way people experience your culture.

In many ways, Learnership is not new. One of its great strengths is that it clarifies and crystallises much of what we have always strived to achieve in schools. We've always wanted students to be effective learners, so you'll find aspects of Learnership already exist in your school community. Where you find aspects of Learnership in your existing culture, double down on them. You're not sweeping aside everything that has gone before. Focus on the aspects that are working well and celebrate them.

A New Zealand school I worked with many years ago had a very strong culture of celebrating outstanding achievements, both in the school and in the wider community. The leadership team wanted to introduce the Habits of Mind into the school culture. They recognised they had always valued the Habits of Mind as part of celebrating outstanding achievements. They just hadn't named them or done it explicitly. So the leadership team simply made this connection explicit.

The beauty of this approach was twofold. First, it helped the school community recognise that the Habits of Mind were something they already valued. This helped reduce the feeling that it might be an extra or add on. And second, tying the Habits of Mind to an existing tradition in the school cemented their place in the community's life.

To one degree or another, Learnership – or aspects of it – is already part of your school culture. Where you find it, breathe life into it. Show how it's already helping you reach your goals, and use the clarity of your new understanding of Learnership to enhance it.

Of course, not all your existing structures and practices will neatly reflect the culture of learning and growth you are seeking to establish. Many will need to be realigned.

Realign

When you read the previous chapter, you probably had moments when you recognised the things you couldn't see – positive practices that currently exist in your school that, in the absence of a focus on growth, weren't quite hitting the mark. They are practices that are good, but would be better if …

These are the parts of your culture that need to be realigned.

The goal of realignment is to bring together all the experiences in your school community in a way that brings your vision and aspirations to life. This eliminates inconsistency and contradictions in your community and reduces friction. Most importantly, it builds an internal coherency and consistency. And each time a practice or policy is realigned, it makes realigning the next one easier.

One challenge you'll face as you realign is that your existing culture might push back. The existing internal consistency and coherency that will ultimately make your culture strong is the very thing that makes it hard to change. This is where you need to give the existing practices in your school a nudge in the right direction.

Recall our discussion about growth nudges from part II. These were little reminders that help you create growth messages, where there was a risk that you could create fixed messages. You can apply these nudges across your school to help realign your culture.

For example, consider a typical school awards night. Within the performance and teaching culture in our current system, awards are often based on achievement, either for reaching a particular standard (the students with the top marks) or for getting the highest standard (a winner). What we are seeing being valued is achievement. And while this is good, it could be better. What we want to see valued is the learning and growth that lead to the achievement.

The nudges we can use to reshape these awards towards a more learning and growth orientation are, 'Assessment is about where you are, not who you are', and, 'Value the backstory'. These nudges help us change the meaning of the awards and create a culture of growth and learning, while still valuing achievement. In this way, the awards night focuses on improvement and growth and *how* this was achieved, not just *what* was achieved.

Consider how the messages of traditional awards might be nudged towards learning and growth if the final award at your next award night was introduced like this:

> I'd like to introduce our next award. This is our final and major award of the evening. The highest honour in our school community. This award goes to the students who have achieved the greatest growth in the past 12 months. This award is open to students at all year levels and at all standards. These are students who exemplify what it means to be a skilful learner.
>
> This, our most esteemed award, does not necessarily go to the students who have achieved the highest standards or received the

highest grades. In our learning community, we understand that the standard you are at today is a temporary thing. We all improve. Your best is only your best when you measure by yesterday's standards. By tomorrow's standards, it will be your second best. While we celebrate today's achievements, it is the growth and the actions you take to achieve growth that will ultimately bring about your greatest achievements, so it is this that we value most.

But please, do not be confused. This is not an alternative to extraordinary achievement. Many of the students who are about to walk onto this stage and receive this award are students who have excelled in their studies this year, precisely because of the way they have engaged in their learning and the growth they have achieved. We recognise their achievements result from the backstory of how they went about learning.

We invite all members of our learning community here tonight to recognise what can be achieved as we apply ourselves to becoming better learners and achieving more growth.

Please welcome on stage …

Imagine being a student sitting in the audience. What you'd experience is people being rewarded for what they have done, not who they are. A recognition that we are all changing, growing and getting better. The – most important – awards are going to students who are getting better at getting better.

GETTING BETTER, OR JUST GETTING BUSY?

Of course, it's not just your work with students that might need a nudge to be realigned. There are many practices teachers experience that can and should be realigned, too. Consider, for example, the process of annual reviews and teacher evaluations, the values they communicate, and how we might nudge them towards being more growth oriented.

Most schools I work with have some type of annual review process for teachers. This process is intended to drive continuous growth.

However, in my experience, most fail to do a good job of this. In the prevailing teaching and performance culture, they tend to drive performance instead.

Although the details might vary, most annual review processes look broadly like this. Each year, teachers sit down with a mentor and review their performance for the year. This often takes the form of measuring performance against documents like the Australian Professional Standards for Teachers. This is usually to demonstrate (and provide evidence for) the quality of their teaching.

The next part of the meeting is to set goals for the coming year. Think about the goals teachers commonly set. In a culture of performance, teachers know the most important thing to demonstrate at next year's meeting is that you've achieved your goals. That you can tick the boxes. So many teachers are inclined to set *easy goals* that are in their comfort or performance zone. Goals they know they will be able to achieve.

In a culture of performance there is little or no reward for sitting down at next year's meeting and discussing the things you tried that were beyond your current abilities, explaining how much you learnt, but that you haven't achieved your goal yet. In a culture of performance, the most important thing is achieving the goal.

Within the culture of learning and growth we seek to develop, we recognise standards are important but we place more value on growth and the actions teachers are taking to achieve growth. We are more interested in encouraging and valuing action to maintain a trajectory of growth than the maintaining of a static standard. The review process should be a time to demonstrate growth, not simply standards.

The nudge to your culture is to ask the question are teachers 'getting better, or just getting busy'? This nudge reminds you that in a culture of growth, learners need to be stretching and challenging themselves by setting goals in their learning zone, to achieve growth.

Ask yourself who you would rather employ: the Highly Accomplished Teacher who has consistently demonstrated his abilities for the past five years? Or the Proficient Teacher who, only three years into her teaching practice, has demonstrated significant growth over those three years? Who's the better investment?

Like the awards ceremony above, the realignment to make here is to shift from measuring standards alone to measuring the change in standards and the process of improvement – each teacher's backstory. As you work on both, these come into alignment and strengthen your culture overall. Teachers and students are both being valued for the same things.

PROVIDING SPACE FOR GROWTH

Nudging your culture can be complex, and the knock-on effects of each nudge need to be thought through. If all you did was change the process of the review meeting so teachers were setting challenging goals, it's likely that not much would change. Outside that meeting, teachers are still rewarded for doing a good job, all day, every day. There's little space for growth. So you need to provide the space for growth to take place as well.

I recommend you watch Eduardo Briceño's excellent TED Talk, 'How to get better at the things you care about'. Eduardo echoes that growth occurs in the learning zone. The challenge we have in schools is teachers feel they spend nearly all their time in their performance zone.

To counter this, Eduardo talks about how, as leaders, we need to create islands of safety in what is otherwise a high-stakes environment. We must create opportunities for teachers to go into their learning zones, where the consequences of failure are low and the opportunity for feedback is high. Remember that many of your teachers may have spent many years in their comfort and performance zones and forgotten what it's like to be in their learning zone. Eduardo's latest book *The Performance Trap* further elaborates on this idea and is another excellent resource.

Often the reason we do something one way in a culture is simply because it fits with the way we do something else. Connections within a culture have grown up together. While this consistency and coherency can make it hard to change a culture, you can also use it to your advantage. The self-referencing nature of a culture means that one part of the culture can affect many others. Pick the right part to nudge and there can be a knock-on effect, bringing other elements into alignment with your vision.

DEALING WITH TOXINS

Some practices require a little bit of a nudge to realign them. Others might need more of a shove. But some might need to be removed altogether. These are the toxins in your culture. You might already recognise a few of these. If you can't see them now, they'll become apparent as you try to realign around them. Their influence will be far-reaching, and they will undermine your efforts to realign other aspects of your culture.

The most toxic elements of your culture as it relates to learning will almost always be founded on fixed mindset beliefs – structures and practices that were established on the idea that people are fundamentally and unchangeably different will always undermine the work you are doing to create a culture of learning and growth. These are often practices that label students in a permanent way, creating self-limiting beliefs based on perceived fixed abilities or inabilities.

One of the embedded practices teachers often challenge me about has to do with the practice of streaming students. Teachers resonant with the growth mindset ideas I discuss, but have that 'yeah … but' moment for streaming and 'ability groups'. They want to stream, but don't want to label students. Streaming seems to reinforce the idea of fixed abilities, which makes them uncomfortable.

Is streaming toxic? Does it need to be removed? Or can it be realigned? The answer is … it depends.

The problem is not with the practice itself. The problem is with fixed messages that are carried with the way it's often implemented. The basic concept of streaming is to have every student working in their learning zone. This is a good thing because it's where growth can happen. It's also where we can get students to understand what their learning zone feels like, develop their Habits of Mind and come to be 'comfortably uncomfortable' with the struggle that leads to growth. So in this sense, streaming is in alignment with our culture of learning and growth.

However, what sometimes happens, and sometimes on a significant scale, is that students come to be labelled as *having* high or low abilities, aka the 'smart kids' and the 'dumb kids'. This is particularly true when the composition of groups remains static over time, and the labels remain attached to students. Implemented this way, streaming would work against our culture of learning and growth. The way labels remain constant masks any growth that may occur. Students are still in the 'same group'.

The two nudges that can have a powerful effect here are that 'assessment is about where you are, not who you are', and to 'attach time stamps to performance'. This leads us to change the messaging we attach to streaming. Labels are now attached to the levels students are currently working at, not the students. So students see themselves moving through the levels, improving. The levels now represent a point in time in the student's development, their current abilities, not their 'fixed' abilities.

The question you need to answer to determine if any practice is toxic is, how deeply embedded are the fixed messages associated with the practice and how much are they influencing other practices in the school?

Whether a structure or practice needs to be realigned or removed depends on how deeply entrenched it is in the current culture and the way it influences the alignment of other structures and practices. You may discover there are no real toxins in your current culture that can't be reshaped with a good nudge. That would be an excellent base to be working from!

Your culture can cope with some inconsistencies. Our education system, and the way it's discussed in the wider community, contains many fixed messages, most of which we have little control over. The way students are ranked at the end of secondary school is a good example. It's something the system imposes on us, and something the wider community associates with 'smart kids get good results'.

We can try to counter these messages by applying nudges such as recognising the backstory that has gone into achieving particular specialities and results, emphasising that the end of year 12 is a point in time, not a judgement of ability, and many more. But we probably can't remove the practice altogether. A strong culture will cope with this.

NEW CAPABILITIES – DEVELOPING LEARNERSHIP

Doubling down on your strengths, realigning where possible and dealing with toxins as necessary all focus on aspects of your culture that already exist. The next part of establishing your culture of learning and growth is to add new capabilities. You can't develop a culture that values skilful learning without teaching your community how to become skilful learners! It's not enough to just tell students you expect them to be skilful learners. The development of Learnership needs to be an explicit focus in classrooms and the wider life of the school.

In the next chapter, I explore what implementing a program for nurturing a growth mindset and developing Learnership can look like in your school.

PART VI KEY TAKEAWAYS

- Culture is 'the way things get done around here'. It's the default set of behaviours you see in your school.
- Your school's learning culture is driven by a set of often unspoken beliefs about learning.
- Your learning culture is both a reflection of, and driving factor for, the development of different levels of Learnership. These are:
  - Avoidance culture – Non-Learners
  - Activity culture – Beginning Learners
  - Performance culture – Performance Learners
  - Teaching culture – Directed Learners
  - Learning culture – Independent Learners
  - Growth culture – Agile Learners
- The Learnership Diagnostic will help you identify your school's learning culture.
- Although there are many positive elements to a school's learning culture, what is often missing is a focus on growth.
- Developing a growth culture requires you to:
  - Aspire – be clear about the culture of growth you want to achieve
  - Amplify – take every opportunity to share your vision
  - Adapt – leverage the elements of a growth culture that are already present
  - Realign – use nudges to realign your culture towards growth

Use the space below to add some of your own part VI key takeaways.

- _____
- _____
- _____
- _____

DISCUSSION AND ACTION

- Which of the learning cultures most closely resonated with you and your school?
- Identify elements of your school culture that are already aligned with growth. How might you amplify these?
- Identify elements of your school culture that might need a nudge to realign them with growth.
- Watch Eduardo Briceño's TED Talk 'How to get better at the things you care about' with your team. What, if anything, is stopping you from creating more opportunities for growth in your school?

Use the space below to add some of your own discussion and action items.

- _____
- _____
- _____
- _____
- _____
- _____
- _____
- _____
- _____
- _____
- _____
- _____

WHERE TO FROM HERE?

Having identified the growth culture that will allow you to achieve your short-term educational outcomes and reach your long-term goals for your students, it's time to make that happen. You can't do this on your own. Your job is being a leader, so it's time to lead. In the next section we look at how we get teachers who are already overworked and often resistant to change on board with Learnership. We then answer the all-important question of how we actually develop Learnership in our students.

Part VII
Building a learning community

By now you have a clear vision of the learning community you want to create – one that focuses on Learnership. Where the status of learning has been raised from an act to an art. Where you have a culture based on learning and growth. Where you raise the aspirations and outcomes of the young people you serve. Where you meet the long-term goals of your learners, as well as exceeding the short-term outcomes of the system.

But the reality is you can't do this on your own. School improvement relies on the teachers in your school buying in to your vision. So in this part we come to the perennial question: how do you get teachers on board?

There's no doubt about it – it's a tough time to be a teacher. Increases in workloads, higher expectations, greater scrutiny, and an intense focus on the profession as a whole means the role is more demanding than it has ever been. Teachers are frustrated to the point that many want to leave the profession.

The good news is that in the culture of learning and growth you seek to build you actually make teachers' lives better. Teachers want to do a good job. Your focus on Learnership helps them achieve that, while at the same time addressing many of their deepest sources of frustration.

In the following chapters I show you how to address common teacher frustrations, showing them how they can meet (and exceed) the demands of the system while simultaneously increasing their satisfaction and decreasing the pressure they feel. I show you how to get teachers on board by showing them how focusing on Learnership will make their lives easier, not harder.

Chapter 25
Addressing the needs of teachers

Learnership makes teaching fun again!

SHARING THE RESPONSIBILITY FOR LEARNING

It is a tough time to be in the teaching profession. According to Monash University's 'Australian Teachers' Perceptions of their Work in 2022' survey, most teachers feel the public does not respect teachers and that the teaching profession is underappreciated. Teachers feel overburdened with administration and data collection tasks.

Teachers are also sick and tired of copping the blame for things that are outside of their control, such as poor funding or a boring curriculum. It's unfair, and they rally against it. Teachers feel they are carrying all the responsibility for learning and are being unfairly blamed when outcomes are not being met, even when the reasons are outside their control.

So when teachers are first exposed to the idea of Learnership, it comes as a breath of fresh air. Finally, they have a way to articulate the responsibility students have toward how they engage in the learning process. It also gives teachers a way to describe learning that is multidimensional. Learning is no longer something that students are expected to merely do, it's something they can learn to do well! Learnership gives them the solution to the problem they couldn't quite see or define for themselves.

Learnership lifts the burden of absolute responsibility for student performance that has been unfairly placed on teachers' shoulders. In doing so, it helps address some of our teachers' biggest frustrations. It relieves some of the pressure. Learnership gives voice and clarity to what teachers have always known – that students must share some of the responsibility for their own learning through how they engage in the learning process.

> ❝ Learnership lifts the burden of absolute responsibility for student performance that has been unfairly placed on teachers' shoulders.

Of course, Learnership is not a blame-shifting exercise. It's not an invitation to the media and politicians to blame students for poor performance. It is a recognition that teachers aren't solely responsible for learning outcomes. It's a recognition that the picture painted by media and politicians is an oversimplification. Teachers play an important role, and we want quality teaching. But, in at least some contexts, we don't have a teaching problem; we have a learning problem.

While Learnership unburdens teachers of the sole responsibility for learning, it also empowers them to help guide students towards achieving even better results. It helps them do a better job. Teachers understand quality teaching. Learnership gives them a way to understand quality learning. They use this to guide students towards becoming better learners and, as we'll see in a moment, to achieve more.

RAISING THE STATUS OF LEARNING

One solution to these challenges that was offered by teachers in the Monash University study was to have higher expectations of students and parents. Learnership helps to achieve this.

Learnership raises the expectations for students who have come to expect to simply be *taught* by the teacher. Learnership clarifies how they should be *learning*. For parents, who in the recent past have been fed a regular diet of 'teacher quality equals student outcomes', Learnership clarifies their child's role in the learning process. Instead of blaming teachers for poor performance, it raises the expectations placed on parents to partner with schools in helping develop their child as a skilful learner. It allows parents to be better partners in their child's education.

The clarity that Learnership brings to understanding how all members of the school community engage in the learning process raises the status of learning from an act to an art. Learning is no longer seen merely as the outcome of teaching. Learning is a skilful process, one that must be developed over time. Yes, teachers have a role in helping students develop this skill, and students have a responsibility to develop these skills.

> ❝❝ The clarity that Learnership brings to understanding how all members of the school community engage in the learning process raises the status of learning from an act to an art.

Learnership helps to decrease the pressure, responsibility and blame being directed at teachers. Decoupling the close association between teacher quality and student outcomes allows teachers to celebrate being a quality teacher while recognising they are not solely responsible for learning outcomes.

GIVING TEACHERS BACK THEIR ENERGY

We all know teachers are exhausted. If there's even a hint that your focus on Learnership is going to add to their workload, you're never going to get them on board. The good news is that Learnership will not add to their workload at all. You're going to get them on board by showing them how Learnership is going to *reduce* the amount and *increase* the quality of their work.

Almost every experienced teacher will tell you that simply being in a classroom, engaging in their core business, is more exhausting now than it has ever been. This is in large part due to how students are (or aren't) engaging in the learning process. Our classrooms are filled with students who have low levels of Learnership.

These students not only need to be led through the learning process, they need to be cajoled and coaxed the entire way. Teachers must constantly scaffold learning. They are identifying students' mistakes for them, and then showing them how to correct them. Teachers are constantly providing feedback, often to find students don't act on it. Students are often demotivated and reluctant to take on challenges, so teachers need to engage or even entertain students to get them to complete work. Many teachers feel they spend their days *dragging* students through the curriculum.

Our focus on Learnership gives teachers back some energy. As students develop a growth mindset and increase Learnership, more of the learning load is being lifted by the students. They require less coaxing, less scaffolding, less correcting of mistakes, less keeping on task. The more students develop Learnership, the more they take charge of the learning process for themselves.

> ❝ As students develop a growth mindset and increase Learnership, more of the learning load is being lifted by the students.

This makes teachers' lives better in several ways. First, teachers spend more time leading students through learning, and less time dragging them through it. Although the amount of effort might be similar, the reward is greater. Second, as students develop Learnership it opens up a range of exciting teaching strategies.

MAKING TEACHING FUN AGAIN!

Teachers want to make their lessons interesting and challenging for students. They want to engage students in rich, open-ended tasks.

Every teacher loves seeing students engaged in deep problem-based learning or inquiry-learning tasks that challenge them to think deeply. Teachers want students to negotiate and contribute to how and what they are learning. This is the type of curriculum that most teachers find most exciting, engaging and rewarding. As leaders, it's also what we would like to see more of in our classrooms. We know these types of rich learning experiences provide some of the best outcomes for students.

The trouble is, most times, these types of rich learning experiences either take enormous effort from the teacher or simply don't work with some students. This is because students rarely have the required level of Learnership to participate effectively.

Imagine giving an open-ended task to a Beginning Learner. They won't generate questions. They are unlikely to be genuinely curious. They aren't going to try to construct their own understandings. They want to be told. For them, learning is an activity. They'll look for the shortest route to any solution so they can finish by the end of the lesson.

Of course, teachers can and do engage students in these rich learning experiences at all different levels of Learnership. But it's hard work and leaves teachers exhausted. As a result, teachers often find it easier just to tell students what to do. What teachers would like to do gives way to what students are willing and able to do.

The issue is that a certain degree of Learnership is the entry price for this type of engaging, rich, open-ended curriculum. A focus on developing Learnership improves the lives of teachers because it makes this type of teaching possible. It makes their day-to-day practice so much more energising and rewarding.

> ❝❝ The issue is that a certain degree of Learnership is the entry price for this type of engaging, rich, open-ended curriculum.

In the eyes of many teachers, we measure the quality of their work through student achievement of short-term learning outcomes. The system asks teachers to ensure students achieve 'one year's growth in one year's time'. It measures learning outcomes and applies benchmarks that are reported on regularly. Schools are constantly asked to demonstrate that students are 'at standard'.

The challenge is that the quickest and easiest way to achieve these short-term results so often undermines long-term goals. When quality teaching is so closely linked to improved (short-term) learning outcomes, why wouldn't teachers seek recognition and reward for this?

Herein lies the issue. As school leaders, we have long-term goals for students. We are seeking to raise their aspirations and set them up to thrive in a rapidly changing and increasingly complex world. We want success not just this year, but for life beyond school. Most teachers share this desire. But pressures to achieve short-term outcomes, and the rewards associated with them, can be at odds with our long-term goals.

Teachers who are understandably focused on short-term outcomes can develop Learnership to help them achieve those outcomes, and as increasing Learnership helps students achieve and eventually exceed short-term learning outcomes, their job satisfaction and recognition increases.

HELPING TEACHERS DO A BETTER JOB

The quickest way to kill any initiative is to tell good teachers they are doing a bad job.

Many teachers are weary from the constant changes in education. On top of that, the negative portrayal of teachers in the media and the common inference of poor teaching quality has sensitised teachers to potential criticism. For some teachers, particularly those who might be towards the fixed end of the Mindset Continuum, the mere mention of the need for change is interpreted as criticism. Growth becomes another way of saying you're not doing a good job.

The beauty of Learnership is we can honestly celebrate teachers for doing a good job. Our focus on Learnership is not about changing teacher practice, it's about student practice. It will improve learning outcomes, but, for the first time in a long time, that will not mean more work or large changes for teachers.

Teacher practice *will* change. But in terms of getting teachers on board, the change is about the students. Teachers will teach students to be better learners.

MAKING TEACHERS' LIVES BETTER

There is no magic bullet that will solve all the challenges teachers face in our modern educational environment. However, a focus on developing Learnership is certainly not an added burden. Instead, it will help improve teachers' professional status and the day-to-day working life of teachers.

The key to getting teachers on board is to ensure they see how this work is going to improve their lives. Many will see the value to students' lives. Like you, they'll want to engage in this work because they'll recognise it as one of their long-term goals of education. The altruistic nature of many teachers will mean they want this to happen. We all got into teaching to help kids. And there may have been a time when simply showing teachers the value this work will add to the lives of students would have been enough. But not now.

> ❝❝ The key to getting teachers on board is to ensure they see how this work is going to improve their lives.

Right now, a large majority of teachers are planning to, or would like to, leave the profession. They love teaching. They love kids. They simply feel they can't do it anymore in the current environment. So getting your teachers on board means showing them how this benefits them.

When teachers recognise how this work is going to make their lives better, as well as their students' lives, it becomes a win–win. It makes the decision to focus on Learnership a no-brainer. With everything you know now, how could you *not* focus on Learnership? The win for you as a leader is it becomes easier for teachers to decide to do it than to decide not to do it.

Chapter 26
Showing teachers the future

Imaging teaching *skilful* learners.

LET THEM SEE FOR THEMSELVES

It is tempting to simply tell teachers how developing Learnership is going to improve their lives. You could run a staff meeting and present all the information we've just discussed. However, that's perhaps not the most effective strategy for getting teachers on board. A more effective way to get teachers' support is to let them discover it for themselves. Instead of inviting them on board, let them ask to come on board.

Teachers know how their students are engaging in the learning process. They see it every day. The problem is they lack a framework to capture, describe and understand those behaviours. They are left with frustratingly vague concepts like 'work ethic' or asking students to 'work harder', hoping they will engage more effectively.

Learnership gives them the framework they didn't know they didn't have. It suddenly captures and explains what it is about some students' behaviours that mean they achieve while other students struggle. It's nothing they didn't already know, in a vaguely ill-defined way. But the affirmation and clarity that comes from the Learnership Diagnostic is powerful. Importantly, it gives teachers deep, practical and immediate insights into how to improve student learning.

The Learnership Diagnostic gives teachers a new way to see into their classrooms and understand their learners. And just like it gave you the opportunity to see how Learnership impacted the culture of your school, this time your staff can complete the diagnostic and interpret the results through the lens of the teacher. Allowing your teachers to complete and interpret the Learnership Diagnostic has at least three powerful outcomes.

> 66 The Learnership Diagnostic gives teachers a new way to see into their classrooms and understand their learners.

Ownership

Gathering teacher observations gives teachers ownership of the results. It's not someone else telling them what types of learning behaviours they have in their classroom – it's their collective observations. There is little to debate about the results. Teachers provided the data. The diagnostic just graphed it for them. The only question is, what they can do about it?

Clarity

The Learnership Diagnostic makes Learnership visible. As we discussed in chapter 23, the Diagnostic doesn't tell you the number of different types of learners. It's about the frequency of behaviours associated with each type of learner being observed by teachers. The results bring Learnership into sharp focus. When teachers see the behaviours graphed in this way there is often a collective nod of agreement – there's the issue!

Empathy

The Learnership Diagnostic also provides a description of the types of challenges teachers face at each level of Learnership. Many trials have shown that the descriptions accurately reflect teachers' classroom experiences. These are universal challenges, shared by teachers in many different settings. Let teachers spend some time with those descriptions.

At this point, teachers are usually becoming convinced that Learnership accurately captures both how students engage in the learning process and that this explains many of their frustrations in the classroom. It validates the concept in their minds. The question becomes, what next?

TAKE ME TO THE FUTURE

The shift that gets teachers on board and committed comes now. Look at the diagnostic results, then refer to part V and share the descriptions of the two highest scoring categories with your teachers. Now ask teachers this simple question: 'How would your work life and the results of your students change if we could move that graph to the right?'

This is a remarkably powerful question.

Teachers have already recognised Learnership describes the behaviours they see in their classroom. They've agreed it explains many of the challenges and issues they face on a day-to-day basis. They've validated the concept through their own experiences. Now you can simply paint a picture of the future and ask, do you want to go there?

I recently did this exercise with a group of 50 primary school teachers. They completed the Learnership Diagnostic and got the results shown on the next page. The bulk of the behaviours they were observing in the classroom were below the bar. Teachers were feeling exhausted from constantly needing not only to manage the learning process for students, but also encourage students to engage in it. There was constant pressure to help students get better results.

Learnership Diagnostic results

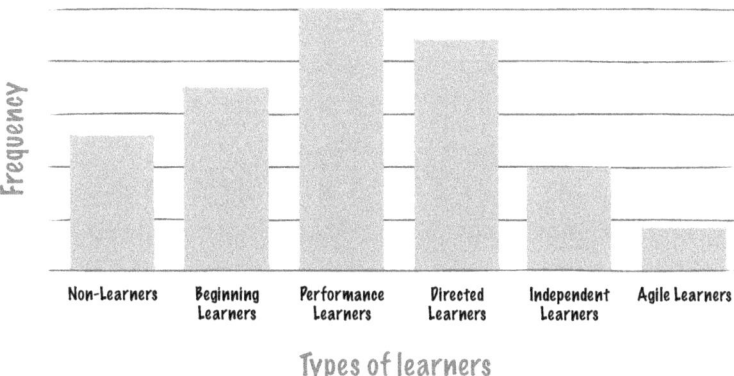

I then asked them to imagine what their classrooms would be like if they instead had learners who engaged in learning like this:

Learnership Diagnostic results

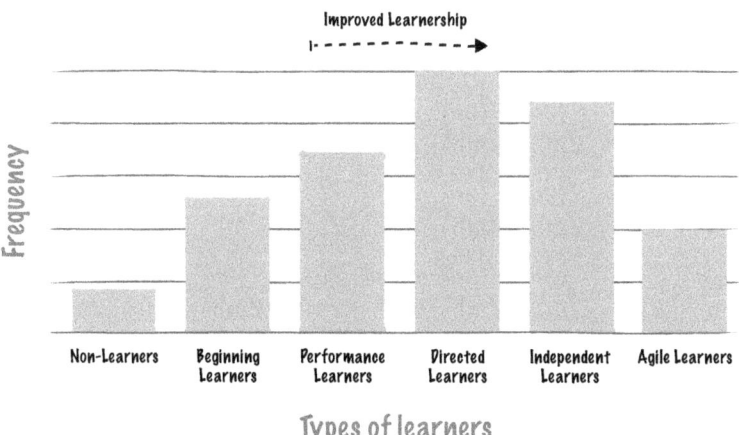

There was an audible gasp in the room.

Shifting your graph just one step to the right makes a vast difference to teachers' lives. They would rather be in that environment than the one they are in now. There is never any argument.

I wasn't promising them a school full of Agile Learners – yet. Just a shift. But that new world was so much better than their current one.

Shifting your results one step to the right is realistic and achievable. You are inviting them to consider a school where every student is just a little better at learning. I've never met a teacher who doesn't want this. For nearly all teachers, it's a no-brainer. They are in.

Of course, you're going to need to reinforce all the ideas we've discussed throughout this book. You'll continually mention the Learning Equation, and how to magnify the impact of skilful teachers as they develop skilful learners. You'll talk to your school community about how the school is focusing on the role of the learner, as well as the role of teacher. You'll raise the status of learning from an act to an art. You'll continue to connect many of the day-to-day challenges teachers experience with the need to increase Learnership. All of that helps to keep teachers on board.

The only question that remains, and the one that might still stop a few teachers from being fully committed, is, how do we achieve that change? That's the question we answer in the next section.

PART VII KEY TAKEAWAYS

- The key to getting teachers on board is to show them how Learnership will make their life better.
- Learnership:
  - helps lift the unfair burden of teachers being solely responsible for achieving learning outcomes
  - clarifies what it means to be a skilful learner
  - gives teachers back their energy
  - allows teachers to engage in more exciting pedagogy
  - helps teachers be more successful at their job.
- Using the Learnership Diagnostic gives teachers a glimpse into the future.

Use the space below to add some of your own part VII key takeaways.

- _____
- _____
- _____
- _____
- _____
- _____
- _____
- _____
- _____
- _____
- _____
- _____

DISCUSSION AND ACTION

- As a leadership group conduct a thought experiment. How might the lives of teachers, students and leadership be different if your Learnership program could move the results of the Learnership Diagnostic one step to the right?
- Go to www.learnership.app and enter the code 'from an act to an art' (without the quotes) and follow the instructions sent to you to conduct a Learnership survey with your entire staff body.

Use the space below to add some of your own discussion and action items.

- _____
- _____
- _____
- _____
- _____
- _____
- _____
- _____
- _____
- _____
- _____
- _____
- _____
- _____
- _____

WHERE TO FROM HERE?

You've come a long way. We've made the case for Learnership, understood what it looks like and taken a snapshot of the level of Learnership in your school. We've explored what a culture of learning and growth looks like. And now you know how to get teachers on board. All that's left is bringing it to life and teaching your students how to be more skilful learners.

Part VIII
How to develop Learnership

Teachers not only need to be brought onboard, they also need to develop skills in supporting students to develop Learnership.

Schools that successfully build a culture of learning and growth recognise that developing Learnership takes time and planning. Learnership is not something that can be taught in a 'learning to learn' program in the first few days of the school year. And it can't be left to chance. It requires a sustained, planned and integrated approach. Learnership is developed every day, not just in the first days of the year.

Just like any other area of expertise, learners need to incrementally build and consolidate the skill of learning. This means starting with the foundations, and then building the deeper and more complex learning skills over time. Just like learning a martial art starts with the basic skills at white belt level, which are then consolidated and built on towards black belt, so too do we build Learnership. This will be developed through the years of schooling and beyond, and requires that learners progress through a carefully thought out scope and sequence.

Chapter 27
Teaching for Learnership

Developing Learnership in every classroom, every day.

A LEARNERSHIP CURRICULUM

In this chapter I sketch out the broad details of this scope and sequence to illustrate the pathway towards developing expertise in learning. We will consider three elements:

- An outline for the scope and sequence for each element of Learnership.
- How those elements can be woven together as part of the school's culture.
- Implementing and sustaining a successful Learnership program.

That sounds like a massive undertaking, and you might be wondering how you can possibly fit a Learnership program into your already crowded curriculum. Before we go into the details, let me first reassure you that this is not going to be a burden on teachers, and I'm not advocating for large amounts of time to be taken out of the curriculum. Second, remember that your focus on developing Learnership is an investment. Skilful learners are better at getting better, and gain more out of every learning opportunity. So the small time investment you'll make will be returned many times over as learners gain more from every lesson. This scope and sequence has been tested and implemented by schools in Australia, New Zealand and Singapore.

> 66 ... your focus on developing Learnership is an investment.

SCOPE AND SEQUENCE FOR LEARNERSHIP

As you saw in part IV there are five essential elements of Learnership. There is a logical sequence of development for each of these elements, which I describe below. This is a sequence that builds upon itself to create more skilful learners.

Obviously, this is only an outline of the scope and sequence for developing Learnership. A thumbnail sketch of what's involved and the major landmarks on that journey. There is a great deal more detail, nuance and richness in completing the journey.

Understanding the scope and sequence of Learnership helps you recognise common gaps and blocks many students in your school have in their level of Learnership. As we outline this scope and sequence, I'll illustrate how our failure to systematically address the development of Learnership has undermined some common teaching and learning strategies in our schools.

Nurturing a growth mindset

Unlike the failed teaching 'about' mindsets approach, there is a logical progression for developing students' understanding of themselves as learners that both challenges existing fixed mindset beliefs and helps learners build a more growth-oriented understanding of themselves.

Our curriculum begins by helping students identify the greatness gap, and focuses on identifying and valuing the backstory. This is done at both a personal level and also to help understand the backstories of those who have developed expertise. This foundation highlights that *becoming* comes before *being*.

We move onto addressing some of the more common fixed beliefs that pervade our community, such as the idea that we have (fixed) strengths and (limited) potential. We help learners understand they are in charge of developing their strengths and that learning is a way of creating their potential. We build a solid understanding that learning is about creating abilities, not discovering them.

After learners develop a sense of themselves as creators of their abilities, it's time to help them understand learning as a skill. Learning is not something they simply do, it's something they learn to do well. Students learn about the qualities of skilful learners and unpack the Learnership Matrix, recognising how they, and others, engage in the learning process, how that impacts their learning and growth, and ultimately how to develop Learnership.

While it is helpful, we do not need to establish a growth mindset before we develop other aspects of Learnership. The process of becoming a skilful learner nurtures a growth mindset. So every time we focus on developing Learnership, every time we talk about learning as a skill, every strategy we teach for becoming a better learner, every time we value growth and the backstory and every time we recognise and celebrate how students are engaging in the learning process, we are creating growth mindset movers. In effect, our whole Learnership program is a growth mindset mover.

Building an understanding of challenge

The scope and sequence for developing a learner's understanding of, and relationship to, challenge begins with recognising that not all learning is the same. We teach students to recognise their comfort, performance, learning and aspirational zones. As they become familiar with each zone, they are taught the different expectations and behaviours required in each. These understandings, scaffolded by the teacher, allow students to be far more intentional about learning as they move in and out of each zone during learning.

An essential component of developing a healthy relationship with challenge is for students to understand their learning zone. Learners are explicitly taught what it feels like, and that it's a normal part of learning. And to distinguish their learning zone from other zones of learning.

The zones of learning help learners better understand the nature of challenge. They recognise why some challenges are easier than others. Why some lead to growth in abilities, while others only to breadth of understanding or improved reliability and consistency of performance. This allows learners to begin to bring a deliberateness and intentionality to how they approach challenges.

Building on their understanding of the nature of challenge, learners develop a richer concept of how to practise effectively. Students refine the skills of deliberate practice, distinguishing between unproductive practice, rehearsal, purposeful practice and deliberate practice, and refine how they use the three F's of practice (Focus, Feedback and Fix it).

As learners develop a deeper understanding of challenge, they build a value of challenge as the pathway to growth. They come to appreciate how challenge increases the size of their comfort zone. They learn how to target their own challenges, and eventually to embrace challenge as a means of futureproofing themselves.

> ❝❝ As learners develop a deeper understanding of challenge, they build a value of challenge as the pathway to growth.

As you review this quick sketch of a learner's development in their relationship to challenge, it becomes apparent why some common approaches to student goal setting have been less effective than we'd hoped. If students are encouraged to set goals before they understand the zones of learning, they may choose easy goals or avoid goal setting altogether. They may trade the short-term satisfaction of completion for the long-term benefit of growth.

It's also easy to see how this sequence leads learners to a place where embracing challenges makes sense. When students can recognise that not all challenges are the same, they understand their learning zone and how to respond to it, and appreciate how challenges allow them to hone their Habits of Mind, why wouldn't they embrace a challenge? However, the chances of convincing a learner to embrace challenges without first going through the steps outlined above would be close to zero. Yet that's the path often attempted in schools – to simply *tell* students they should be embracing challenges.

Developing Habits of Mind

The Habits of Mind help to greatly expand a learner's language for learning. The habits become the cognitive anchors which allow them to meaningfully reflect on their learning behaviours. This forms part of the foundation for understanding many aspects of their learning.

Building on this foundation, we teach students about how the Habits of Mind help them succeed in the learning zone. They are taught to recognise which Habits of Mind will help them solve different types of problems. This allows them to shift their focus from *what* they are learning to *how* they are learning as they step into their learning zone.

As students develop an understanding of how to improve their Habits of Mind, they understand they can learn to behave more intelligently. This gives them insights into how they can make hard things easier. Both of which are powerful growth mindset movers.

Students gain even greater insights and take control of the development of their Habits of Mind by assessing their habits through the Learner Profile. They become more aware of their Habits of Mind, and more targeted and intentional in their development.

Clearly developing Habits of Mind requires much more than simply putting posters on the wall and teaching students the language of the Habits of Mind. At each step in this sequence we deepen and enrich both their understanding of the Habits of Mind and their relationship with them.

Using the language of the Habits of Mind gives clarity and consistency to how students reflect on their learning behaviours. Teachers understand the importance of reflection for improving learning. However, strategies that ask students to reflect on their learning behaviours without first clearly defining those behaviours in a consistent and coherent way are ultimately less effective than we would hope. The developmental aspect of the Habits of Mind makes those reflections more actionable.

Again, you'll immediately recognise how this pathway goes well beyond telling students the habits are important and they should 'use' them. It carefully builds a deep understanding, appreciation and valuing of the Habits of Mind and leads students to a point where they will want to nurture them as their greatest asset.

Mistakes and feedback

Many learners go through school with only the most basic understanding of mistakes and feedback. Their understanding is limited to mistakes being an indication you got something wrong, that they are part of learning, and they are meant to help you learn. Feedback is something you are given that tells you what to do next time.

The first step to developing a richer, more productive relationship with mistakes is to recognise that not all mistakes are the same. Several primary schools I work with have decided to begin developing this aspect of Learnership by differentiating between careless mistakes, performance mistakes and stretch mistakes. This teaches learners that some mistakes are helpful, others unhelpful, and others are to be avoided. They move onto unpacking confusion mistakes, aha moment mistakes and eventually design mistakes.

Students further develop Learnership by learning to recognise the different behaviours associated with each type of mistake. Increasingly mistakes become about information and action, rather than judgement.

Learnership is further developed as learners build an understanding that the value they receive from feedback depends not on what they are given but on what they do with it. They come to recognise it's their actions that count.

As students recognise mistakes and feedback as sources of information, and it's how they gather and act on that information that drives them forward, they can become less reactive and more proactive in generating that information. They learn how to tailor feedback and design mistakes. They shift from habitually and reactively asking for feedback or correcting mistakes after the event to proactively knowing what information they'll need and priming a person to give them that feedback.

Again, we can see how failing to recognise the nuance and developmental understanding of feedback and mistakes has hindered learning in the past. Teachers who have simply said 'mistakes help us learn' and 'mistakes are part of learning' have failed to address the fact that not *all* mistakes help us learn – some should be avoided, and the learning comes not from the mistake but from the action students take to correct the mistake.

Enhancing effective effort

Most learners have only a basic understanding of effort. They believe effort is equal to the amount of time and energy they spend on a task. The scope and sequence I've mapped out guides students to initially recognise effort as the cost of growth – the price paid for crossing the greatness gap.

We further develop students' understanding of effort as we introduce them to the Effective Effort Matrix. This ability to differentiate between different types of effort helps them become increasingly discerning about how their time and energy is being spent. They begin to shift from time management to effort management.

Once again, we see how when we carefully build learners' understanding of effort it leads to more mature and more effective understanding. Compare the likely results of this sequence to the more common pleas from teachers for students to 'put in more effort!'

WEAVING THE ELEMENTS TOGETHER

Understanding the scope and sequence outlined above is just the first step. The next step is to create a program to deliver those outcomes in a coherent and sustainable way.

When implementing a Learnership program, I advocate that you weave the elements of Learnership together – just like we understand language in terms of reading, writing, listening and speaking, and we weave those elements together when teaching language. Each year we build upon each element, and each element supports the development of the others. Learners are taken on a journey that weaves the elements of Learnership together to help them become better learners.

> ❝ I have developed a program that breaks the scope and sequence above into stages, each with a slightly different focus that captures all five elements, building on the skills developed in the previous stage.

I have developed a program that breaks the scope and sequence above into stages, each with a slightly different focus that captures all five elements, building on the skills developed in the previous stage. The schools I work with have found it very powerful to sequence and deliver Learnership in these five broad stages:

1. Beginning
2. Developing
3. Extending
4. Mastering
5. Expert.

The focus for each is described in the following pages.

Beginning: we are learners

This foundation of developing Learnership focuses on helping students understand themselves as learners. Significant attention is given to moving students along the Mindset Continuum. Students come to understand learning as a process of creating their abilities. They build a language for learning, including an understanding of the Habits of Mind and an ability to recognise the different zones of learning. We also give attention to shifting learners' understanding of assessment from being about who they are to being about where they are.

Developing: becoming skilful learners

From understanding themselves as learners, the Learnership curriculum moves on to understanding what skilful learners do. Students explore the concept of Learnership and reflect on how well they currently engage in learning. We introduce students to their Habits of Mind Learner Profile and use this to reflect more deeply on their learning behaviours. They build on their understanding of the zones of learning to recognise different types of challenges. This allows them to recognise different types of effort, focusing on where and how their time and energy are spent.

Extending: taking charge of learning

At this level of Learnership students take charge of their learning. They refine how they engage in practice, making explicit use of the three F's of practice (Focus, Feedback and Fix it). They use the insights gained from their Habits of Mind Learner Profile to understand how to take charge of developing their Habits of Mind. They set their sights on the top level of the Learnership Matrix, understanding how Agile Learners behave.

Mastering: becoming Agile Learners

At this level, we guide students in developing the skills of an Agile Learner. They explore the importance of becoming an Agile Learner, not just in the short-term goal-oriented world of school, but also in the world at large. Students are guided in the practice of embracing challenges and how to leverage those challenges to cultivate their Habits of Mind. They develop their ability to design mistakes and tailor feedback. The deep insights they have gained into themselves as learners allow them to work on refining their motivation calibration.

Expert: self-direction

At this level students are being mentored by teachers as they independently set goals for developing Learnership. They are encouraged to reflect deeply on their Learnership, identifying areas for growth. These are individual, and include how they develop specific Habits of Mind, improve their motivation calibration, refine how they tailor feedback and work on other elements of Learnership.

IMPLEMENTING LEARNERSHIP

Now that we have a way to weave the Learnership program together and develop more skilful learners, it needs a place to live in your school.

Learnership is obviously not a 'learning to learn' program conducted in the first few weeks of school and then forgotten. The scope and sequence I outline makes it clear this will take time and sustained effort. So where does Learnership 'fit' in your school? How is it delivered?

The schools I work with have found it useful to assign the stages outlined above to different year levels within the school. This gives different teachers the responsibility for developing different aspects of Learnership.

In several primary settings, the P–2 teachers have taken on the responsibility for the Beginning stage. The 3–4 teachers have taken on the responsibility for the Developing Stage. The 5–6 teachers have taken on the responsibility for the Extending stage, with the flexibility to go beyond.

In secondary schools it's been common to cover the Beginning stage in the first year, with each stage following a year after that, culminating in the year 11s and 12s focusing on the Expert stage. Obviously this would change if you had significant numbers of students coming from a primary school that has been implementing this program.

Exactly where these levels sit in your school will vary depending on the age and prior learning of the student, and how quickly you move students through each level. The most important aspect is that a level of Learnership is attached to a year level or stage of learning. This gives teachers at that year level an understanding of prior learning, what they are expected to do, and what they are preparing learners for. Most importantly, it gives them ownership over that part of the program.

Arranging Learnership by stages of learning gives a horizontal focus, with all students at a particular age or stage of learning sharing a similar focus. However, there is another complementary way to organise your Learnership program that has proven to be particularly powerful – creating a focus for each term.

MAKING LEARNERSHIP 'HOW THINGS ARE DONE AROUND HERE'

One of our goals is to build a culture based on learning and growth. To make Learnership part of 'the way things are done around here'. This means building it into not just the curriculum of the school, but the life of the school as well.

For better or worse, schools cycle through four terms each year. And every year the cycle repeats. Attaching Learnership to these cycles is a powerful way to weave it into the culture of the school.

I've arranged my Learnership program so there is a common theme each term, as follows:

- Term 1: Understanding learning
- Term 2: Developing Habits of Mind
- Term 3: Embracing challenges
- Term 4: Achieving growth (effort).

This means all members of the school community are focused on the same aspect of Learnership at the same time, although they'll be looking at it from different levels of complexity.

Every teacher at a given year level knows the aspect of the Learnership program they are responsible for delivering. And every term, every teacher in the school is focused on building a common element of Learnership. This has an enormously powerful effect on making Learnership 'the way things are done around here'.

This means Learnership can be woven into other school activities. A principal told me her school incorporates each term's Learnership theme into their newsletters and assemblies – which also makes it easier for her to decide what to write and speak about for each. Each of these actions makes Learnership more and more a part of 'the way things are done around here'.

One school I work with was using this approach as the basis for a common professional learning meeting for all staff. Because every teacher was going to be focusing on a common element of Learnership that term, they were able to dedicate a staff meeting each term to that focus. Doing this wove another thread to the fabric of making Learnership 'the way things are done around here'.

Another school has been in the pattern of running parent information nights once a term. The purpose of these sessions is to help connect parents with the life of the school and their children's learning. These sessions now take on the Learnership focus of the term. Why? Because that's the way they do things around there. The culture becomes self-referencing and self-sustaining.

> ❝ The more Learnership becomes 'the way things are done around here', the more things around here are done that way.

This type of culture building feeds on itself. The more Learnership becomes 'the way things are done around here', the more things around here are done that way. It drives informal conversations with students. It gets reflected in the feedback teachers write on student work. Backstories start being mentioned when achievements are reached. Teachers focus on their own Learnership. And more.

As students move through school they will spiral through the Learnership curriculum, each term regularly and predictably revisiting the elements of Learnership. Each year will build on the last as they develop. The thread of Learnership weaves its way, subtly and meaningfully, through every day and every aspect of school life.

Importantly, Learnership and its different elements will now be built into the cycles of the school. One term leads into the next. Each year builds on the last. There is a continuity and momentum to Learnership that means the work is recommitted to each year. It becomes simply 'the way things are done around here'.

Scope and sequence for developing Learnership

Key outcomes by level

MASTERING
- Getting better at getting better – futureproofing
- Cultivating your Habits of Mind
- Embracing challenges
- Tailoring feedback for growth

EXTENDING
- Understanding the Agile Learner
- Developing your Habits of Mind
- Purpose practice for achieving growth
- Motivation calibration: investing effort in growth

DEVELOPING
- Discovering the skill of learning
- Creating your Habits of Mind Learner Profile
- Getting to know your learning zone
- Effective effort – the currency of growth

BEGINNING
- Nurturing a growth mindset
- Building a language for learning
- Understanding zones of learning
- Mastering mistakes

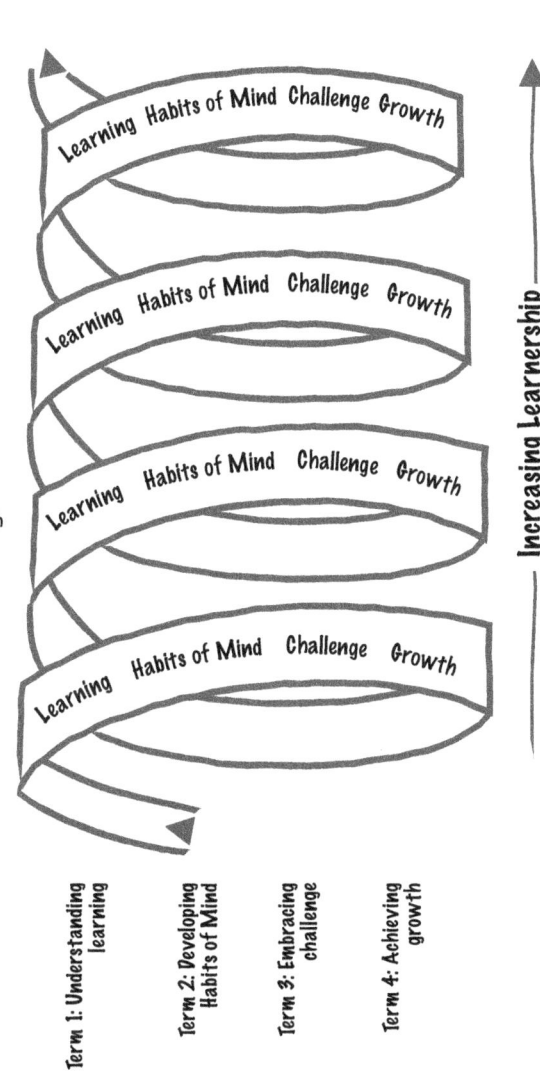

Term 1: Understanding learning
Term 2: Developing Habits of Mind
Term 3: Embracing challenge
Term 4: Achieving growth

FOCUS BY TERM

TEACHING LEARNERSHIP

Finally, we reach the all-important question of when, specifically, do you teach Learnership?

Learnership should be being developed in every classroom, every day. It should be a part of how teachers plan units of work. A part of every lesson. Discussions about how students are learning should become part of the everyday classroom practice. Everything we've talked about in this book helps this occur.

> ❝ Learnership should be being developed in every classroom, every day.

The last thing I'd want to see happen is for Learnership to suffer the same fate as our early attempts of 'teaching' a growth mindset. Where mindset became something to be taught *about*. Learnership should not be a 'lesson in a box'. It's not a topic to be taught. It's a skill to be developed, continuously.

However, the curriculum scope and sequence I've outlined requires that certain lessons are taught. Someone will need to explain the zones of learning to students. Lessons will have to be given to introduce the language of the Habits of Mind. Instruction will need to be given on identifying the different types of effort.

Leaving it to teachers to squeeze the explicit teaching of Learnership into the curriculum is unlikely to be successful. I suggest you create a specific time, and responsibility, for the direct teaching of Learnership. How much time you dedicate to this will be a school-based decision. But it doesn't have to be much. Two or three lessons a term has proven to be sufficient. This keeps the ball rolling without being burdensome on teachers.

There are very good reasons for creating space in the curriculum for explicitly teaching Learnership. It shows the school community Learnership is valued. It gives space for some explicit skills to be taught, and most importantly, it provides a point in time for teachers to reconnect with Learnership.

Valuing Learnership

Time is one of the most valuable, and scarcest, commodities in a school. The simple act of putting Learnership on the timetable reflects the value the school places on it. Learnership is not something extra teachers are being asked to do. You are carving out the time to make it possible. Giving time to Learnership on the timetable, making it part of a teacher's load, is respectful to teachers. Plus, it's a way to amplify your growth culture.

Many schools already have a space in the timetable Learnership can slot into. In some schools Learnership becomes part of the pastoral care program. In others a separate subject – two or three lessons a term – is created. In one school I worked with, the responsibility for the explicit teaching of Learnership lessons was rotated through different faculties.

As you're well aware, teachers are time poor and the curriculum is overcrowded. Additionally, teachers are not experts at developing Learnership in their classroom. Even the most committed teachers are likely to find it difficult to know how to develop Learnership under these circumstances. Even after you conduct staff training in Learnership, many teachers will struggle to recall exactly how to develop it in their day-to-day lessons. That's why the most important part of the explicit Learnership program I've developed is not the content taught to students; it is the way it requires teachers to reconnect with Learnership.

The most important part of the Learnership program

The most valuable part of building your Learnership program into the timetable, and making it an explicit part of the teaching program, is not the opportunity it provides for student learning. Most of that will happen as an integral part of every lesson. Its true value lies in the opportunity it creates for ongoing teacher learning.

You now recognise that teaching and learning are separate skills. Being a skilful teacher does not automatically make you a skilful learner. And as we discussed in chapter 9 on challenges, in many professions, including teaching, there is a tendency for people to become adequate in their job, and then remain in their comfort and performance zones for long periods. Eduardo Briceño's excellent TED Talk that I directed you to earlier does a great job of explaining this.

The consequence is that many of your teachers may have forgotten what it feels like to be in their learning zone. Few have deeply reflected on how they develop their Habits of Mind. And many carry unexamined fixed mindset beliefs with them. The truth is that although they might be great teachers, they may not be great learners, so many will be ill equipped to lead students in becoming better learners. As one leader I worked with eloquently put it: 'The I do, we do, you do model for learning is limited by the "I do" part.'

Recall also that the number one strategy for changing students' mindsets is to change teachers' mindsets. This doesn't happen as the result of one professional learning day, or simply showing teachers the Mindset Continuum. Just like students, teachers need constant nudges along the continuum before they can reprogram their autopilot, become more growth oriented in their mindset, and begin to fill classrooms with growth mindset movers.

Clearly, as your school embarks on a Learnership journey there will be a need for teacher professional learning. A full day (or two) of professional learning is a great way to kick off your Learnership journey, communicate key ideas and build a strong foundation and commitment to the work. However, sustaining that journey, and building teacher capacity, requires more. Let's face it; in term four, how many teachers remember what you did on the first day of term one?

To create and sustain a culture of learning and growth we need professional learning that is timely and relevant to their needs right now. We must give teachers the opportunity to revisit key ideas, and consolidate their understandings. Their thinking and practice needs to be challenged regularly. They must have the opportunity to implement, reflect and change their practice. So professional learning must be spaced throughout the year, drip fed in small, manageable amounts, and delivered 'just in time' so it can be applied immediately.

Having a key focus for each term helps with this. As I mentioned above, some schools use the Learnership theme for the term as the focus of short professional learning at the start of the term. This is an excellent way to cover key ideas and refocus everyone. Key nudges can also be revisited at this time.

> 66 To create and sustain a culture of learning and growth we need professional learning that is timely and relevant to their needs right now.

The individual Learnership lessons provide an excellent opportunity to provide even more focused, just-in-time professional learning. Although there's a common focus for the term, each year level is concentrating on a different stage of Learnership. For example, using the model I've described above, term three's focus is Challenge. At the Beginning Learner stage the specific aspect of challenge that is focused on is the zones of learning. At the Developing stage the focus is on understanding different types of challenges. By the Extending stage the focus is on understanding different types of practice. So the lessons that need to be prepared are different at different year levels.

As teachers prepare for the short Learnership lesson we inject short, highly targeted and relevant professional learning. Using online tools, teachers can revisit key ideas, develop a short lesson for students, and be reminded how to apply and model those ideas in their day-to-day teaching. In this way the Learnership lesson is not simply about teaching Learnership to students, it's about embedding Learnership into teacher practice.

This type of drip-fed, just-in-time professional learning also helps to respond to staff turnover and new teacher induction. New teachers don't need all the upfront professional learning. The combination of each term's themes, coupled with some short whole-staff learning at the start of the term and the resources associated with the specific aspect of Learnership they are focusing on, gradually builds their skills over time.

In real terms, the time required to explicitly teach Learnership is small. Although it's important and it illustrates the value the school places on Learnership, these are not the most important reasons for putting Learnership on the timetable. The most important reason is that having it on the timetable creates a point in time for teachers to regularly revisit, reconnect and refocus on Learnership. In this way Learnership becomes simply the way things are done around here, in every lesson, every day.

Where to now?

Well, you made it.

Choosing to focus on the skill of learning is not simply a good thing to do, or a means for improving student learning outcomes. It is something we *must* do. It is how we raise the aspirations of students, and help them create a better world for themselves and the community at large. If we claim to want to set students up for life, not just for school, choosing to develop Learnership in our students is the socially responsible thing to do.

We've talked a lot about preparing students for the world they are going to live in. But we sometimes forget we are living in this world too. Education is being impacted by these changes just as much as the rest of our community. We don't sit separate to our wider community. We are a part of it.

If Learnership was just about the students, this book would have been solely about curriculum and pedagogy. A simple how-to guide to teach students to become Agile Learners. But this book is so much more. It's about creating a true learning community. It's about building a culture, a way we do things around here, that's founded on learning and growth. That's because it's not just students we are talking about. It's the teachers as well. And you.

When you looked at the Mindset Continuum, you no doubt recognised that you and your staff don't always have a highly growth oriented mindset. When you did the Learnership Diagnostic, I'm sure you reflected on how skilfully you and your staff engage in learning, and recognised room for improvement. The fact that being a great teacher does not mean you are also a great learner can be a painful truth.

In chapter 1, I spoke about students having multiple careers. Working in industries that might not exist yet. Solving problems and using technologies that haven't been invented. This is not a future that's 50 years away. It's happening now. You are leading an organisation in a world that is rapidly changing and increasingly complex.

When you came into the education profession, it's likely that being a teacher, or at least being in schools, was something you thought you'd do your whole career. Like many of our generation, you're a 'lifer'. But increasingly, that's not the case. More and more young teachers expect teaching to be a part of their working life, not *all* of their working life. They expect to move on to other careers.

And we are seeing more people coming into education as a second or third career. These people aren't expecting to start at the bottom. Many have industry experience and expect that experience to be recognised.

Then there are the broader societal changes rolling through that continue to impact education. When I went to school we had one room of computers, with bulky green monitors and a flashing curser for the next input. A few years into my teacher career, in the early '00s, I returned to university do a post graduate diploma in computer education – a degree that didn't exist when I left school. The first mobile phone I used was a loaner given to me by my school when I took some students on an excursion. And let's not forget that, probably like you, I was alive before the internet existed!

Change and the impact of that change continues to accelerate. Over the last few years we've had the impact of COVID-19 and the shift to deliver education online. In just the past 12 months, we've seen the early impact of technologies like AI. Layer into this all the new roles and responsibilities that principals have taken on. The latest curriculum changes. The new state and national priorities. Principalship is no longer only about being an educational leader, you're a psychologist, business leader and town planner too! Like the wider community, schools are becoming increasingly complex places, and increasingly difficult to lead.

And we see the impact of this change every day. Just as resilience has become a focus for our students, so has staff wellbeing become a focus for our staff. People aren't coping with the challenges.

Insurance companies are moving to protect themselves from rapidly increasing mental health claims.

If our school communities are going to thrive, and not just survive, in this world, students, teachers and school leaders will also need to become Agile Learners. In that respect schools are no different from any other organisation. That's why it's our whole community that needs to be focused on developing Learnership, not simply students. Just as we are asking our students to do, every member of our school community, including teachers and school leaders, needs to move beyond resilience and become antifragile by leveraging the challenges to our advantage.

A growth mindset is the foundation of your learning community. It is the invitation to grow. The understanding that you are capable of growth. But it is not the growth. To achieve the growth you must take action. That's what Learnership is about. Once you understand your capacity to grow, Learnership is the process of becoming an expert at achieving that growth.

Every member of your school community needs to understand themselves as a learner. Fundamentally, that's what a growth mindset is all about. It's a recognition that, through effective effort, you can change your most basic characteristics. As Anders Ericsson said, 'talent is not the cause of something, it's the result. It does not create a process, it is the end result of that process'. Someone with a growth mindset understands that if they want to be talented, they don't go looking for their talents, they go to work creating them.

Your next job in building a culture of growth and learning is to raise the status of learning in your school from an act to an art. Be in awe of how skilfully expert learners engage in the process of learning. Celebrate as you see your community becoming increasingly skilful learners. Talk about it with your teachers. Help them recognise that they are not solely responsible for student learning outcomes. We don't want to lose sight of the skill of teaching, but, like figure skaters Torvill and Dean, it takes two. Done well, what happens in the classroom, the dance between skilful teacher and skilful learner, is a thing of beauty. Use these ideas to amplify your message and enhance your culture.

Talk about Learnership in the same way you'd talk about any area of expertise. Expertise takes time to develop. The Beginning Learner builds their skills, developing an increasingly rich and nuanced understanding of how they engage in the art of learning. They develop a complex language for learning that allows you to have rich conversations about how they build talents and abilities.

Developing Learnership is an investment, not an expense. It shouldn't be seen as a burden or as another layer of complexity in an already complex and challenging school environment. Exactly the opposite. Guiding students to become more skilful learners makes teachers' lives better! The more skilful the learner, the less the cognitive load needs to be lifted by the teacher, and the richer and more engaging the curriculum and our pedagogy can be. Learnership gives teachers back their energy and makes teaching more rewarding. It helps teachers get back to why they got into teaching in the first place, and fall in love with teaching, and learning, all over again.

For you, Learnership helps you become a better leader. By building a Learnership culture, you set up a way of doing things in your school that will outlast your tenure as a principal. You step beyond the current culture of performance and teaching, and infuse into the school a set of guiding principles built on learning and growth. In doing so, you impact not just the students in your school today, but also those who will come in the future. By raising the status of learning in your school from an act to an art, you are doing so much more than preparing students for the tests of school. You are preparing them for the tests of life.

Want some more
James Anderson
in your life?

If you've got great value from James's latest book, there are a number of ways you can work with him. Check out the information in the following pages, or visit his website at

www.jamesanderson.com.au

And you can connect with him on LinkedIn to keep up to date with his latest offerings.

Would you like to work with James in your school?

James Anderson partners with schools all over the world to help build cultures of learning and growth. With a powerful blend of in-person and online training, resources, coaching and mentoring, James fosters partnerships that respect the unique context of each school he works with.

James tailors engaging, thought-provoking and practical professional learning experiences that drive meaningful growth in your school.

The best place to start is by contacting James directly to set up a call to find out what you need and how best he can help.
Email: **james@jamesanderson.com.au**.

www.jamesanderson.com.au

Deep Dive Teacher Workshops

Empower educators, enrich classrooms, and fuel student success with James Anderson's teacher workshops. Topics cover everything from Learner Agency to Growth Mindset and Learnership and are packed full of practical classroom strategies.

James offers live, virtual and hybrid workshops. With a professional studio and a knack for connecting across platforms, he ensures teachers have an engaging experience and leave with practical strategies that they can implement immediately in their classrooms to improve student learning.

By working with James, teachers will help students to:

- Nurture an increasingly growth-oriented mindset
- Develop greater learnership
- Increase Learner Agency.

To find out more about how your teachers can attend one of James Anderson's workshops please visit **www.jamesanderson.com.au**.

www.jamesanderson.com.au

The Learnership Program

Bring the scope and sequence for Learnership to life in your school. This extensive online resource is your complete professional learning and cultural change package.

What's included:

- **Detailed Scope and Sequence:** Chart a clear path to nurturing Learnership throughout the stages of learning.
- **Continuous Professional Learning:** Access on-demand, just-in-time, bite-sized video lessons for teachers, promoting ongoing growth and professional development.
- **Classroom Resources:** Equip your educators with a rich repository of activities and pedagogy to cultivate Learnership in students.
- **Nudges for Growth:** Nurture a Growth Mindset and foster a culture of growth within your school community.
- **New Staff Induction:** Ensure that Learnership becomes a sustained and integral part of every classroom, every day, even with new additions to your team.

Reach out to James Anderson to explore how the Learnership Program can work for you. Email: **james@jamesanderson.com.au**.

www.jamesanderson.com.au

Are you looking for a world-class speaker for your next live or virtual event?

James Anderson delivers keynotes, presentations and workshops to audiences all around the world. A masterful storyteller, James engages his audiences, gently challenges them to think differently, and leaves them empowered and inspired to take action.

Tailored to your specific needs, his keynotes explore important aspects of Learnership, Growth Mindsets and Learner Agency. Helping the audience understand the skill of learning, and the importance of developing a culture of learning and growth in schools.

James is an industry leader in virtual speaking. Delivered from his Melbourne-based multi-camera professional studio, he powerfully leverages, and seamlessly integrates, technology to masterfully engage his audiences.

To find out more about getting James to speak at your next event, either face to face or virtually, email **james@jamesanderson.com.au**.

www.jamesanderson.com.au

Would you like to interview James Anderson?

Over the past 20 years James has been interviewed across all types of media. He is as comfortable in front of a camera on TV and online summits as he is behind a microphone for your podcast, or being interviewed for your feature print publication.

James can talk with authority and insight on the following:

- **Learnership** – developing the skill of learning to thrive in a rapidly changing world
- **Mindset** – cultivating an understanding of yourself as a learner
- **Learner Agency** – becoming the master of your circumstances and powerful in the face of change
- **Parenting** – how to raise children that are futureproofed
- **Habits of Mind** – learning to be smarter, making hard things easy
- **All things learning.**

If you'd like to interview James about any of the above or his latest book, **Learnership: Raising the status of learning from an act to an art in your school**, please email james@jamesanderson.com.au.

www.jamesanderson.com.au

Are you looking for the perfect gift for an educational leader?

There is no doubt that the insights and strategies James shares in **Learnership** have great meaning, relevance and value to educational leaders at all levels. In **Learnership** James opens a new chapter in education, a chapter that focuses on the skill of learning. The way he raises the status of learning in schools from an act to an art, is a crucial message that every educational leader needs to hear.

It's not surprising that thoughtful educational leaders are choosing Learnership as the perfect gift. Principals often purchase sets for their leadership teams to encourage shared professional development through group reading. Associations find it to be a meaningful gift for their members, and conferences provide copies for every delegate.

If you're in search of an excellent gift for a fellow educational leader, James Anderson's **Learnership** is one of the most valuable gifts you could choose. Share the wisdom of learning and inspire growth within your educational community.

If this sounds like the ideal gift for your team, please email **james@jamesanderson.com.au**.

www.jamesanderson.com.au

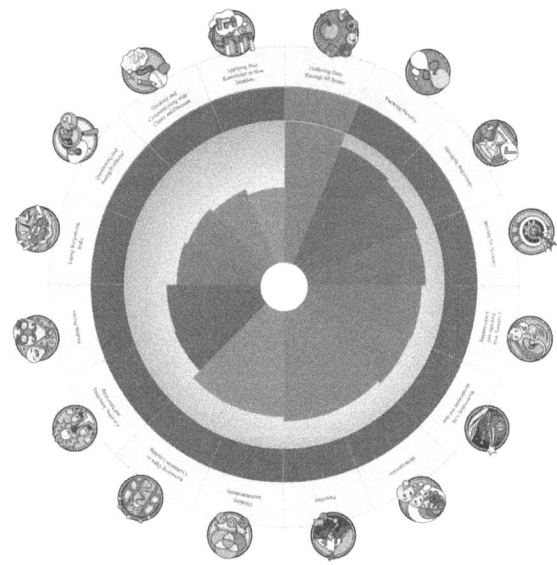

Habits of Mind Learner Profile: A Unique way to Assess and Nurture Learning Dispositions

Unlock the power of the Habits of Mind Learner Profile, a unique tool that empowers schools to assess, nurture and report on students' learning dispositions like never before.

With the Learner Profile, you can:

- **Create a Language for Learning:** Establish the Habits of Mind as a shared language for learning within your school community
- **Foster Meaningful Learning Conversations:** Create rich discussions about students' Habits of Mind between students, teachers and parents
- **Drive Growth in Habits of Mind:** Promote continuous improvement and development of students Habits of Mind
- **Lead students to Embrace Challenges:** nurture students relationship with challenge
- **Increase Learnership:** Equip students to become more skilful, more effective learners
- **And much much more.**

The Learner Profile is fully customisable, able to meet the unique needs and existing language of your school. It seamlessly complements your existing assessment and reporting systems. Importantly, when paired with a Habits of Mind Problem Profile, it drives a pedagogy that is focused on the how of learning.

If you'd like to find out more about how the Habits of Mind Learner Profile can enhance learning and assessment at your school please email james@jamesanderson.com.au.

www.jamesanderson.com.au

www.ingramcontent.com/pod-product-compliance
Lightning Source LLC
Chambersburg PA
CBHW051534010526
44107CB00064B/2725